PELICAN BOOKS

A156

BRITISH MUSIC OF

OUR TIME

D1323972

BRITISH MUSIC OF OUR TIME

EDITED BY
A. L. BACHARACH

PENGUIN BOOKS
HARMONDSWORTH · MIDDLESEX

PUBLISHED IN PELICAN BOOKS 1946
NEW EDITION 1951

MADE AND PRINTED IN GREAT BRITAIN
FOR PENGUIN BOOKS LTD
BY HAZELL, WATSON AND VINEY LTD
AYLESBURY AND LONDON

Contents

Editor's Preface

*

LET us make no bones about it: this book is unabashed propaganda. We have it, I think, on the authority of the Brains Trust that propaganda is not good or bad in itself, but only by virtue of what it aims at doing. What is it, then, that the twelve of us, here in conspiritorial collaboration, have attempted? Is it a good thing and have we succeeded? The answer rests, as it always must in such circumstances, with the reader, and anything that an editor has to say by way of explanation may well be regarded as an admission of failure. All the same, and realising the risk, may I as question-master of this invisible and inaudible musical brains trust be permitted at least a few words in which to introduce its members to the invisible and inaudible public, whose questions I have tried to sense and pass on to the team?

A good many years ago a friend of mine wrote in an undergraduate magazine: 'What we need in criticism is, above all, clarity ... ' But the compositor knew a better one than that. Unconsciously, or slyly, he changed a letter in the last-quoted word, and my friend was left to go down to posterity as demanding *charity* – the last thing, I fancy, that he meant to ask for. Yet perhaps the printer was right. Of literary criticism I do not hold myself qualified to speak, but I must confess that I have often wished for a little more of the milk of human kindness when I have listened to what many a self-confessed 'confirmed music-lover' has had to say about new compositions of British composers, showing themselves in this matter less open to new ideas than professional musicians and critics, which is perhaps to be expected. For if by charity you understand, as I do, not a willingness to overlook incompetence or perversity, but a sympathetic attempt to understand just what the other fellow is trying to do, a willingness to admit that he is entitled to try to do it and to praise him if he has succeeded, our musical writers of to-day are by no means devoid of charity or perhaps of the two lesser virtues that should go with it.

The eleven essayists who appear in this volume are all agreed with the editor about one thing, that charity, as I have defined it, begins at home. Each man of them is, as you may easily observe, an enthusiast for his subject. What matter if the result is some slight measure of contradiction? If Mr A gives first place to Dr W and Mr B has an equally extreme admiration for Sir X Y, while Mr C insists that Z is the outstanding British composer of the last fifty years – may they not all be right? For it is surely even less permissible to say dogmatically who is the best of our contemporary composers than to pick out any of the great ones of the past as the supreme master, be it Bach, Mozart, Beethoven, Handel, Schubert, or whom you will.

What is really important is that the writer should himself sincerely admire and enjoy the music of the composer whose work he is trying to help the reader to understand. The publishers of this book, as well as the contributors and the editor, are profoundly convinced that tens of thousands, maybe hundreds of thousands, of concert-goers and listeners, are asking for, and will derive immense and increasing enjoyment from, well-informed and honest advice about how to approach the music written by composers of their own time and their own country. And that is what the contributors hope, and the editor believes, that they have given in the pages that follow. Read them and see. Or I should perhaps more wisely have written 'Read them – and listen'.

The list of extant gramophone records in the appendix is lamentably short. If the result of producing this book should be to stimulate something more than an unspoken wish for further recordings of 'British Music of Our Time', and to cause you to put your requests in writing to the recording companies, well, the companies may regard the voicing of your wants with mixed feelings, but the writers of this book will probably not – and the composers will certainly not. It is hoped in any later editions found possible to keep the list of records up to date.

I cannot conclude these 'chairman's introductory remarks' without some expressions of genuine gratitude. First and foremost to all the contributors, who have so clearly understood the kind of book I wanted to edit and, whether it was entirely *their* idea of a book or not, have so accommodatingly, each in his own different way, helped to write it. Secondly, to the publishers, who have left me a completely free hand as to the way the subject of this book should be attacked and the forces I might mobilise to attack it. Thirdly, to Mr F. S. Clough, who has checked the list of records, for compiling which I am very much indebted to Miss Valentine Britten. And last, but by no means least, to two of the contributors in particular, Gerald Abraham and the late Ralph Hill: with them I discussed the general plan of the book, the relative allotment of space – calling for *very* tricky and at times almost invidious distinctions – and the particular enthusiast to approach as author of this chapter or that. I know that they have helped me to avoid many snags, if not even the giving of active offence, and they must take their share of credit for whatever success the book may have. But for its faults you have only to blame the editor.

The above words, with a few alterations and deletions, are substantially what were written five years ago, when this book first appeared. Meanwhile, numerous readers have written to express their appreciation of what we have tried to do or their disapproval of our failure to do what they wanted. Fortunately most of our critics' views cancelled out. There was, for example, one indignant Celt who held that our use of the word 'British' was unjustifiable, seeing that we had written of none but English composers:

his views nicely counterpoised those of the abusive gentleman who said, among other things, that the editor must certainly be a foreigner who was ashamed of the word English; otherwise he would have used it, instead of throwing sops to Scots and Welshmen!

Although on this and a number of other matters the editor and the publishers both remain unregenerate, they are well aware of certain respects in which this reprint could have been much improved, had it been possible to replace it by a complete revision. There is the need to discuss important works produced since 1945, and several more young composers have meanwhile implemented their earlier promise to an extent that would secure their discussion in any similar book written to-day. Again, even the wisest critic – perhaps, indeed, especially the wisest critic – will wish to revise certain of his judgments of contemporary composers after five years' intense musical activity.

It is our conviction that a revised edition of this book should be indeed published as soon as practicable and it is our intention to arrange for this to be done. Meanwhile we trust that new readers of this reprint will pardon any anachronisms in it and find the book as a whole still to have the value indicated by the fact that the first impression has for some time been out of print. And at least we have kept our promise to bring up-to-date the list of available gramophone records.

A. L. BACHARACH

Hampstead
  London NW3
    December 1950

CHAPTER I

The Roots and the Soil:
Nineteenth-Century Origins

SCOTT GODDARD

*

AT the turn of the century, when the leisurely nineteenth gave way to what now seems the hectic twentieth, two significant events took place. In 1900 Sullivan died and Elgar's *Dream of Gerontius* was performed for the first time.

These were big events in British music. Almost unnoticed, an event at least as significant had happened. 'I saw poor old "G.'s" coffin lowered deep into an ugly comfortless corner in an ugly crowded cemetery.' The writer was Hubert Parry and the coffin was that of George Grove. His life had been more important for the future of British music than even Sullivan's. For while Sullivan was a creative artist of great ability, Grove was a teacher; and it was teachers with vision, which Grove undoubtedly had in fortunate conjunction with organising ability, that British music most needed.

The position of British music during the latter half of the nineteenth century had been precarious. The state of music in general was sound enough: there was always a large and fairly intelligent audience available, as much in this country as in any other. But the state of British music in particular was weak through lack of support. Historians have been inclined to lay this at the door of what has been conveniently but inexactly called the Mendelssohnian hegemony. In reality three main causes had brought it about. There was the apathy of the intelligent, who mistrusted music because it appealed to the emotions, which indeed was all they allowed it to do. There was, too, the supine policy of the Churches, who never seemed to realise the paralysing effect their badly written, ill-performed music was having on their congregations, and even had they wished to change things they would hardly have turned for help to native talent. Lastly there was the general snobbery of 'society'. For them music was fair game because of its immediate sensuous appeal and strong entertainment value. Their dislike of music the words of which conveyed anything definite to them, that is to say English vocal music and therefore English opera, they were liable to carry over into a general suspicion of any music written by a British composer. Light music, as far as the drawing-room ballad, was excepted. Oratorio also was exempt, probably because biblical tales were already so well known that they could be taken for granted and the words hardly listened to. And since these works had to be sung by English choral societies they had to be sung in English. With these oratorios went a number of attendant cantatas, which shared the exemption. And it is significant that the beginnings of the 'new music' are said to date from the performance of a cantata, Parry's *Prometheus Unbound*.

The result of this mid-Victorian attitude to the music of British composers was a continued rise in imported music and musicians. This was inevitable, and, ridiculous though the cause may now appear, the situation had its value since it made possible the visits of men such as Mendelssohn, Dvořák, Berlioz, Wagner, Tchaikovsky, all of whom brought their own splendid music with them. But it was a situation inimical to music born here, that could have come into being only in such adverse circumstances, it might be feared, in a self-conscious spirit of protest. The danger was that this spirit would wholly occupy men's minds. By an almost inexplicable miracle this danger was avoided.

Protest there was but it came more often from performers, annoyed that an English name should command lower fees than a foreign. Composers mainly followed another course, they worked. And by the time the next generation was ready at the opening of the twentieth century to demand equal rights of performance with Mendelssohn and the later continental visitors, or with Schumann and the other great names that figured in the programmes of the Monday Pops at St James's Hall, it was too late for British music to be affected by social stupidity or political nationalism in the way that French and Austrian music was later to suffer. The music of this country was already securely enough founded in a number of notable works; so that, protest as the younger generation might against what they considered an unfair preponderance of foreign works in programmes of the great concert-giving organisations, at least they could support their protest by producing music already of a strong character and an individual quality.

These younger men, from the time of Parry's and Stanford's pupil Vaughan Williams onwards, were by then becoming aware of their particularly rich heritage. For art and science there was Tudor music, for instinct and the autochthonous emotion there was folk-music, both being treated with pious respect by scholars who were busy handing on these things to the creative musicians of the day. On that rather than on an indignant emulation of continental models, they based their ideology, if they ever had one, and upon that they based their work. It was a sound outlook, and they owed it to the stolid virtues of their teachers, the men of the generation working at the turn of the century.

George Grove, who was an omnivorous student, had by then given fresh impetus to musical research in England through his visit to Vienna in 1867, when he and Sullivan unearthed the parts of the ballet music for *Rosamunde*. His programme notes for Manns's Crystal Palace concerts seemed for the first time to presuppose intelligence in audiences; they were masterly, original, and prophetic essays in the art of stimulating the listener's understanding before playing upon his emotions. Grove, in the programme notes, in his *Beethoven and his Nine Symphonies*, and eventually in the great *Dictionary of Music and Musicians*, was intent on educating the public. In him Parry and Stanford found precisely the right man with whom to work as the first Director of the Royal College of Music, when that institution was founded in 1882. When to all this is added the great *Dictionary* which first appeared in 1879, it will be seen that Grove's death in 1900 was as significant a loss to British music as Sullivan's five months later.

When Arthur Sullivan (1842–1900) died he had wonderfully succeeded in comic opera, where none thought he could or indeed should, and failed in his cherished ideal of becoming England's foremost composer of serious, that is festival, music. Like the next great popular figure in British music, Edward Elgar, he stands apart from the young movement that was reviving creative music. His reasons for this aloofness were other than Elgar's, however; Sullivan was himself one of the elder musicians, and since he was no teacher he could have no part in the movement such as Grove played. There was a further difference, in Sullivan's instinctive desire to help younger men, shown in his impulsive sympathy towards the early efforts of the most gifted among them.

His instincts in music were towards order and symmetry. Nothing gives such clear evidence of Sullivan's Englishry as that he should have shaken off the Mendelssohnian manner that came easily to him and dug his roots deeper into Handel and even Purcell. Had Gilbert been a less smooth versifier with a finer ear for rhythm, caesura, and internal assonance, Sullivan would almost certainly have by-passed Handel and come into closer touch with Purcell, with results for us to-day that might have been valuable. As it was he remains one of the lesser masters of music, securely possessed of a small corner of the field. His right to it will never be questioned, for he brought into comic opera an exquisite tact, a superfine technique, and a rare gift for good tunes. So good is the music that the musical listener must perforce regret lost opportunities. Yet Sullivan's contribution to the revival of interest was notable. In a sense he too prepared the way. Had he been able to appeal to a more thoughtful audience (not with the ponderous touch of *Ivanhoe* or *The Golden Legend* but with the wit and grace of *Princess Ida*), he might have prepared the way for Stanford's songs, perhaps even his operas.

When Hubert Parry (1848–1918) succeeded Grove at the Royal College of Music, he had written his best symphonies, the *Cambridge* and the *English*, his finest short orchestral work, the *Overture to an Unwritten Tragedy*, and the greatest of his cantatas, the setting of Milton's *At a Solemn Music*, now always known as *Blest Pair of Sirens*. The succeeding years seemed as though they would justify the growing suspicion that this composer, who promised to be among the most inspired of his day, had been swamped in the teaching and administration which were making Parry into one of the most influential guides of the rising generation. Undoubtedly his music, though it never altogether lost its individual melodiousness and breadth, became noticeably the product of a mind too occupied with the minutiae of existence to think consecutively in creative art, at least to think itself out of the rut of musical sequences. Yet the *Symphonic Variations for Orchestra* (1897) still had the imaginative energy of the earlier Parry, the man of the *Unwritten Tragedy* overture, with the addition of more musical subtlety and greater expertness; and the cantatas (or short oratorios) *Voces clamantium* (1903) and *The Love that Casteth out Fear* (1904) showed no decrease in Parry's power to produce noble settings of English, nor any loosening of his grasp upon original and effective design. Indeed his songs, which at first had charm but smelled of the drawing-room, became subtler and more refined until they reached the characteristic and fully individual *Tenth Set* of the *English Lyrics*. Parry's songs are uneven but comprise exquisite things. It is a loss now that the finest of them (at the least generous count, half of them) are neglected. As much may be said for his part-song compositions, in which delicate craft he was a master.

Nevertheless his professional duties took an increasing amount of his time and energy, a situation from which posterity has benefited, since it gave rise to one of the most notable studies of J. S. Bach ever written (1906), and to the stimulating *Style in Musical Art* (1911) founded on Parry's lectures while Professor of Music of Oxford University. At the end the creative composer in him was remarkably vindicated by a series of *Choral Preludes* and *Choral Fantasies* for organ, culminating in the *Wanderer Toccata and Fugue*. Finally the six *Songs of Farewell* for various dispositions of unaccompanied voices set the seal of high and complete achievement on his creative work. They set also a new standard for unaccompanied vocal writing. Not since Purcell had there been anything in our music of this peculiarly penetrating quality.

Parry was the product of Eton and Oxford. His social background was the secure life of the country squire, the man of means and leisure. After Shelley and Byron had broken loose it had become less abnormal for a youth to turn from the Services or the Church to the practice of the art of letters; but that the art should be music and that it should be seriously studied was still an innovation. The urge to create must have been compelling and the vision have had strong poetic impulse that could overcome the traditional tendencies inherent in the average young man of Parry's position. From such tendencies Parry turned first towards the hazardous difficulties and delights of creative music, at which he began to work while a school-boy, and later to the exacting duties of teaching and administration at which he overworked for the main part of his life. His sympathies widened (while some of his antipathies in art and in life remained too deep for him to reach their roots, which he never tired of trying to do), and at length he became one of the most inspiring men of his age.

It is in the later choral works, such as the two cantatas mentioned above, that the intrinsic quality of Parry's art and the trend of his philosophy became apparent. There was in him an element of the mystic, crossed with a hearty, bluff Englishry that blew through the spiritual essence of his work in sudden gusts of impetuous feeling that threatened to tear its fabric to shreds. These works are purposeful, idealistic and earnest. They enshrine Parry's philosophy as a teacher and in an equal degree his downright, not primarily subtle, musicianship. Such qualities were to become suspect; the fashion for them went out with the Armistice in the year of Parry's death. Inevitably Parry's cantatas, which are the essence of his mature work, must lie apart until audiences can once more bear admonitions and exhortations without feeling irked. He was at such moments often his own librettist, and it is in these works that he achieved his most original designs. To realise the individual quality of his utterance in these peculiarly individual works the hearer has to allow himself to be carried onward to the climax of Parry's towering sequential perorations. *Voces clamantium* ends with one of these to the words 'O man' (Handel's rising fourth of 'I know' in *The Messiah*) 'look upward where the skies are clear'. Such sentiments, and such assured, splendid motion in the music, are still a memorable experience for anyone sympathetic enough to the tradition to understand it. Parry's cantatas are an episode in British music that the historian may not ignore.

Charles Villiers Stanford (1852–1924), the most distinguished and capable British composer of the end of the nineteenth century and the musician whom many (including himself) thought of as Grove's successor at the Royal College, was a perfect example of the Irishman in exile. Like George Moore, he never seemed at peace in the land of his birth, and like Mr Bernard Shaw he reserved to himself the ineluctable right to live in England and criticise to the full extent of a lively wit and an acrid tongue the men and their observances in the country of his choice. He was penetrated absolutely with Irishry (which he put to exquisite use in the orchestral *Rhapsodies*), and, Ulsterman that he was, the first German War found him a patriot more acute, though less tenderly sensitive, than even that greatest of all modern exiles, his contemporary Henry James.

Stanford's stock was that of well-to-do Dublin intelligentsia. He took to music early and after Cambridge studied in Germany. His Irish blood may be said to have saved him from complete teutonicising; the keenness of his wit made it impossible for his music to take on the air of pomposity paraded by many of the foreign imitators of German classicism. He played an important part in the musical life of the country and was without any doubt one of the greatest influences among the pioneers of modern British music. As a teacher, both at Cambridge, where he was Professor of Music, and still more so at the Royal College of Music, he exercised his discriminating powers of analysis in a way that left its mark on many composers of the next generation. Where with Parry it was the immense vision of music's ennobling properties that influenced the man and through him his pupils, with Stanford it was the cool beauty of music's science that he laid bare before his pupils' gaze. His mind was as active as his brain was fertile, and in his own music he could call on these attributes at will.

Stanford wrote voluminously in practically every genre. His work was always musicianly, often splendidly so and sometimes sheer magic. This last quality, which can be suggested by means of no more adequate synonym for the incalculable and the poetic, exists in works, of which some are still current (the song *The Fairy Lough*, the part-song *Heraclitus*, the *Fourth Irish Rhapsody* are instances). Some are now left unheard through the mischances of fashion (the *Irish Symphony*, with a slow movement that is a great example of the easy confluence of folk-lore and art), or are shelved because, as with the eight operas, presentation of such works is peculiarly hazardous. English opera has always led a hard life. In Stanford's day its circumstances were more necessitous and bleak than during the revival of enthusiasm in this century. Then, to write opera at all demanded an extreme degree of courageous foolhardiness and the faith of an idealist. Stanford had his ideals, largely centred in the art of fine musicianship, and he had faith in himself. He was, in fact, singularly free from that self-questioning which lames a man's spirit and forms both the smallest and the greatest creative artists. But the critical acumen of the alert craftsman never deserted him, and, although he over-wrote, his work was at its driest never banal. He ended by having proved his claim to be considered a composer capable of sustaining with complete ability, and often with the most entrancing poetry, the larger designs of symphony and opera.

That Stanford's ambitions should have led him towards opera was fortunate in view of the pleasure posterity still has, or might more widely have, in *Shamus O'Brien*, *The Travelling Companion*, perhaps *The Critic*, which is of a delicious subtlety, and just possibly *The Canterbury Pilgrims*. Contemporary opinion was divided between his admirers, who regretted what they thought was a needless expense of great gifts, and his detractors, who, though they denied him the possession of any gift for creative work, were equally certain that his operas were waste of the public's time. Both were wrong, as has since been proved by the Vic-Wells revival of *The Travelling Companion*, which was discovered to be not only dramatically effective (this was not surprising) but intensely moving.

The significance of Stanford's operas, like that other and different importance of Parry's cantatas, has to do with the contemporary attitude to home-made music, which made musicians produce their works too much

under the stress of protest; so that Parry's gestures sometimes become exaggerated and Stanford's insistence on
recognition sometimes has the character of the unbeatable
Irishman fighting the fog. After the success of *Shamus*,
which beat Sullivan at his own game and then was itself
surpassed by the realism of Synge, nothing but failure
came to his work in opera. It is interesting that a composer
should have thought it necessary, or indeed worth the
immense labour and almost inevitable defeat, to write
operas in English at the turn of the century. The glamour
of the stage, which Parry acknowledged and shunned, may
have held Stanford as, to a lesser extent and in a less significant manner, it held Mackenzie. Stanford provided
incidental music to Tennyson's *Queen Mary* and *Becket*.
There is a strong dramatic quality in cantatas such as *The
Revenge* and *The Voyage of Maeldune*, also in one of the few
persisting works, the *Songs of the Sea*. European opera was
in a state of high vitality and with Europe Stanford, who
in art was no isolationist, kept close contact. His description of the first performance of Verdi's *Falstaff* remains one
of the liveliest pieces of reporting in existence.

But, whatever the causes of Stanford's hopeless storm-
ing of the operatic citadel, the effect was valuable for the
twentieth-century British composer. Stanford showed, as
no composer had done since Purcell, that the English language could be used in opera as fluently as any other and to
as powerfully dramatic effect; also that an English situation
provided as effective a plot as any. (Newbolt's version of
Hans Andersen made *The Travelling Companion* into a
delightfully British gallimaufry of Sir Galahad, St George
and Tom Brown.) Stanford, in fact, vindicated the British
composer's position as an operatic writer in the eyes of the
next generation who, whether they know it or not, now
benefit from his pertinacity.

In 1879 Stanford published the first of his church services, the famous *Stanford in B flat*, known now to all
choirs. This aspect of his music was to have as lasting an

influence as his song-writing and as great an importance in the development of British music as his operas. He recovered for a mainly unheedful Church the lost tradition of the Wesleys, and founded a new one of his own in which noble diction and grandeur of musical design blended. As in every aspect of Stanford's music, one is left with the impression of an incomparably rich talent which, for all that may be said of his having overwritten himself, was fortunately kept ready for the flashes of his genius.

Of the academic trinity presiding over the destinies of music in Britain at the end of the last century, the Scotsman Alexander Mackenzie (1847–1935) was the most well-tempered musician. With none of the abundant aspirations of his English counterpart, nor any of the acute, wayward temperament of his Irish colleague, Mackenzie instead steered a medium course, did valuable work as a teacher, and as a composer upheld tradition. He was an ideal principal for the Royal Academy of Music.

His artistic sympathies were of the more liberal teutonic type. Where Parry's may be said to have centred in J. S. Bach and Stanford's in Brahms (each statement a convenient over-simplification), Mackenzie owed allegiance partly to Mendelssohn and mostly to Liszt. He came of decent burgher stock and of a family with a long musical tradition, had good average schooling as a child in Edinburgh, came to early proficiency in music, and was studying in Germany before his teens.

As a composer Mackenzie, whose works are even less performed to-day than those of his two chief contemporaries, showed talent, taste, and no hint of latent genius. He had learned his craft well and achieved thereby a compact capability. Thus he unfalteringly produced works in many of the main branches of music that were, if not distinguished, at least freer than most from those banalities rife during the latter half of the century among native composers. Hearing Mackenzie's *Scottish Pianoforte Concerto* (1897, Paderewski) to-day, one sees that what he lacked was not talent or even inspiration of a restricted character, but acute poetic vision. Something of the humorous nature of the man, as it appeared in his dealings with his fellows, shows through in the Burns cantata *The Cottar's Saturday Night*. The Scottish rhapsody entitled *Burns* should be recalled to life, and possibly the opera *The Critic on the Hearth*, which is well spoken of by the few who have heard it. Mackenzie wrote no symphony. Among shorter orchestral forms there are the overtures, of which *Britannia* should interest the connoisseur for the curious echo, almost prophetic, of Rowlandson's sailors and their doxies dancing on Portsmouth Point.

A year after Mackenzie's *Britannia*, Edward Elgar (1857–1934) finished his first oratorio, *The Light of Life*. Already he had written the two *Wand of Youth* suites, the overture *Froissart*, the *Chansons de matin* and *de nuit*, all of which music still lives, as well as his first cantata *The Black Knight*. Within four years Richter brought out the *Enigma Variations* and Elgar moved to the top of the profession. His early attempts to get learning sufficient to his needs, like the early struggles to make a living, which forced him to fend for himself, were preparations which resulted in his becoming a lone figure in music. He made an immense name that never became attached to any forward-looking movement. Neither teacher nor leader nor guide, he fulfilled rather the accepted traditions of the dedicated artist. His self-regarding singleness of aim he justified in the splendour of his finest music, the two great symphonies, the two concertos, the three later oratorios, and the tone poem *Falstaff*. Most of these works belong to the twentieth century, and Elgar is seen now as the most apt representative of the Edwardian period.

Like Sullivan he stood apart from the revival of his country's creative music. In his late years, when he had become one of the most distinguished Elder Statesmen of music, he was made an object of veneration and a rallying-point of protest by the younger men. There was no sign of his welcoming their adulation, still less of any sense of gratitude at being made the centre of a storm, or that he was flattered at being placed on precisely that pedestal. If his early years were a hard struggle (there were to be more bitter examples of that among his younger colleagues), he was fortunate in his friends among the Roman Catholic community of which he was so distinguished a member. The significance of Elgar in the new movement is that of an aloof figure whose example could not be ignored. In relation to Parry and Stanford, both of whom saw his worth and were instrumental in getting him a hearing, he stands as a much greater technician than the former and in orchestral music than the latter. As for vision, Elgar's was less heaven-assaulting than Parry's and more generously human than Stanford's.

In an age such as the present, where music written in this country has frequent performances and new works by known, and hardly less by unknown, composers can count on being brought quickly to a public hearing, it is instructive to realise the much smaller opportunities of performance that existed in the time of Parry, Stanford and Mackenzie. In London regular concert-giving organisations, actively interested in British music, were still a dream of the future. The Royal Philharmonic Society, meeting with the same regularity and frequency it always affected from the time of its jubilee season in 1862 up to the present day (an average of seven concerts in the year), seems to have been practically unaware of the new music being written in England. Manns at the Crystal Palace, his interest stimulated by Grove, was beginning to include such music in his programmes. Parry's early concert overture *Guillem de Cabestanh*, completed in short score during 1878, received its full orchestral performance at the Crystal Palace six months later. From then onwards the Sydenham programmes contain a growing number of native works; but it was a full eighteen years later that a new extended work by an English composer could be

performed in London within thirteen months of its
appearance in Hanley, and thereafter have at least four
other performances during that same year. The work was
Elgar's *King Olaf*, and by that time not only had the
interest in British music increased but with that had come
greater opportunities for performance in London and the
provinces.

In the nineteenth century a young composer had to rely
on the Three Choirs' Festival in the West of England to
give his work a hearing: and since there was only a single
concert of secular music at each Meeting, his chances
were further reduced if he wrote a symphony rather than
a cantata. In London the Festival of the Sons of the Clergy
in St Paul's, which had moved Haydn to tears and aroused
Berlioz's interest in massed choral effects, had not yet
decided to countenance the newer music, as the London
Church Choir Festival was to do to Vaughan Williams's
O praise the Lord when Walford Davies was in charge.
The big triennial festivals at Leeds (when Stanford was
conductor), Sheffield (the scene of Henry Coward's
training activities, which resulted in one of the most expert
of all festival choruses even in the north), Norwich, and
Birmingham then began to show practical interest in new
British works as useful, and with time as keen, as that
previously shown in works by Mendelssohn and Dvořák.
The field was becoming wider. With the possibility of
performance there came an increased incentive to compose.
In the meantime the Competition Festival movement had
grown swiftly since its inception in 1885, when it was
started by Mary Wakefield in Sedgwick. This first Westmorland festival, begun in a private house through the
personal enthusiasm of one musician and transferred to the
neighbouring town of Kendal in the next year, was the
beginning of a movement that was to affect the whole
countryside. In a short time Competition Festivals were
being held up and down the land, drawing in musicians of
every type and standard of attainment as competitors and

judges. It was not to be long before other countries, chiefly in the British Empire and the United States, followed, and distinguished personages were invited to come from Britain to act as judges. The movement was typically British in the modesty of its beginnings, the tentative nature of the undertaking, the amateur character of the young organisation. In later years, when festivals had become fast and the management of them a thoroughly professional business, the movement met with some criticism; it was feared that the spirit fostered was not so much liberally educational as tending towards pot-hunting and the greed for diplomas. But as seen originally by Mary Wakefield, an amateur singer of remarkable talent, a song writer, and one of the most gifted lecturers of her day, the movement was designed to raise the whole standard of popular appreciation of music, not in performance alone. This it succeeded in effecting. It was essentially a provincial undertaking, and, although the great cities drew it into their orbit, its best work was, and still is, done in the small towns and villages. Its value has been immense as a humanising force, bringing the professional element (the judges) into intimate contact with the competitors drawn from the huge reserves of amateur effort which in the final estimate form the effective musical life of a country and exercise the grim function of making public opinion. To have begun to bridge the dangerous gap between these two elements, neither of which can exist for long or for any good purpose without the other, and to guide public opinion in the direction of intelligent appreciation of the whole art of music, was the notable contribution Mary Wakefield made before her death in 1910. Her movement had started ten years before the Proms.

It was in 1895 that Robert Newman initiated the Queen's Hall Promenade Concerts, with Henry Wood as his conductor. In the early years of this notable venture there was little to suggest what it was to mean to British

music in general and the young composer in particular.
The early programmes give only the barest hint of that.
But within a few years, the rush of new music having
developed strength, the Prom season became a central
point to which composers and audiences alike turned for
the latest news about contemporary British music. Newman and Wood had cause to be grateful to far-seeing
amateurs like Mary Wakefield, and to teachers such as
Parry, Stanford, and Mackenzie. For the Prom audience
was largely drawn from people who had come under the
influence of such leading figures in the musical life of the
country and so had become aware of the opportunities
presented by this later movement centred during each
autumn in Queen's Hall. All these – the annual and
triennial festivals, the amateur festivals which started in
Westmorland to cater for the villages, and the Proms in
London begun as the venture of an impresario and gradually developed into concerts for popularising the best old
and new music – were an opportunity for the younger
generation of composers to obtain performances as well
as audiences of some critical ability and intelligence, the
one as necessary as the other.

During the last years of the century there emerged the
new generation of musicians, for the most part pupils of
Parry and Stanford. They were in general men twenty
years younger than Elgar; he, true to his wonted singular-
ity, held a course half-way between the elder musicians
and their followers, and by the same token his name, in the
final period of the last century, was already made. The
Enigma Variations had appeared under Richter in 1899. In
years and attainment Elgar was already ahead of the
younger men. Certain of these composers shall be considered briefly here, either because they belong in feeling
to the waning century or because their promise, which
should have been fulfilled in the coming century, was cut
short.

Coleridge Taylor wrote at least one remarkable choral

work and never lived to make what would have been a still more noteworthy and valuable contribution to the world's musical development: the collection of the native music of his own land (his father was a West African) and the handing down of that music to the outside world through the personal medium of his very competent art. And if it is objected that this is not the proper medium, the fortunes of the music of West African descent in Harlem can hardly be upheld as a better model. Coleridge Taylor's technique would at least have retained some of the pristine purity and dignity of the music. His own models were Mendelssohn, Grieg and Dvořák. From Stanford he had learnt precise craftsmanship. What he made of his gifts was unlike anything Stanford would or could have done. The warmth and frank emotionalism of the *Hiawatha* trilogy, which Sullivan welcomed and Stanford is said to have mistrusted, were new in serious British music then, and it has always kept a slightly exotic air. Coleridge Taylor was forced early on to earn a living with his pen. Inevitably he overwrote. The *Bamboula* rhapsody shows the excellence of his technique when at its best; and the *African Romances* (songs), the *African Suite* (orchestra) and the *Negro Melodies* (pianoforte) suggest the measure of the loss his early death may well have been to the art of his native country that he never found time to visit.

Edward German sailed for so long under the flag of Sullivan, whose follower he became in popular estimation, that his work has never got free from that connection. And since his operas must inevitably suffer by comparison with the Gilbert and Sullivan set, owing to the inferiority of their libretti and the inherently weaker constitution of their plots, German's music in this style has gone dead with the passage of the years. But the *Welsh* rhapsody and the *Norwich* symphony suggest that he was a more subtle artist and a musician of wider sympathies than Sullivan. *The Princess of Kensington* and *Merrie England* are German's most successful operas, and they do not bear the comparison they court with Sullivan's. The incidental music to *Henry VIII* contains dances that still hold the tea-shops enthralled. They are psychologically in a moribund tradition of imitation Tudor and have generated a rachitic progeny of background music to documentary films.

Two late-Victorian composers must be mentioned here, the one for her creative work as a composer, the other for his on the borders of music. Ethel Smyth's opera *The Wreckers* appeared in 1906. It was followed ten years later by *The Boatswain's Mate*. The first was a three-act work of grand-opera proportions, the second a two-act comic opera with a libretto written by the composer after W. W. Jacobs's tale and an overture containing the tune of her *March of the Women*, at once a reference to her advocacy of the cause of women's suffrage and to the masterful character of her heroine. Ethel Smyth was always the centre of a storm, largely self-engendered. Opinion differs as to whether she should be considered one of the first, most capable composers of her time or the greatest female composer of all to date. In regard to this latter aspect she was her own clamorous publicist, insisting in a series of brilliant books of reminiscence upon the hardships of her lot and the crass male obstructionism which, in common with a minority of her readers, she considered to have militated against her chances. There is a further division of opinion as between the significance of her literary work on the one hand and her music on the other.

Two years before Smyth's *The Wreckers*, Walford Davies produced his cantata *Everyman* at the Leeds Festival. Its success was immediate and it was not only wishful thinking that rated high the music of this young organist of thirty-five who had been one of Parry's men and one of Stanford's most gifted pupils. But his fame was to be based on other matters than composition. He was one of the first talented musicians to realise the possibilities of broadcasting as a means of publicising his ideals for educating what he styled the 'ordinary listener'. This part of his work was a brilliant success, and the historian is forced to look upon it as a twentieth-century portent. He had a strong sense of moral values, inherited perhaps from Parry, but in that case without Parry's breadth of vision. Unlike Parry he was a Churchman first, religion coming some distance behind. Like Ethel Smyth he had the crusading spirit, which sent him, as it did her, to another medium for the propagating of a cause.

CHAPTER II

Frederick Delius

1863–1934

RALPH HILL

*

DELIUS was one of the most isolated and remote figures in the history of music. As a composer he belonged to no school, nor did he derive from one: his style was practically the result of pure genius. The best part of his life was spent at his country house in Grez-sur-Loing, near Paris, where he worked at his compositions utterly indifferent to money, honours, and the applause of the crowd. He did not even bother to become acquainted with the influential musical circles of Paris, which in their turn refused to recognise him as a composer. His residence in France and his equal lack of interest in the musical circles of England might have resulted in his being completely ignored by his countrymen, had it not been for the championship of a small and select circle of musicians headed by the redoubtable Sir Thomas Beecham. As it is, Delius's music is heard only at rare intervals, for it is too subtle, delicate, and elusive for the type of baton we rear in Britain.

Born at Bradford in 1863, Delius came of a German family of Dutch extraction. His father, a woollen merchant, was a typically harsh nineteenth-century disciplinarian with a kind heart. Although he took an interest in music he refused to entertain the idea that the musical profession was fit for a gentleman. I am not sure that he was wrong. However, according to family testimony the

ream vision of ineffable beauty, the source of which
some indefinable region beyond the world of logic
ason; the moment you bring reason to bear upon it
sion begins to fade'. Except for certain slight in-
s of Grieg in Delius's early works, his music defies
cation: it owes little or nothing to any particular
n or country and it is uninfluenced by the current
al and aesthetic movements of his time.

Fenby tells us in his book that Delius believed
hould be a simple and intimate thing, direct and
ite in its appeal from soul to soul, a thing of in-
ther than of learning, of the heart rather than of
l. Fenby quotes a revealing conversation with
vho said: 'You can't teach a young musician to
any more than you can teach a delicate plant how
but you can guide him a little by putting a stick
d a stick in there. Composition as taught in our
is a farce. Where are the composers they pro-
ose who do manage to survive this systematic
teaching either write all alike, so that you can
is lot belongs to this institution, this lot to that,
e us the flat beer or their teachers, but watered

Delius had no time for the intellectual appeal of
approach to music was essentially emotional.
asion he said to a follower: 'My dear fellow,
ing in counterpoint. I have done all that stuff
may take it from me that it leads nowhere.'
intellectual power is the very thing that
d. This is noticeable in the very direction
ct is most needed in composition: in his
ecture Delius's form is essentially rhapsodic,
en in his beautiful and well-contrived tone
s *Paris*, *On Hearing the First Cuckoo in Spring*,
rise, and *Eventyr*.

ncertos (for piano, 'cello, violin and 'cello,
l of lovely music as they are, are rhapsodies

young Delius learned to play the violin well and mastered
enough piano technique to improvise at the keyboard.
But the more he became infatuated with the idea of making
music his career, the more his father put obstacles in his
way. Having tried his hand in the woollen business (which
at least provided him with a trip to Scandinavia and the
Riviera) and failed, Delius prevailed upon his father to
buy him an orange-grove in Florida.

Recalling those days, Delius told Eric Fenby that when
he left Bradford for Florida he was demoralised: 'You can
have no idea of the state of my mind in those days. In
Florida, through sitting and gazing at nature, I gradually
learnt the way in which I should eventually find myself,
but it was not until years after I had settled at Grez that I
really found myself. Nobody could help me. Contemplation, like composition, cannot be taught.'

Then Delius struck up a friendship with an organist and
music teacher named Thomas Ward, from Jacksonville.
Ward was invited to stay at the orange-grove, with the
result that a course of composition appeared to Delius a
more fruitful occupation than growing oranges.

As this essay is not intended to be biographical save in
so far as such details may have a direct bearing on the composer's music, I will pass over the events of the next year
or two, which finally forced Delius's disillusioned father
to send his son to study at the Leipzig Conservatorium.

According to Fenby, Delius said: 'It was not until I
began to attend the harmony and counterpoint classes at the
Leipzig Conservatorium that I realised the sterling worth of
Ward as a teacher. He was excellent for what I wanted to
know, and a most charming fellow into the bargain. Had
it not been that there were great opportunities for hearing
music and talking music, and that I met Grieg, my studies
at Leipzig were a complete waste of time. As far as my
composing was concerned, Ward's counterpoint lessons
were the only lessons from which I ever derived any benefit.
Towards the end of my course with him – and he made me

work like a nigger – he showed wonderful insight in helping me to find out just how much in the way of traditional technique would be useful to me. ... And there wasn't much. A sense of flow is the main thing, and it doesn't matter how you do it so long as you master it.'

Then came more family upheavals, which were overcome by the influence of Grieg, who persuaded Delius's father to allow his gifted son to pursue the career of a musician. Finally Delius settled in Paris, where, disdaining musical society, he associated freely with painters and writers, such as Gaugin and Strindberg. In 1897 Delius married Jelka Rosen, an artist, who devoted herself to his interests for the rest of his life. They went to live at a charming house in the romantic village of Grez-sur-Loing, near the Forest of Fontainebleau. Robert Louis Stevenson in his *Essays of Travel* has given a vivid description of Grez. 'It lies out of the forest,' he says, 'a cluster of houses with an old bridge and an old castle in ruin, and a quaint old church. The inn garden descends in terraces to the river; stableyard, kailyard, orchard, and a space of lawn, fringed with rushes and embellished with a green arbour. On the opposite bank there is a reach of English-looking plain, set thickly with willows and poplars. And between the two lies the river, clear and deep, and full of reeds and floating lilies. Water-plants cluster about the starlings of the long, low bridge, and stand half-way up upon the piers in green luxuriance. They catch the dipped oar with long antennae, and chequer the slimy bottom with the shadow of their leaves. And the river wanders hither and thither among the islets, and is smothered and broken up by the reeds, like an old building in the lithe, hardy arms of the climbing ivy.' The ruined castle and the old church adjoined Delius's house, which had a long garden sloping down to the quiet river and beyond that the open country.

Delius lived in this lovely, secluded spot until he died in 1934. The scene is important, because he composed the greater part of his finest work there, and therefore Grez

was to him what Dorset was to Thor or fertiliser of his inspiration. The e beautiful natural scenes and soun was enough to start the flow of D And there is no doubt that it was that those lovely tone poems *In Hearing the First Cuckoo in Spring, River* were first conceived.

Philip Heseltine (to whom all music must be for ever indebted f pathetic book on the composer first thing one must realise abo is the outcome of a profound therefore completely at varianc 'the modern spirit in music'. 'I continues Heseltine, 'to descr one who, instead of writing to nature (and even Nietzsch most irreligion is mere re religion that would destroy the very nature of religion. of the same order as the c to the sun's apparent moti

Delius's music is perha write about at length b there is so little variety its technique. Delius re stable who confines hi colours that are restric and nuances. In terms Hardy in so far as th his novels are centr Thus to know and teristic works is virt

Delius is a com musical art. Edwin way to enjoy his

as a lies i and r the v fluenc classif traditi technic

Eric music s immedia stinct ra the head Delius, compose to grow, in here a academies duce? Th and idiotic say that th or they giv down.'

Indeed, music: his On one oc there is noth myself. You

Sustained Delius lacke where intelle musical archi as may be se poems, such a *Song Before Su* Even his c and violin), fu young Delius learned to play the violin well and mastered enough piano technique to improvise at the keyboard. But the more he became infatuated with the idea of making music his career, the more his father put obstacles in his way. Having tried his hand in the woollen business (which at least provided him with a trip to Scandinavia and the Riviera) and failed, Delius prevailed upon his father to buy him an orange-grove in Florida.

Recalling those days, Delius told Eric Fenby that when he left Bradford for Florida he was demoralised: 'You can have no idea of the state of my mind in those days. In Florida, through sitting and gazing at nature, I gradually learnt the way in which I should eventually find myself, but it was not until years after I had settled at Grez that I really found myself. Nobody could help me. Contemplation, like composition, cannot be taught.'

Then Delius struck up a friendship with an organist and music teacher named Thomas Ward, from Jacksonville. Ward was invited to stay at the orange-grove, with the result that a course of composition appeared to Delius a more fruitful occupation than growing oranges.

As this essay is not intended to be biographical save in so far as such details may have a direct bearing on the composer's music, I will pass over the events of the next year or two, which finally forced Delius's disillusioned father to send his son to study at the Leipzig Conservatorium.

According to Fenby, Delius said: 'It was not until I began to attend the harmony and counterpoint classes at the Leipzig Conservatorium that I realised the sterling worth of Ward as a teacher. He was excellent for what I wanted to know, and a most charming fellow into the bargain. Had it not been that there were great opportunities for hearing music and talking music, and that I met Grieg, my studies at Leipzig were a complete waste of time. As far as my composing was concerned, Ward's counterpoint lessons were the only lessons from which I ever derived any benefit. Towards the end of my course with him – and he made me work like a nigger – he showed wonderful insight in helping me to find out just how much in the way of traditional technique would be useful to me. ... And there wasn't much. A sense of flow is the main thing, and it doesn't matter how you do it so long as you master it.'

Then came more family upheavals, which were overcome by the influence of Grieg, who persuaded Delius's father to allow his gifted son to pursue the career of a musician. Finally Delius settled in Paris, where, disdaining musical society, he associated freely with painters and writers, such as Gaugin and Strindberg. In 1897 Delius married Jelka Rosen, an artist, who devoted herself to his interests for the rest of his life. They went to live at a charming house in the romantic village of Grez-sur-Loing, near the Forest of Fontainebleau. Robert Louis Stevenson in his *Essays of Travel* has given a vivid description of Grez. 'It lies out of the forest,' he says, 'a cluster of houses with an old bridge and an old castle in ruin, and a quaint old church. The inn garden descends in terraces to the river; stableyard, kailyard, orchard, and a space of lawn, fringed with rushes and embellished with a green arbour. On the opposite bank there is a reach of English-looking plain, set thickly with willows and poplars. And between the two lies the river, clear and deep, and full of reeds and floating lilies. Water-plants cluster about the starlings of the long, low bridge, and stand half-way up upon the piers in green luxuriance. They catch the dipped oar with long antennae, and chequer the slimy bottom with the shadow of their leaves. And the river wanders hither and thither among the islets, and is smothered and broken up by the reeds, like an old building in the lithe, hardy arms of the climbing ivy.' The ruined castle and the old church adjoined Delius's house, which had a long garden sloping down to the quiet river and beyond that the open country.

Delius lived in this lovely, secluded spot until he died in 1934. The scene is important, because he composed the greater part of his finest work there, and therefore Grez was to him what Dorset was to Thomas Hardy, the source or fertiliser of his inspiration. The emotional effect of the beautiful natural scenes and sounds of the countryside was enough to start the flow of Delius's musical semen. And there is no doubt that it was in such circumstances that those lovely tone poems *In a Summer Garden*, *On Hearing the First Cuckoo in Spring*, and *Summer Night on the River* were first conceived.

Philip Heseltine (to whom all writers on Delius and his music must be for ever indebted for his thoughtful and sympathetic book on the composer) has rightly said that the first thing one must realise about Delius's music is that it is the outcome of a profoundly religious nature, and is therefore completely at variance with what is glibly called 'the modern spirit in music'. 'It is considered paradoxical,' continues Heseltine, 'to describe as a religious composer one who, instead of writing anthems and services, turns to nature (and even Nietzsche) for his inspiration; and yet most irreligion is mere reaction against a pretence of religion that would destroy religion, a misconception of the very nature of religion, a confusion of ideas which is of the same order as the credulity of the senses in regard to the sun's apparent motion round the earth.'

Delius's music is perhaps the most difficult of any to write about at length because, comparatively speaking, there is so little variety or contrast in either its mood or its technique. Delius reminds one of a painter like Constable who confines himself to landscapes conceived in colours that are restricted to a limited range of half-lights and nuances. In terms of literature one thinks of Thomas Hardy in so far as the characters and their background in his novels are centred around one corner of England. Thus to know and to love one of Delius's most characteristic works is virtually to know and to love all.

Delius is a composer who upsets all our canons of musical art. Edwin Evans observed that there is only one way to enjoy his music and that is 'to let it float past you as a dream vision of ineffable beauty, the source of which lies in some indefinable region beyond the world of logic and reason; the moment you bring reason to bear upon it the vision begins to fade'. Except for certain slight influences of Grieg in Delius's early works, his music defies classification: it owes little or nothing to any particular tradition or country and it is uninfluenced by the current technical and aesthetic movements of his time.

Eric Fenby tells us in his book that Delius believed music should be a simple and intimate thing, direct and immediate in its appeal from soul to soul, a thing of instinct rather than of learning, of the heart rather than of the head. Fenby quotes a revealing conversation with Delius, who said: 'You can't teach a young musician to compose any more than you can teach a delicate plant how to grow, but you can guide him a little by putting a stick in here and a stick in there. Composition as taught in our academies is a farce. Where are the composers they produce? Those who do manage to survive this systematic and idiotic teaching either write all alike, so that you can say that this lot belongs to this institution, this lot to that, or they give us the flat beer or their teachers, but watered down.'

Indeed, Delius had no time for the intellectual appeal of music: his approach to music was essentially emotional. On one occasion he said to a follower: 'My dear fellow, there is nothing in counterpoint. I have done all that stuff myself. You may take it from me that it leads nowhere.'

Sustained intellectual power is the very thing that Delius lacked. This is noticeable in the very direction where intellect is most needed in composition: in his musical architecture Delius's form is essentially rhapsodic, as may be seen in his beautiful and well-contrived tone poems, such as *Paris*, *On Hearing the First Cuckoo in Spring*, *Song Before Sunrise*, and *Eventyr*.

Even his concertos (for piano, 'cello, violin and 'cello, and violin), full of lovely music as they are, are rhapsodies rather than concertos. Of the four the most successful is the Violin Concerto, which consists of one continuous movement that falls into three sections in contrasted *tempi*. Although the whole conception of this work is unorthodox, as is that of the other concertos, it is perfectly adapted to the composer's intimate and contemplative style. There is little or nothing about the solo part that is showy, but plenty that is decorative. From a purely technical point of view this concerto may not be as effective as other concertos of lesser musical importance, but those who love Delius's music give it a high place among his works, for it is full of the composer's peculiar nostalgic sweetness and bitterness.

The simplest form in musical composition, and perhaps the most completely satisfying, is the theme and variations. Of course, I mean 'simplest' in the general outline of structure rather than in the details of its sectional treatment, for within the limits of a single variation the utmost subtlety and complexity of technique and expression can be exploited. Nevertheless there could be nothing more simple than the basic idea of a theme being repeated a number of times with elaborations and modifications so that it is presented in a series of new guises (or 'fancy dresses'). The possibilities of fresh patterns are as unlimited as those of a Persian carpet. Delius proved this in his very individual and masterly treatments of variation form in his *Dance Rhapsody No. 1*, *Brigg Fair* and *Appalachia*.

Appalachia: *Variations on an old Negro Song*, for orchestra and chorus, was composed in 1902. Appalachia is the old Indian name for North America, and according to the composer the music is intended to mirror 'the moods of tropical nature in the great swamps bordering on the Mississippi river which is so intimately associated with the life of the old Negro slave population. Longing melancholy, an intense love for Nature, childlike humour and an innate delight in dancing and singing are still the most characteristic qualities of the race.'

The work consists of a long introduction (in which the three main themes are introduced), fifteen variations on the Negro song, and a choral epilogue based on the themes of the introduction. Except in the thirteenth variation, which is for unaccompanied chorus, and in the epilogue, the chorus is used (wordless) as a section of the orchestra. *Appalachia* is one of Delius's most beautiful and impressive works and shows exceptional resourcefulness in the handling of the material, particularly from the point of view of harmony and orchestration.

In *Brigg Fair*, which was composed three years later, Delius again gives symphonic continuity to variation form in order to express a poetic idea that is, however, less explicit than in *Appalachia*. The theme is that of an old Lincolnshire folk-song, the words of which tell the story of the simple and true love of a country lass and lad. He vows that should he prove false to her 'the green leaves they shall wither, and the branches they shall die'. The first two verses of the lines prefixed to Delius's score are as follows:

> *It was on the fifth of August,*
> *The weather fine and fair,*
> *Unto Brigg Fair I did repair,*
> *For love I was inclined.*

> *I rose up with the lark in the morning,*
> *With my heart so full of glee,*
> *Of thinking there to meet my dear,*
> *Long time I wished to see.*

Delius has called this work an 'English Rhapsody'. The music sets out to evoke the emotions of the lovers and to give an impression of the quiet beauty of the countryside. It is constructed after the style of a *passacaglia*, which falls into six main but connected sections: an introduction, the theme and six variations, a middle section based on a new theme, eleven more variations on the original theme, and a coda. The introduction is pure impressionism and creates the atmosphere of the peaceful, sun-bathed countryside. Perhaps the most beautiful and moving part of the whole work is the middle section, which Philip Heseltine has described as 'the passionate contentment of a happy love-song sung in the fields to the accompaniment of a softly murmuring wind'. The delicate and expressive scoring has more than a touch of genius about it.

The *Dance Rhapsody No. 1* dates from the same time as *Brigg Fair*, and follows the same kind of constructional plan. As in *Appalachia* and *Brigg Fair*, the theme is continually being repeated in varied harmonic colours of a richly chromatic character, giving the effect of a musical kaleidoscope. Delius's style throughout the whole range of his music is essentially harmonic, and often his melodic ideas derive from harmony.

I have often heard people say that Delius was essentially an English composer and expressed the very spirit of the people. Before making such precise statements it is worth remembering that Delius was a true cosmopolitan, which is shown in some of the subjects of his works: the lovely *North Country Sketches* are mood pictures of the seasons in the Yorkshire countryside; *Appalachia* and the operas *Koanga* and *The Magic Fountain* were inspired by his sojourn in Florida; the tone poem *Paris: A Song of a Great City* is an impression of Paris at night; the orchestral ballad *Eventyr: Once Upon a Time* is intended to evoke the atmosphere of the fairy-tales of Asbjörnsen, the Norwegian writer; and *Song of the High Hills* was inspired by a summer night in the mountains of Norway.

Except for the *North Country Sketches* and *Brigg Fair*, Delius's tone poems that bear pastoral and imaginative titles were inspired by his musings in his own picturesque garden and on the little river that adjoined it at Grez-sur-Loing. I would say that, generally speaking, his music is no more concerned with the English countryside than it is with the French – it is an expression of his own emotions and those alone.

There is, however, one very curious link with Britain, which is that Delius's melodies show certain affinities in style with Celtic folk-song, notably Hebridean. That these affinities were purely unconscious and therefore co-incidental is proved by the fact that Delius knew nothing about Hebridean folk-songs at the time he was forming his own very personal melodic idiom, for they were neither collected nor published until some years later.

Even the tune of *Brigg Fair* is characteristic of Delius, and we find its offspring in that lovely little tone poem *Song before Sunrise*, which was written in 1918 for Philip Heseltine. It is delicate, evocative music scored for a small orchestra in which the strings are treated with typical richness of effect. Both in character and in scale *Song before Sunrise* might well be grouped with those other two masterpieces for small orchestra, *On Hearing the First Cuckoo in Spring* (of which, by the way, the second part of the principal theme is divided from a Norwegian folk-song) and *Summer Night on the River*.

Delius excelled in his use of massed voices as he did in his handling of the orchestra. In most of his choral works the chorus is treated with the same subtle sense of colour as the orchestra: neither one nor the other is predominant – they are fused into a perfect whole. Two of Delius's greatest choral works are *A Mass of Life* and *Sea Drift*.

A Mass of Life, written during the years 1904–5, may be considered a musical confession of faith. It is based on the more lyrical and poetic passages in Nietzsche's *Thus Spake Zarathustra*, and it is, in fact, a hymn in praise of life and all it has to offer rather than of a future life and hope of salvation. It opens with an exhortation to the Will to be strong and inflexible and prepared for triumph. Laughter, song, and dance shall predominate and joy prevail. Zarathustra, the superman, who proclaims the power of laughter, encourages the higher mortals to revelry and lightheartedness. But a note of restlessness creeps in when Zarathustra is assailed by thoughts of love. In the glowing heat of summer noon he sinks into rapturous sleep. In the evening his melancholy returns: the secret sorrows of night are revealed to him and he realises that 'Joy craves eternal, never-ending Day'.

Delius has lavished some of his most beautiful and inspired music on this work. It is infused with a quiet melancholy and wistful resignation, which are a faithful expression of one side of Nietzsche's own personality and philosophy. The *Requiem*, which is a pendant or sequel to the Mass, has been described by Fenby as 'the most depressing choral work I know'.

In the music of *Sea Drift* an impressionistic technique is employed with beautiful and moving effect. The actual writing of the vocal parts is indeed masterly, for each is calculated with unerring judgment, so that one might say that Delius has 'scored' for his vocal forces much in the same way as he has scored for the orchestra. *Sea Drift* has perfect organic growth moving forward to its end, suggesting and underlining the moods and ideas of the poem with rare understanding and subtlety.

Delius's *Sea Drift*, for baritone solo, chorus, and orchestra, is based on the greater part of 'Out of the cradle endlessly rocking', the first of the eleven poems comprising Whitman's *Sea Drift*. The poem tells a tragic little story of two birds who built their nest in a lonely part of the seashore, and a boy who watched them at mating time, 'every day, cautiously peering, absorbing, translating'. One day the she-bird disappeared and was never seen again. 'And thenceforth all summer in the sound of the sea, and at night under the full of the moon . . . I saw, I heard at intervals the remaining one, the solitary guest from Alabama.' The telling of the story is shared by the lonely boy (baritone) and the chorus, which also personifies the he-bird crying out to the wind and the stars to bring back his mate.

Philip Heseltine said, 'It is impossible without quoting the whole poem to give an adequate impression of the wide range of its emotion, and the way in which the passion of the words and music rises and falls with a perfection of poise and cadence that seems to echo the very sound of the sea itself, uniting the story and its setting in a single vision that grips the imagination with an almost uncanny tenacity. In this music we seem to hear the very quintessence of all the sorrow and unrest that man can feel because of love. It is the veritable drama of love and death, an image of the mystery of separation.'

Another beautiful work for chorus and orchestra is *Song of the High Hills*. 'I have tried to express,' said Delius, 'the joy and exhilaration one feels in the mountains, and also the loneliness and melancholy of the high solitudes, and the grandeur of the wide, far distance. The human voices represent Man in Nature – an episode that becomes fainter and then disappears altogether.' To hear this work is for me one of the most moving experiences: it possesses a grandeur, ecstasy, and ethereality that place it among the most beautiful things in the art of music.

It is scored for chorus and a large orchestra, including six horns and a sarrusophone. The chorus, which is treated purely colouristically and therefore may be considered as a part of the orchestra, enters at a section of the work headed 'The wide, far distance – the great solitude'. The vocal parts are wordless throughout, and the singers are instructed to sing on the open vowel best suited to the character of the music. The general effect of this device is indescribably lovely.

Space will permit only passing mention of such beautiful works for unaccompanied chorus as *To be Sung on a Summer Night on the Water* and *On Craig Dhu*, both of which are fine examples of Delius's original treatment of ensemble voices.

Of Delius's six operas (*Irmelin*, *The Magic Fountain*, *Koanga*, *A Village Romeo and Juliet*, *Margot la Rouge*, and *Fennimore and Gerda*) only *A Village Romeo and Juliet* and a few excerpts from the other operas, such as the Prelude to

Irmelin, La Calinda from *Koanga,* and the Idyll for soprano, baritone, and orchestra based on material from *Margot la Rouge,* continue to be heard occasionally. *A Village Romeo and Juliet* and *Fennimore and Gerda* are the only two operas that have been published in their entirety.

Delius's masterpiece in opera is undoubtedly *A Village Romeo and Juliet.* It was composed to a libretto based on Gottfried Keller's novel, and the story concerns the tragic love of a young Romeo and Juliet who suffer through the bitter enmity of their parents. Sali and Vreli are the children of two rich farmers of neighbouring estates. They have played together since childhood, but are forbidden to see each other again after their fathers have quarrelled. They meet again after a cruel separation, and, determined to have one day of pleasure together, they go to a neighbouring fair, happy in each other's company. There they are recognised and worried by importunate questions. Anxious to be alone, they leave the fair and walk to the Paradise Garden, which is 'an old, dilapidated little country house with a rather high veranda, situated in a beautiful garden run wild. Everything shows traces of bygone beauty. In the background a river flows by, and a barge full of hay is moored to the bank. The garden overlooks a long valley through which the river winds its way. In the distance are the snow mountains.' The lovers, however, are not allowed to be alone, for the Dark Fiddler, the evil genius who is an important character in the drama, interferes with them. They finally cast themselves adrift on the barge and scuttle it, with the result that it sinks and they are both drowned.

It is a tragic little story full of mysterious atmosphere, and the music paints the scene and evokes the moods of the characters with a magical charm and accuracy. Between acts five and six comes the exquisite orchestral interlude 'The Walk to Paradise Garden', which is the epitome of the whole drama.

A few words remain to be said about Delius's songs,

piano music and chamber music. He composed a fair number of songs, of which the best, such as *Black Roses*, *Autumn*, *I-Brasil*, and *To Daffodils*, ought long ago to have become established in the repertoire of the great songs of the world. An important characteristic of Delius's style of song-writing is the way the melodic line and the harmonic background are so closely interwoven. Apart from settings of English poems, Delius set poems by Verlaine, Nietzsche, Ibsen, Björnsen and the Danish poet, Jacobsen.

Delius's piano music is practically negligible: a Dance, originally written for harpsichord, and three little Preludes possess charm, but nothing very distinctive in keyboard style. His chamber music, which includes three Sonatas for Violin and Piano, a Sonata for 'Cello and Piano and a String Quartet (No. 2), contains much beautiful music. These works are tone poems rather than sonatas and pay merely lip-service to what we call sonata-form. The music is essentially lyrical and rhapsodic and flows with that ease and continuity so characteristic of the composer's style. But I do not think there is any question that Delius's true medium, in which he showed the full stature of his genius, was the orchestra and the chorus.

Towards the end of his life, when Delius was blind and paralysed, he laboriously dictated to Eric Fenby a number of works, such as *A Song of Summer* for orchestra, the Violin Sonata, No. 3, and *Songs of Farewell* for double choir and orchestra, which was an astonishing feat of concentration and imagination.

I suppose Delius's music will never be widely appreciated. I know no other great composer who is so essentially subjective in appeal. Either you like his music or you do not, and all the study and argument in the world will not help you to come under its magical spell unless the peculiar style of the melody and flavour of the harmony appeal to you from the first. In other words, first reactions count more than with other composers.

Despite the fact that Delius wrote a number of master-pieces, his works are rarely performed, because, unless a conductor is in absolute sympathy with the inner spirit of the music, both he and his orchestra are liable to succumb to a state of boredom that is devastating to the integrity of the music and to the enjoyment and understanding of the audience. The many subtleties of phrasing, colour, and texture make a Delius score one of the most difficult and exacting things to interpret as a vital organic whole.

Delius was the last of the great full-blooded roman-ticists, and most of his finest works are introspective and imbued with a certain sadness and melancholy – nostalgia is probably the more apt term. At these moments one is reminded of 'those dreams whose gossamer is spun out of the invisible threads of sorrow'.

CHAPTER III

Gustav Holst

1874–1934

GERALD ABRAHAM

*

IT is already clear that, like Berlioz, Holst belongs to that small but intensely interesting class of composers about whom there can be no general critical agreement, who are indeed predestined by the nature of their art to be the subjects of very sharp critical disagreement. All intelligent critics are agreed that Haydn was a great composer, Mendelssohn something less than a great composer, Grieg an altogether minor but strikingly individual master; there may be considerable variation of intelligent opinion within those general verdicts, but to disagree with the verdicts as a whole would be to advertise oneself as a born eccentric, a deliberate paradox-monger, or an ass. (All three are species of the same genus.) But one can consider Berlioz as either a highly original genius or an uninspired dullard who handled the orchestra with remarkable dexterity, and in neither case forfeit one's claim to be considered a sane and balanced judge of musical values. The ability to appreciate him is a divine gift, somewhat capriciously distributed; and the distribution has been so severely restricted that the happy recipients dare not dismiss the less fortunate as mere eccentrics. Berlioz is a sort of legitimate 'blind spot'. So is Holst. There is the widest divergence of opinion even about what ought to be demonstrable facts. Some of us – I am one – consider the mature Holst one of the most truly 'original' and individual

composers of the twentieth century; meaning by that, not
that he was without musical ancestors, not that he was
immune from all sorts of influences – if he had been, he
would have been a most undesirable freak – but that in his
best and most representative work these influences, these
traces of ancestry, have been completely and tracelessly
dissolved and absorbed by the quasi-chemical action of
his own creative mind. Yet according to Cecil Gray (*A
Survey of Contemporary Music*) 'his style is a compendium or
pastiche of the styles of nearly all representative modern
composers, which he has equally failed to make his own.
He has no more originality of outlook than any of the
composers mentioned above [Stanford, Parry, Cyril
Scott, Holbrooke, Bantock, Goossens, Bliss, Berners]; if
anything he has less'. Mr Gray would, I think, even deny
Holst the one gift hostile critics usually allow both him
and Berlioz: mastery of the orchestra.

The parallel with Berlioz – beginning with brilliantly
luminous orchestration and continuing through types of
melody that are to some listeners exquisitely sensitive,
to others utterly commonplace, and harmony that is at the
same time simple, forthright, and startlingly unorthodox –
is tempting to work out in some detail. But it is one of
those temptations that have to be resisted if one's
critical object is anything more serious than the filling
of paper with an amusing intellectual game. We shall
learn what Holst really was, not by comparing him
with anyone else, but by looking steadily and concen-
tratedly at *him*.

First of all let us see how he became 'him', tracing
the various stages of his artistic growth through the
pages of his daughter's book.[1] As a foundation we can
postulate thorough familiarity with such classics and

Gustav Holst, by Imogen Holst. O.U.P., 1938. This is so far almost
the only source of biographical material, though it is valuably supplemented for the period 1893–1908 by Fritz Hart's 'Early Memories of
Gustav Holst' in *The R.C.M. Magazine*, Vol. 39, Nos. 2 and 3.

then-contemporaries as would be heard all day and every day in the house of a professional musician in Cheltenham in the 1880's; but only with those. The first personal taste of which we hear was 'a passion for Grieg', and we know that at twelve or thirteen he read Berlioz's *Treatise on Instrumentation* from cover to cover. On the non-musical side he was exposed to theosophy in his stepmother's drawing-room. The earliest composition of which we know anything, the operetta *Lansdowne Castle*, written early in 1893 when Holst was not yet nineteen, according to Fritz Hart 'owed much to two of his earlier loves – Sullivan and Grieg. Sullivan, because *Lansdowne Castle* was a comic opera, and Grieg because he was probably the most approachable of Gustav's boyish gods'. But Hart also speaks of a number 'the melody of which was based on a series of rising fourths', which struck him 'as being more original than it probably was' and melodies or melodic patterns in series of rising fourths[1] were to become a marked feature of Holst's mature style (cf. *Jupiter* in *The Planets*, the finale of the *Choral Symphony*, etc.). The first serious impact after Holst came to London to study at the Royal College of Music was that of Wagner in general and *Tristan* in particular, and Hart tells us that Holst's setting of 'a number beginning "Don your garbs of withering fury, O ye hags of night"' in the children's operetta *Ianthe*, written at this time, 'was something between "The night-wind howls" from *Ruddigore* and the opening music of the *Walküre*, but with quite a dash of himself, I must admit'. *The Idea*, another children's operetta dating from about 1894–5, is unmistakably Sullivanesque – as anyone may see who cares to hire a vocal score from Novello's; for, despite Miss Holst's omission of the very name of the work from the list of her father's compositions, it was published and has not long

[1] According to Edmund Rubbra (article in *The Monthly Musical Record*, July 1935), 'successive melodic fourths' are a noticeable feature of the first movement of the *Cotswolds* Symphony (1900).

been out of print. An opera, *The Magic Mirror*, dating from 1896–7, was condemned by the composer himself as 'all Wagner' and destroyed.

Grieg, Sullivan, Wagner, and a little later Bach and Purcell: and to those we must add in these student and post-student days Stanford's influence as a teacher of the craft of composition and the practical experience of being a trombonist on Brighton Pier, in Wurm's White Viennese Band, with the Carl Rosa Company, and in the Scottish Orchestra. Nor must we overlook the imponderable effect of the friendship with Vaughan Williams, and the more obvious results of successive discoveries in the world of non-musical thought: William Morris (to whose memory Holst dedicated the slow movement of his *Cotswolds* Symphony), Walt Whitman, and (more important even than Whitman) Sanskrit literature. It may be argued that literature and religious philosophy can have no influence on musical style, and that is true generally and with most men; but I cannot help feeling that the teaching of the *Bhagavad Gîtâ*, with its emphasis on 'doing without' and on ignoring the opinion of the world, not only intensified the uncompromising directness of his later work but was to some extent responsible for its bone-dry economy of texture.

The love of Whitman was, musically, the slighter but more lasting influence, manifested first in the unpublished *Walt Whitman* overture of 1899, again in the setting of *The Mystic Trumpeter* for soprano and orchestra (1904), and after that only in two mature works: *A Dirge for Two Veterans* set for male voices, brass, and drums in 1914 in immediate response to the outbreak of the First World War, and the exquisite *Ode to Death* for chorus and orchestra, dedicated to the memory of the young composer Cecil Coles and other friends killed in action (1919). The group of 'Sanskrit' works is more important, larger, and more concentrated in time; it includes the three-act opera *Sita* (1899–1906), the symphonic poem *Indra* (1903), the nine solo *Hymns from the 'Rig Veda'* (1907–8), the little chamber opera *Sāvitri* (1908), the fourteen choral *Hymns from the 'Rig Veda'* (1908–12), *The Cloud Messenger* for chorus and orchestra (1910), and the *Two Eastern Pictures* for women's voices and harp (1911). Yet although one can speak of Holst's 'Sanskrit period' in a biographical sense, one cannot do so in a musical sense, for these Sanskrit works cover the whole of his evolution from Wagnerian discipleship to the attainment of full artistic maturity. The grandiose three-act *Sita*, on which Holst worked for seven years and which lost the Ricordi prize for the best English opera to E. W. Naylor's *The Angelus* in 1908, was a failure. Years later Holst used to speak of it as his 'Wagnerian opera', 'good old Wagnerian bawling'. 'So it was, to a certain extent,' comments Professor Hart,

yet at the time of its making he was so steeped in his Sanskrit studies that there was a most un-Wagnerian element in its spiritual conception. Wagner with his feverish mental activity seized upon any philosophy that would serve his creative needs at the moment, but Gustav had absorbed the spirit of the *Bhagavad Gîtâ* so deeply that it had become an essential part of himself, and was always to remain so. Thus, though it was obvious that Gustav had assimilated much of the Wagner of *The Ring*, including something of the Wagner of its more grandiose moments, there was still a great deal – in my opinion – of what was the genuine Holst in *Sita*, especially in those passages which were expressive of his blunt, direct and sometimes even rather gauche sincerity.

Moreover, *Sita* 'helped him to get Wagner out of his system and thus made it possible for him to write the beautiful *Sāvitri* two years later'. Certainly no opera could be less Wagnerian than *Sāvitri*, lasting just half an hour, with three characters and practically no scenery ('This piece is intended for performance in the open air, or else in a small building', says a note in the score), with an orchestra of two string quartets, a double-bass, two flutes, a cor anglais, and a female chorus vocalising on a single vowel. There is no prelude, though one of the choral *Hymns from the 'Rig Veda'* – the *Hymn of the Travellers* for female voices and harp – may be used if one is required, and for the first forty-two bars the voices of Death and Sāvitri are heard unaccompanied. The work ends similarly with the unsupported voice of Sāvitri dying away in the distance. No opera could more austerely discard everything that appeals to an audience; *Sāvitri* flouts every operatic convention since the Florentine primitives of 1600. The physical action could hardly be simpler – the coming of Death to the woodman Satyavān and his defeat by the devotion of Satyavān's wife Sāvitri – and the heart of the thing lies in what the characters say. Every word must be audible and Holst was content to set the words to a sort of melodic recitative (tracing its ancestry from Purcell rather than Wagner), freely rhythmised and supported by only the most transparent accompaniment. There are few attempts at sensuous beauty of sound, though those few – such as the choral background when Sāvitri greets Death, *Welcome, Lord, Thou art called the Just One* – are memorable. *Sāvitri* is an opera for spiritual and intellectual aristocrats, for such audiences as those that gathered at the house of Giovanni Bardi, Count of Vernio, at the end of the *cinquecento*.

What was responsible for this return to the spirit and almost the manner of Peri's *Euridice*? Partly, of course, the more deeply working influence of Hindu thought, but much more, I believe, the musical influence of English folk-song. It was only about 1905 that Holst had become aware of its existence. Love of the English countryside had always been an important part of his make-up; he used to boast that he was 'a Cotswold man'; but apparently the unpublished *Cotswolds* Symphony of 1900 had no connection with folk-song. Now he discovered it and discovered that it corresponded to his own musical ideals. (We tend to forget that in a sense a creative artist 'chooses' his influences; an influence cannot make itself deeply felt unless it corresponds to something in himself.) Now, his daughter tells us, he found that the tunes had the simplicity and economy that he felt to be essential in any great art. They combined an emotional beauty with an impersonal restraint. The words and the music had grown up together, and there was a spontaneous freedom in the rhythm that made each phrase sound inevitable. Like most other people who come under the spell of folk-music, he was soon saturated in the sound of the Dorian and Aeolian modes, and for a time he found that open fifths and flattened sevenths were a necessary part of his life. He tried setting several of the tunes, but his piano accompaniments were not always a success, for it was difficult to grow out of the chromatic habits of the last twelve years. But folk-songs finally banished all traces of Wagner from his work.

The first obvious fruits of the new enthusiasm were the *Two Songs without Words* (*Country Song* and *Marching Song*) for small orchestra (1906) and the *Somerset Rhapsody* for orchestra, dedicated to Cecil Sharp (1906–7), and it is amusing to observe how 'the chromatic habits' and Griegish harmonies peep out here and there in the *Rhapsody* (cf. pp. 5, 15, and above all 22–3 of the miniature score). But traces of imperfectly absorbed Grieg survive in Holst's music as late as the coda of the *Intermezzo* of the *St Paul's Suite* for strings (1913). Holst continued to arrange folk-songs and weave them into his compositions in later years – the *Second Suite* in F, for military band (1911), the *St Paul's Suite*, the *Six Choral Folk-Songs* (1916), the finale of the *Fugal Concerto* for flute, oboe, and strings (1923), the Falstaff opera *At the Boar's Head* (1924), the handful of piano pieces written during 1924–7, and the arrangements of *Twelve Welsh Folk-Songs* (1930–1)[1] – but he can hardly be described as belonging to the 'folk-song school', for folk-songs or imitations of folk-songs constitute only a very small proportion of his output, and even that proportion is smaller than might appear from the little list just given; three of the tunes arranged as the *Six Choral Folk-Songs* had previously been used in the F major

[1] He also introduced genuine exotic themes in his two Oriental suites, *Beni Mora* (1910) and the *Japanese Suite* (1915).

Suite for military band – and the finale of the Suite, the *Fantasia on the Dargason*, was transferred bodily to the *St Paul's Suite*. No; the most valuable results of the enthusiasm for English folk-song were the purification and simplification of style, the spell of the modes and the new flexibility and freedom of vocal line. It is thus less a parodox than it may at first appear to suggest that *Sāvitri* was composed under the influence of English folk-music; indeed, there are a few traces here and there of more direct folk-influence on the melodic shapes of *Sāvitri* (for instance, Satyavān's *Farewell, friend, until the morn; To a fairer love I go* at his first appearance). Similarly, I fancy I detect a trace of sublimated Grieg melody in Sāvitri's *Thy thoughts are mine, My spirit dwells with thee*, which again is echoed in the *Intermezzo* of the *St Paul's Suite*.

Sāvitri was Holst's first really characteristic work, and practically everything he wrote after that is marked by his personal methods, if not always by his inner personality. The compositions of the next five or six years are truly Holstian in what they exclude rather than what they include. Delightful as some of them are – notably the two military-band Suites and the *St Paul's* – they are not very important, though they are thoroughly characteristic of Holst's practical, workmanlike attitude to the craft of music-making, – the attitude later revealed in his willingness to make even his most ambitious scores more easily playable by cueing in substitute instruments. The most notable works of this period are extensions of the thought-world of *Sāvitri* in various media: *The Cloud Messenger* for chorus and orchestra, and the seven 'groups' of *Hymns from the 'Rig Veda'*, three for solo voice and piano, one for mixed chorus and orchestra, one for women's voices and orchestra, one for women's voices and harp, and one for men's voices and string orchestra with brass *ad lib.*, twenty-three hymns in all. It is significant that perhaps the finest and musically the most Holstian, if one must choose a 'most', is the *Funeral Hymn*, the third of the first choral 'group':

> *Away, O Death, thy work is ended now,*
> *Far from us on thy lonely path go thou,*
> *The path on which no other God may tread,*
> *This mound we raise doth part us from the dead.*

The idea of Death, Death as an awful yet not unkind Being, 'lovely and soothing death, serenely arriving', always fascinated Holst and drew from him some of his best music: in *Sāvitri*, in the later *Ode to Death*, and in this solemn but triumphant *Funeral Hymn*.

But the works on which Holst's reputation mainly rests, the first works of full maturity and those whose greatness is least open to question, are those of the decade 1914–24: above all, *The Planets*, a suite for large orchestra (1914–16), the *Four Songs for Voice and Violin* (1916–17), *The Hymn of Jesus* for two choruses, semi-chorus, and orchestra (1917), the *Ode to Death* for chorus and orchestra (1919), and perhaps the one-act comic opera *The Perfect Fool* (1918–22) and the *Choral Symphony* (1923–4), though some would put them in the 'questionable' class. It happens that the beginning of this period coincides with what his daughter describes as his 'wild excitement over the re-discovery of the English madrigal composers', particularly Weelkes, whom he considered 'the real musical embodiment of the English character in his fantastic unexpectedness'; but I say 'happens' advisedly, for I can detect no immediate reflection of this excitement in his own music.

The Planets resulted from Holst's interest in astrology, then recently heightened by a holiday with Clifford Bax in the spring of 1913. In a letter quoted by his daughter in her biography, he wrote:

As a rule I only study things that suggest music to me. That's why I worried at Sanskrit. Then recently the character of each planet suggested lots to me, and I have been studying astrology fairly closely. It's a pity we make such a fuss about these things. On one side there's nothing but abuse and ridicule, with the natural result that when one is brought face to face with overwhelming proofs there is a danger of going to the other extreme.

It has often been said, and Miss Holst repeats, that 'once he had taken the underlying idea from astrology, he let the music have its way with him'. But a passage in an article by Marion M. Scott[1] suggests that Holst may have allowed himself here and there to be guided not only by the general astrological significance of the particular planet but by some specific property of its influence.

Turn to *Uranus, the Magician*. According to ancient beliefs in the lore of numbers, 16 was called 'The falling tower', or 'Uranus number'. Its unpleasant property was that just when everything was going splendidly and seeming on the point of fulfilment all would be dashed away and the victim left with nothing but his misery. Listen to the last bars of Holst's *Uranus* where the old Magician works up his enchantment into a terrific chord that blazes through the whole orchestra and then suddenly collapses into a moan and nothingness. Surely there is the Uranus number!

All the same *The Planets* are in no sense programme music. One must accept them as seven pieces of 'absolute' music, individually and collectively among the most remarkable and individual compositions of the twentieth century. There may still be traces here and there of not wholly absorbed influences: Holst might not have hit upon the staccato bassoon colour near the beginning of *Uranus* if Dukas had never associated staccato bassoons with magic in *L'Apprenti Sorcier*; the white loveliness of the serene alternating chords of *Venus, the Bringer of Peace* (or the bleaker, alternating ninth chords of *Saturn, the Bringer of Old Age* – like the similar alternating-chord passages in *The Hymn of Jesus* and *The Perfect Fool*) may derive at second-hand through the end of Vaughan Williams's *Sea Symphony* from passages in Elgar's *Gerontius*, and the truly jovial *molto pesante* tune for strings and horns in *Jupiter, the Bringer of Jollity* carries an echo of Sullivan's Private Willis. But it would be preposterous to base on these recollected

[1] In *The Listener*, 18 May 1944.

particles, each three-quarters dissolved in the alembic of Holst's creative imagination, a charge of unoriginality. Each movement of *The Planets* is based on material that could have been conceived by no one but Holst, and treated as no one but Holst could have thought of treating it. The treatment may sometimes be open to criticism. Holst had a somewhat square and primitive conception of formal structure and he makes no effort to conceal his joins; he sometimes cuts technical problems, instead of solving them, as in the escape from the magnificent central melody of *Jupiter* (which anyhow gives one the impression of not really belonging to the movement) back to the bustle and jollity. But that very squareness and downrightness is Holstian.

It is equally wrong to dismiss *The Planets* merely as a series of brilliant essays in orchestration. Each *Planet* is an experience – for those capable of experiencing Holst. The unsusceptible can talk only about things like the mercilessly incessant 5/4 rhythmic figure of *Mars, The Bringer of War*; they seem to miss the emotionally shattering effect of the terrible, hollow, wind chords that surge up against that figure. And each movement is a completely different experience; it is not merely a play on words to say that each transports one to a different planet, a different air. Air – that is the element common to all *The Planets*; a sense of vast timeless space, of air exceedingly pure and rarefied. To show how Holst achieves this would require a lengthy technical dissertation with numerous music-type examples, but if I were asked to name the one characteristic that is more Holstian than any other I should say 'the relentless, undeviating continuation of opposed lines and patterns': the brutal opposition of rhythms in *Mars*, the opposition of chords of the seventh on different instrumental groups moving against each other in the third bar of *Venus*, the opposition of 6/8 and 3/4 in *Mercury* (and its inferior companion-piece, the *Dance of the Marionette* in the *Japanese Suite*), the opposition of sharply-defined orchestral patterns in *Jupiter* and *Uranus* or of utterly nebulous ones in *Neptune, the mystic,* which shares with *Saturn* the distinction of being one of the most remarkable purely impressionistic, practically non-thematic pieces of music ever written.

In *The Hymn of Jesus,* a setting of the composer's own translation of words from the apocryphal *Acts of St John,* again with a very large orchestra, the same technique of relentless pattern-drawing produces effects of blinding mystical revelation. 'Mysticism' in music commonly reveals itself – at any rate in modern times – in terms of luscious emotionalism (Franck, Skryabin, Elgar). Holst's ascetic mysticism is totally different. There is a celebrated passage in *The Hymn of Jesus* where, at the words 'To you who gaze, a lamp am I: To you that know, a mirror', one choir reiterates a chord while the other moves down semitonally, so that on 'gaze' and 'know' the two choirs are dwelling in a longish *crescendo* on two full chords a semi- tone apart. One has the sensation – which I take to be what is known as 'a mystical experience' – of momentarily piercing through this muddy vesture of decay to a glimpse of some infinite truth. To Tovey, on first reading the score 'the words seemed to shine in the light and depth of a vast atmosphere created by the music'. And he admirably de- scribes Holst's technical eclecticism in the *Hymn* (and all his other most typical works):

The resources of its style range through all the centuries in which music has been intelligible to western ears down to the present day. There is no essential novelty in the musical aesthetics of Strauss, nor in the diametrically opposite musical aesthetics of Ravel, which may not be found in this score, and found in its clearest and simplest form. There is no musical truth known to Palestrina that is not also to be found here, if our analysis is broad enough and deep enough to reach the fundamental prin- ciples. There are older truths still, truths of musical resonance that are older than Palestrina's classical harmony.[1]

[1] *Essays in Musical Analysis*, Vol. V O.U.P., 1937.

Yet one does not get an impression of a mixture of techniques; Holst knew how to get what he needed from various techniques, but he wrote, at the height of his powers, in only one style: his own. Equally in that style are the remarkable *Four Songs for Voice and Violin*, conceived on the smallest scale and with an almost irreducible minimum of resources, which Holst himself considered among his most successful essays in mating words with music. In an important letter to W. G. Whittaker, quoted in Imogen Holst's book, he wrote:

I find that *unconsciously* I have been drawn for years towards discovering the (or *a*) musical idiom of the English language. Never having managed to learn a foreign language, songs had always meant to me a peg of words on which to hang a tune. The great awakening came on hearing the recitatives in Purcell's *Dido*. ... Well, I didn't get very far in *Sita*, I fear. But in the *Vedas* matters improved, and in the *Cloud Messenger* and *Sāvitri*, especially the latter, the words and music really grew together. Since then I've managed now and then to do the same thing with other people's words, especially in the violin songs. (*My Leman* is a good instance of a tune at one with the words.) But in all this there is no conscious principle, no 'ideal', no axe to grind. And I may do something quite different tomorrow.

The *Ode to Death* is a similar essay in the problem of setting English words naturally in an English idiom; Holst solved it with beautiful success, being deeply moved by a favourite theme. If he was less successful in *The Perfect Fool* it was not because the subject was comic, but because in comic opera one must write *tunes* – and by tunes we always mean a more instrumental type of melody. Now there are a number of good tunes in *The Perfect Fool* – Holst did not absorb Sullivan for nothing, as Sullivan himself had not absorbed Schubert for nothing – and there is an enormous amount of skilful handling of colloquial English, but the two tend to get in each other's way: a good tune gets tripped up by good declamation. The well-known ballet music, written a couple of years before the rest of the opera (indeed, one theme of the *Dance of Spirits of Fire* was borrowed, with improvements, from the *Intermezzo* of the *St Paul's Suite*), is the only part of the *Fool* we have opportunities of hearing nowadays, but in a future distant enough to give some sort of 'period' interest to the fourth-form humours of the libretto it will be revived – with Vaughan Williams's *The Poisoned Kiss* – and our grandchildren will rave over the beauties of the score, while solemn German or American scholars will write solemn dissertations on 'the "facetious school" of English opera'. For unfortunately Holst had not absorbed Gilbert for nothing, either, and Gilbert's facetiousness without Gilbert's wit or polish or ingenious paradoxes is enough to sink the most brilliant of scores. Elgar, too, possessed perhaps even more of this peculiarly English, grown-up-schoolboy type of humour, but it is confined to his letters; it never escapes into his music. But I repeat: a generation to whom the libretto is no longer an obstacle will find *The Perfect Fool* a masterpiece of its kind.

In 1923 February Holst fell off a platform at University College, Reading, striking the back of his head and suffering slight concussion. He appeared to recover quickly, but the after-effects of the accident, fully apparent only a year later, were serious and almost indisputably affected his later compositions. What is disputable is whether the accident affected their quality or only their nature, whether its effect was physically to dry up the springs of Holst's imagination or spiritually to drive it in upon itself and intensify its natural austerity and bareness of utterance. The *Fugal Concerto* of 1923 was perhaps the earliest of Holst's works to be described as 'desiccated', and the much more important *Choral Symphony* on poems by Keats, for soprano solo, chorus, and orchestra (1923–4), earned only the 'cold admiration' of such a sympathetic critic as Vaughan Williams. Perhaps that adjective is less disparaging than it sounds; cold can penetrate and thrill. 'My soul has nought but fire and ice' begins the second of the *Songs for Voice and Violin*, and in art as in physics extreme cold is very like extreme heat. In some of his later works Holst seems to be striving toward absolute zero, not through mere negation of emotion but through intense refinement of emotion. Yet the coldest portion of the *Choral Symphony* – the *Grecian Urn* slow movement – is only a few degrees cooler than *Venus* or *Saturn*[1] or *Neptune*, and there are plenty of 'warmer' moments in the symphony, the glittering sonority of the *Bacchanal*, the golden richness of the finale, the free, flexible curves of the solo part, the truly Holstian tunefulness of the setting of *Folly's Song*, which forms the trio of the scherzo. The chords of piled-up fourths in the first and last movements (another modern device 'in its clearest and simplest form') are a natural consequence of the figuration in *Jupiter*. The two superimposed chords a semitone apart, which give us that piercing revelation in *The Hymn of Jesus*, are now so familiar to Holst (not yet to most of us) that he can invent a melody – the theme of the scherzo, 'Ever let the Fancy roam' – on the arpeggio that they make together, as easily and naturally as Wagner invented melodies on the arpeggio of the added sixth. At the beginning of the *Grecian Urn* the cool alternation of the semitone-distant chords directly evokes 'quietness ... silence and slow time' and that far-off world with its loves 'all breathing human passion far above'.

It is this distance from 'all breathing human passion' that disconcerts so many people in the music of Holst's last period. Fritz Hart suggests that this distance was due to the influence of Stravinsky:

It was from Stravinsky he assimilated the notion of music as something which should be dissociated from emotion. Gustav, perhaps, did not go quite so far as Stravinsky; but he once told me, most earnestly, that composers should sternly eschew what he described as the 'domestic' emotions'. On one occasion he said to a common friend for whose integrity I can vouch, 'When

[1] *Saturn, the Bringer of Old Age*, was Holst's own favourite *Planet*.

I sit down to compose it is as though I were a mathematician attacking some absorbingly interesting problem.'

His daughter tells us that he held sentimentality to be 'the supreme crime in art' and that his pupils in consequence 'shied away, not only from sentimentality, but from sentiment itself'. He simplified the original harmonies of the 'nightingale' lines in the finale of the *Choral Symphony*, 'which were too mild and luscious for my taste'. Doubtless his physical state during the last ten years strengthened his natural tendencies. Miss Holst has given us some terrible and moving pictures of her father 'sitting huddled over the fire, sinking lower and lower into a grey region where thought and feeling had ceased to exist, and the spirit itself was numb', and listening to the first public performance of his *Twelve Songs* to words by Humbert Wolfe (1929) 'so weary that he scarcely heard a note. ... His mind was closed in a grey isolation. He had sunk, once more, into that cold region of utter despair'. And she has described, too, how at that same concert he was thawed by the warmth of Schubert's C major Quintet: 'as he listened to it, he realized what he had lost, not only in his music but in his life. ... At the moment, it seemed as if this warmth might be the only thing worth having.'

Nothing, of course, is easier than to represent that 'moment' as a painful glimpse of his own sterility and the works of the last decade as mournful attempts to squeeze something out of that sterility – successful only here and there in the *Seven Part Songs* to words by Robert Bridges (1925–26), which have considerable affinity with the earlier *Songs for Voice and Violin*, some of the Humbert Wolfe songs, or the *Lyric Movement* for viola and orchestra and the *Brook Green Suite* for strings (both 1933), the last a second *St Paul's Suite* in everything but name. But personally I see little in the last works that is not latent in the early ones. (The anti-Holstian, of course, retorts that

Holst always was half-impotent, musically.) Stravinsky's theories may have played their part – his music certainly did not – but Holst was anything but a doctrinaire composer. Illness undoubtedly drove him inward, but only as Beethoven's deafness drove *him* inward. But austerity, economy, everything in him that was truly classical – he was perhaps the first 'classical' English composer since Purcell – that rejected the 'domestic' emotions : all these were characteristic of *Sāvitri* and *The Planets* and *The Hymn of Jesus*. (Even *The Planets* is economical in everything but orchestral resource.) It is only that these characteristics are intensified in *Egdon Heath* (1927), the *Double Concerto* for two violins and orchestra (1929) with its fine 'Variations on a Ground', the Humbert Wolfe songs, the orchestral prelude and scherzo *Hammersmith* (1930), and the *Choral Fantasia*, on words by Robert Bridges, for soprano solo, chorus, organ, strings, brass, and percussion (1930), a sadly neglected masterpiece. No one would claim that Holst was always successful, and one of his undisputed failures was the one-act opera *At the Boar's Head* (1924), an ingenious attempt to mate the unaltered words of the Falstaff scenes of *Henry IV* with English folk-tunes – with unhappy consequences for both words and tunes.[1] The two choral ballets, *The Golden Goose* and *The Morning of the Year* (1926–27), may be counted half-successes, relatively unambitious works looking back spiritually through *The Perfect Fool* almost to the youthful world of the children's operettas. Holst himself seems to have regarded the two-movement *Terzetto* for flute, oboe, and viola (1924) as a mere experiment, for the score disappeared and was published only twenty years later. The experiment is in polytonality – the flute plays in A, the oboe in A flat, and the viola in C – and personally I find the result not only natural but charming, though the work is not an important one: just

[1] Like *Sāvitri*, *At the Boar's Head* opens with an unaccompanied voice – Bardolph's – behind the curtain.

another example of a very modern device used 'in its clearest and simplest form' to produce music that could have been made in no other way – and was well worth making. Holst was much interested in polytonality during the last decade, witness the *Double Concerto*, *Hammersmith*, and the *Six Canons* for equal voices (1932).

But the quintessential Holst of the last period is to be found in the orchestral impression of *Egdon Heath* and *Betelgeuse*, the first of the Humbert Wolfe songs. *Egdon Heath* was inspired partly by the famous opening chapter of *The Return of the Native*, partly by a walk over the Heath itself (Wareham Heath) at Easter 1926. 'He knew for certain that it was the best thing he had ever written', says his daughter. 'It was still his favourite work at the time of his death.' And Hardy's description of Egdon might almost be applied not only to Holst's orchestral piece but to his later music in general:

> Haggard Egdon appealed to a subtler and scarcer instinct, to a more recently learnt emotion, than that which responds to the sort of beauty called charming and fair. Indeed, it is a question if the exclusive reign of this orthodox beauty is not approaching its last quarter. ...

Egdon Heath must be one of the slowest and quietest orchestral pieces ever written. And like most of Holst's compositions it is short: just twenty-five pages of score, playing for less that a quarter of an hour. That prevailing shortness springs from several causes: from the neuritis that had made the physical act of writing music indescribably burdensome all his life, that had obliged him to use amanuenses and had exaggerated his mannerism of *ostinato* bass-figures through the ease with which they could be indicated by repeat-signs, from incapacity for large-scale musical construction (his most serious limitation), but also from his positive gift for saying much in a few notes. Simplicity and compression have seldom been carried farther in English music that in *Egdon Heath*.

So in *Betelgeuse* that already simple but potent device of magic – the juxtaposition of triads a semitone apart – is still further simplified to a juxtaposition of bare fifths a semitone apart. C, F, C, gives out the piano in octaves, and then B, E, B; and we are removed at once to the timeless, spaceless world where

> *the gold leaves hang in golden aisles*
> *for twice a hundred million miles,*
> *and twice a hundred million years*
> *they golden hang and nothing stirs,*
> > *on Betelgeuse.*

Humbert Wolfe's poem is as important as Hardy's chapter in helping us to understand the infinite remoteness of Holst's last period, and the choice of Betelgeuse seems symbolic. Fifteen years earlier Holst had been content to write music for the planets of our own solar system; even there he had seemed sometimes to stretch out as far as musical thought can reach into limitless space, but most of us managed to follow him. But the planets were too near for the later Holst, too closely linked with human destinies – bringing war and peace, and jollity and old age. His mind was set on that distant star where 'there is nothing that joys or grieves ... nor ghost of evil or good', nor birth, nor death,

> *and the God, of whom we are*
> *infinite dust, is there*
> *a single leaf of those*
> *gold leaves on Betelgeuse.*

CHAPTER IV

'Peter Warlock' (Philip Heseltine)
1894–1930

HUBERT FOSS

*

THE act of singing is not confined to the inhabitants of these islands. Yet it is so characteristic of the English (a term I prefer to British, to include the Welsh and the Scots) that unexaggerated truth may say, in general, that the history of English music is found in song. During the darker ages between Purcell and Parry, what trickle there was from the English musical spring flowed either through the dimmer channels of the church or through the brilliantly lit but not much brighter canal of the stage. Singing, as an act, went on. The peoples retained not only a love for singing but a tradition of it, and a thousand candle-lit retiring-rooms sounded to the voice and harp, while a single concert or a forlorn opera was performed before empty benches. To Germany and Naples we look for instrumental music in history: to England we look for song. And (as I have occasionally said elsewhere, in varying words), if you compare them, you will find an instrumental part in Vaughan Williams's *Pastoral* Symphony more vocal in essence than the voice part of, say, Hindemith's song cycle, *Marienleben*.

Yet, ever since Handel, who fostered that desire for 'music from elsewhere' which still besets us, we have been officially taught that English is an unvocal language, awkward and unmaidenly, clipped in consonants and thin in vowels. The great divorce between 'voice and verse', which made Milton acclaim even Lawes as the link between the 'twin-born harmonious Sisters', has been allowed to continue in unnatural severance, largely, I suspect, because of the total ignorance of the English language and the tradition of its verse among many who sing and (later) teach singing. Actually the English language is extremely flexible as a medium for verse, and (in corollary) an admirable medium for song. Who has done better with other languages than Campion, Dowland, and Purcell with their own?

To English song Peter Warlock devoted his main activities as a composer. He was assailed by doubts whether he would not find more success in writing other kinds of music: he essayed, but he stuck, finally, to song. He was right. It would be impertinent, and in myself incredulous of a fundamental truth, not to assume in this book that there has been a revival of musical composition in England since the 1880's. The release of the mainspring of that revival was caused by the 1914–18 war – that precipitation of physical horrors in reaction to the post-Victorian complacency that succeeded the nineties. Warlock came in one way at the right moment. Song was wanted, but unfortunately not Warlock's kind of song. Twenty-five years afterwards, some of us are still wondering why the lessers, the feeblers, the 'let's-go-back-to-ballads', are still standing in the way of Warlock's proper appreciation. Hugo Wolf was ill-hearted in his day, but he was a native of a country that commanded musical attention. There is a complete corpus of Wolf songs. No one publisher in English has been so enlightened, thus far, even by collaboration, as to produce a complete Warlock in handy volumes. I commend the idea as a worthy piece of English propaganda.

A national revival in music, if it be alive at all, must take on a giant's robe, and hope that its failures will be condoned by sympathy and by the appeal of its national idiom. The waste spaces in the bibliographies of Glinka and Smetana and Pedrell are sad reading, while of Parry and Stanford today we never hear a single major work. Those major works had to be written, whether in blood and tears or in the complacent joy of achievement. But the question arises whether we do right to assess a country's music by its major works or by its general musical trend and inclination. We are still the victims of the Industrial Revolution in our desire for the magnificent and magniloquent: the 'kolossal' period may have left us, but we are still impressed by statistics of size. A million or two people mishandled and miserable on London's Underground are still to us of greater significance than a man with his wife and child comfortably and punctually arriving at their destination in a brougham. Under this system of critical regimentation, with the sergeant-major's voice shouting 'Tallest on the right, shortest on the left', we conceive that a bad symphony cannot avoid being better than a first-class song. We have forgotten the thought behind the Bible story which says 'and after the fire a still, small voice'. Debussy, almost silent amid the Wagnerian trumpetings and the heavy texture of Brahms, should have taught us. We still have to learn.

Against this conception of grandiloquence as a virtue, Peter Warlock was completely and naturally in revolt. He had far too much sense of humour, far too much sense of art as a confluence of perfect details, to be impressed by Holst's picture of the Universe, or by Bantock's unvarying scene-paintings of Omar Khayyám and the Song of Solomon, or by Holbrooke's and Howard de Walden's Welsh National trilogy (have I got the number right?). He himself wrote in a letter: 'When I think of the "monumental" composers in present-day England alone, I feel that I would rather spend my life trying to achieve one book of little songs that shall have a lasting fragrance, than pile up tome upon tome on the dusty shelves of the British Museum.' Warlock saw himself, quite clearly, as neither a Delacroix nor a Rubens. In a picture gallery, we do not always measure beauty by the area of the canvas, and Warlock was piercingly, sometimes even bitterly, clear of the size that he could fill to satisfy himself. The canvases, then, are small. We ourselves must discover, as we have with Wolf, whether the musical material is big or whether it is just rapid and transient. For myself I cannot believe that it is not big in Warlock.

Hubert Parry was a very remarkable man, a great teacher, a personality of importance, a musician of vast and ramifying energy. He made it possible for an Englishman to be a musician without being suspected of not being a gentleman. By far the most enduring of Parry's compositions are his smaller vocal works: and of those his songs form a large part. He brought back fine verse into song for its own sake, and in doing so he created a new tradition of song, where in English voice and verse came together, inevitably, again. It was to this new heritage of English music that Peter Warlock brought his incisive mind, his quick reactions, his passion for detail, and his widely ranging emotional experience. He made it live anew.

Warlock's complete musical output was not very extensive; compared with Purcell's, for example, who died at the same young age of thirty-six, or with Schubert's, who lived to be only thirty-one, it is small. That Warlock had not the almost universal range of Purcell is not to be wondered at, for Purcell lived in an age when musicians were, first, practitioners and, secondly, composers. Warlock was no executant, and shunned any thought of being a performer: on the other hand, he was a scholar and critic of a most eclectic type, and that quality of mind, apart from his technical limitations, undoubtedly curbed the rein of his musical fancy. He ground out few bars of music to keep the pot (or tankard) boiling: he was no devotee of note-spinning, of blowing up frog-ideas into bull-like proportions. He had little liking for scene-painting, for the vague sweeping line that means so little, even if seen from afar. Therefore, in looking at his works, we who follow him can be thankful that we are not confronted with acres of musical thistles and bindweed, but can keep within the confines of a comparatively well-ordered garden – of somewhat Elizabethan pattern.

The published works of Warlock actually comprise approximately one hundred songs, a few short choral works, three orchestral pieces, and an odd unclassified work or two. Of the transcriptions from and editions of older music, some short mention will be made below.

Within that small space is encompassed a rare and varied mind; not offering, it may be thought, a very large quantity of crotchets and quavers written down by the hand to sound to the ears of listeners. A glance at a Warlock manuscript will give a different opinion. Warlock wrote with exquisite precision: not only had the figured bass ceased to be an idiomatic shorthand, but also the shape of the note-heads, the uprights, the binds and ties, were of enormous interest to him. He wrote his crotchets and quavers in a handwriting exactly as precise as his ear demanded of the singer and player that they should reproduce his sounds. A Warlock manuscript is a joy to see, and to play from. It has some remote personal quality entirely different from the precision of an engraved score. I have often regretted, as a printer, having to submit such a delicate piece of craftsman-ship as those MSS. of his to the freehand but comparatively mechanical devices of the punch and the graver. That he could not play what he finally wrote on paper is of no con-cern: there he joined the great company of honest com-posers who use the piano when composing (for whatever medium). He played over his own songs with great (if in-accurate) pains, and when he came to a difficult passage he played on, but slower. Others were neither allowed nor expected to follow the composer's lead. As performance by professionals approached, their technical comments and advice were unavailing. The critic part of his mind stepped in, at once. The sounds he wanted were written down, and that is something to say of a composer: they had to be played and sung to please him.

To the cultivation of his small plot of land, Warlock brought quite extraordinary talents. Only in his music, if you, as a reader, become familiar with it, can you cull the flowers. In contrast to his narrow output, Warlock's mind was acutely receptive. He had, as it were, a mind like a funnel – an enormous trough at one end, his mental-receiving end, and a narrow channel for the outlet. Only, there were three channels (at least) – the scholar, the critic, the composer. Each had a nozzle, directed with some force on to the flammable object.

Concerned as we are with Warlock's composer-vent, we must not forget the receiving funnel which supplied the artistic chemicals. While still at Eton, he came under the influence of Delius's music, and thence there sprang up a friendship with the composer, which lasted for many years. Elizabethan literature attracted him when he was at Oxford. A little later, Bernard van Dieren, an astonishing person both in himself and in his music, pulled a third way. Evidence of each influence is amply shown in the music – one can even see the elbow of Grieg showing through the mantle of Delius if one looks at the only and early piano work – *Folk-song Preludes*. But these were impacts, and no more, upon a vitally active mind, turning its course for a time here and there, but never impeding the main stream of developing genius. The sense of English literature developed especially, and it is not to be wondered that those three influences awoke in Warlock an endemic feeling for the remote, the macabre, the 'romantic' in the Hoffman sense. Warlock was no calm liver, no philosophic hermit: a hedonist, he went out to explore life's possibilities, and succeeded in doing so. He was, himself, a curious relic of the nineties. He combined in one person the characteristics of an Elizabethan like Thomas Nashe and a *fin de siècle* Victorian like Aubrey Beardsley. He had the delicacy of the hothouse plant and the ebullience of the willow-herb that grows on ruined bomb-sites. Humour in plenty, shyness of an odd kind, a roaring laugh that would give way to a fit of solitude and melancholy – there was Warlock, the man who exquisitely poised the psychologists' requirements of both introvert and extrovert. Add to this an eclectic taste quite out of the common, an almost desperate sense of precision, and a love of male company over pint pots, and you begin to have the man who wrote the music – the hollow end of the funnel.

Sincerity is a misused word in art, because it is applied, in its artistic sense, only to life. That Warlock had an artistic sincerity denied to Hubert Parry I make no doubt: I am not here to criticise their sincerity in morals and life. The fact remains that what Parry lacked in his songs, Warlock was able to put into his own – the quality of 'bite', of urgency, or, as I would call it, of single-minded artistic sincerity, the quality that makes the thing, or object, the only consideration at the moment of composing. A recent gramophone review in a distinguished paper gave pause to anyone who knows Warlock's songs: it talked of 'boisterous' and 'rollicking' as if those were the two characteristic epithets of Warlock's work. Their use shows ignorance. There is no typical Warlock: he will chivy us from *Twelve Oxen* to *Milkmaids* and back again to Arthur Symons in *Saint Anthony of Padua*, and then from Beaumont and Fletcher's ale-wife *Jillian of Berry* over the hills (and the sea) to Yeats's Eireann fastnesses where *The Curlew* calls – very literally – on the cor anglais.

To each song Warlock brings a sense of style that is impeccable, and it can be imputed to no one but the singers and the critics, certainly not to the composer, that Warlock's name should be synonymous with *Captain Stratton's Fancy*, openly wholehearted as that gay tune is. I cannot find, for myself, that 'the flowing cups' that 'run swiftly round with no allying Thames', in Parry's song to Althea from the prison-bound lover, have quite that whole-souled appreciation of liquor which informed Captain Stratton.

To look at the three Belloc songs is to find some sense of Warlock's sense of style. They are all, it is true, nostalgic, but all entirely different in conception. As Mr Ernest Newman pointed out many years ago, the Wolf of the *Italienisches Liederbuch* is a changed man from the Spanish, or Goethe,

or Mörike Wolf. You could not exchange one song from
one cycle for another from the others without making a
musical solecism. Yet all the songs are individual. So with
the Belloc songs of Warlock – the passionate sadness over
the lost mill and the past splendour in the first, the mystical
feeling in the second, the love for home in the third: each
emotion is variedly and perfectly expressed.

The one example serves: but the collection of Warlock's
songs is before us, and we must seek to find. What shall we
look for? Let us leave the rumbustious Warlock to the last.

A critical study of Peter Warlock's songs, in detail, from
the point of view of the performers no less than the point
of view of the composer and poets, is a task awaiting a
sensitive musician. He must beware of the Nasmyth ham-
mer of a good prose style: he must display, not pin down
upon a board, the delicate hues of the butterflies' wings.
Here there is neither room nor intention to undertake it.
Nor can even a rough classification be made of various
types of song or emotion or poetry, because the uncomfortable little butterflies escape through our coarse nets into
the freedom of life and will not submit to the burden of
types.

But a survey of the chronological list (the only one published) in Mr Cecil Gray's book by one who knows the
scores and their sound is possibly illuminating.

Warlock slips into the outer world of publication with
the *Saudades* of 1916–17. They are remote, nostalgic songs,
in a manner closely akin to van Dieren's, sensitive, atonal,
exploratory. After one poem by Stevenson, the composer's
choice of words for the next twelve songs is the sixteenth
century or thereabouts. He has found one personal style in
As ever I saw, and another in *My ghostly Fader*. Already
Warlock is setting the same words twice, a practice he
never gave up.

Then, with Stevenson as his collaborator again, we find a
touch of genius in the little-known song, *Romance*. There is
spring in the step here, a jaunty air of discovery, and a sense

of beautiful sounds. Two poems by the contemporary Edward Shanks are followed by the superb lullaby, *Balulalow*, which is immediately succeeded by four toper's songs. *Piggesnie* is delicious, and in the same mood *Chopcherry*, which comes in *Peterisms* (first set). *Rutterkin*, in the same book, shows the pattern interest of Warlock's mind, and in the next book, *Lillygay*, we have a kind of Warlock epitome in five songs. *Sleep*, for string quartet originally but later transcribed for the piano – a masterpiece of easy movement –, gives us a modern equivalent of Dowland.

In the middle of this prolific early period comes *The Curlew*, Warlock's most considerable work in length and general conception. It is a series of four 'linked' songs, for tenor voice, flute, English horn, and string quartet, to poems by W. B. Yeats. In the ecstasy of sadness, no work by a living composer can surpass it. Warlock combines here a positive sense of desolation and the extraordinary negativeness of Yeats's words: 'No boughs have withered because of the wintry winds: the boughs have withered because I have told them my dreams.' The expression of that sentiment in suitable music is itself an achievement: the exquisite beauty of the entire work is something not to be realised save in the hearing – which is seldom allowed to us today.

Rest, sweet Nymphs is a melodic song, *Tyrley Tyrlow* a rhythmic song: it appears also as one of the Three Carols for chorus. In *Autumn Twilight* we find contemplation, the opposite in *Lusty Juventus*, and in *Milkmaids* a delicious strophic tune of a pertness proper to the ladies' petticoats of red.

That (if we include the lovely *Serenade for Strings* in honour of Delius's birthday, in an appropriately Delius-like manner) brings us up to 1923. Even so far, there is enormous variety, enough to show what manner of lyrical mind we are considering. Space does not permit an equally detailed account of the rest of the songs, so one or two must be singled out for notice here.

The Shakespeare settings on the whole get more interesting and richer as Warlock goes on, and the later ones are brilliantly successful though difficult to 'bring off'. *Consider* (Ford Madox Hueffer) is planned on a broader vocal scale than most of its fellows, and seems to demand a different kind of voice. For it is a point of interest that Warlock seems mostly to have designed his songs for a high baritone, or middle voice. He disliked the idea of automatic transposition of his songs, preferring to rewrite the accompaniments to suit an altered pitch. Looking down the list of songs, one observes a predilection for carols, and semi-religious or mystical words, with 'jolly shepherds' and 'Tom Tylers' cropping up every so often. A particularly beautiful pair of songs are *And wilt thou leave me thus?* (Thomas Wyatt) and *After Two Years* (Richard Aldington). *The Fox* is a song of hair-raising dramatic declamation – the Warlock counterpart of Schubert's *Doppelgänger*. Nor should one forget the little songs, like *Candlelight* (which are nursery jingles) and *The Sick Heart*.

The concerted pieces include one of Warlock's most delicate inventions – the *Corpus Christi* Carol for soprano, baritone, and string quartet: two of his most experimental works, *The Full Heart* and *Sorrow's Lullaby*: and the Three Carols. *An old Song*, for small orchestra, is indebted to Delius, but has a delightful clinging fragrance of its own, and then there is the *Capriol* Suite, the one and only piece for full orchestra. Ostensibly based on old French dances from Arbeau's *Orchésographie*, the Suite is really an entirely original conception in which one finds the fullest expression of Warlock's flair for bodily movement and exaggerated gesticulation.

In addition to the composed works, there are many transcriptions of vocal and instrumental works of Elizabethan and Jacobean periods, all of them displaying high scholarship and a profound respect for the musical intentions of the original composers (these in addition to a number of piano duet and solo arrangements of Delius's works). As a writer of criticism too, Warlock (under his real name) is responsible for important studies that range from Delius to Gesualdo, embracing the English Lutenists as they pass.

Such, then, is the rather sadly neglected composer, Peter Warlock.

If one looks in these works for a Beethoven, one does not find it – nor, indeed, does one elsewhere with any frequency. One finds another personality, a real one, expressing itself in miniature forms and accomplishing that expression with something near to perfection. Warlock's is not theoretical music but practical material for singer and pianist. It does not flatter, does not try to persuade the listener with the half-truths of reminiscence. Alert itself, this music requires alertness in hearer as well as performer. Taken all in all, Warlock is in the great line of song-writers, and certainly he has no rival of English blood since the death of Purcell. We should learn about this fellow-countryman of our own time, and sing him.

CHAPTER V

Frank Bridge
1879–1941

J. A. WESTRUP

*

IT is the fate of some composers to be known by a single work. Hundreds of music-lovers have heard *Sea Fever*, but few of them know anything else of Ireland's music. Every amateur singer of any pretensions likes to tackle *Love went a-riding*, if he can find an adequate accompanist. But he does not bother to pursue acquaintance. At the most he is aware of Frank Bridge as the composer of one or two effective songs. Of the range of his invention or the scope of his achievement he has no inkling. Perhaps Bridge himself was partly responsible for this. He was a modest, retiring soul, who rarely made any prominent appearance in public except when he conducted as a last-minute substitute for someone else. He was known to connoisseurs of chamber music as a first-rate viola player. But the connoisseurs of chamber music form only a fraction of the music-loving public; and since the composition of chamber music occupied so much of Bridge's energies, it was only natural that here too he had little chance of making a reputation. It is possible that the realisation of this drove him more and more into the closed circle of his own mind and encouraged him in later years to develop an idiom that the ordinary music-lover would find barely comprehensible. That change in his musical speech, though not wholly revolutionary, was at least radical enough to dismay some of those who had hitherto admired and loved his work.

Chamber music was for Bridge the ideal medium. He was a successful song-writer and wrote well for the piano and the orchestra. His mastery of the technique of composition was such that he could hardly fail to do otherwise. But in his chamber music there is more than this. Here he was at home. An expert player himself, he knew the medium from inside, and everything he wrote for it bears the impress of this intimacy. Some of his work in this field was a direct result of the prize competitions organised by W. W. Cobbett; but we may guess that this encouragement merely intensified an inclination that was already formed. His four String Quartets are an epitome of his development. The first, in E minor, which won honourable mention at a competition at Bologna in 1906, is in the tradition of nineteenth-century romanticism. It is warm-hearted, but it is everywhere controlled by that fine craftsmanship which was the hall-mark of Bridge's work. The melodies are expressive, yet the music is never the slave of a lyrical impulse. Bridge was very successful in writing short pieces, but from the first he showed himself fully able to handle larger forms. The form of the *Bologna* Quartet is on fairly conventional lines, but it is not stiff; and the device of recalling the opening of the first movement at the end of the finale gives an emotional unity to the work as a whole. Bridge was clearly attracted by this device. It occurs also in the Piano Quintet, and in the third String Quartet the finale ends with a quotation from the slow movement.

The second Quartet, in G minor, which won a Cobbett prize in 1915, is still faithful to romanticism, though more chromatic in its harmony. Once again one notices the excellent part-writing and the skill with which the whole work is knit together. The slow movement and the scherzo are combined in a single movement. In the third String Quartet, written for the Americanpatr on Mrs Coolidge in 1926, the break with the past is obvious. The work is in no specified key, and its chromaticism is all the time straining against the bonds of tonality. Yet though the language has changed, the impulses behind it have not. The passionate elaboration of the first movement is still characteristic of the composer, and he shows just as much skill in handling the new language as the old. In the fourth Quartet, written in 1937 and also dedicated to Mrs Coolidge, Bridge has taken a further and more decisive step along the road to atonality. The first movement has the same passionate quality as of old, and the end of the finale looks back to the opening of the first movement. This is recognisably a work of the same hand. But the ordinary music-lover, however much he may admit this recognition, is not likely to make rapid progress with a work whose idiom lies entirely outside his normal experience. It is perhaps significant that so many of Bridge's later works were written for a private patron – for conditions, in fact, in which public approbation is of no account and the artist need consider only himself.

The rest of Bridge's chamber music falls naturally into the framework of the quartets. The earlier period of frank and unashamed romanticism is represented by the Piano Quintet, the String Sextet, and the two *Phantasies* – one for piano trio and the other for piano quartet. The *Phantasies* were occasioned by Cobbett's desire to encourage the composition of single-movement chamber works, and the name was borrowed from the 'fancies' or fantasias of the seventeenth-century English composers. Within the limits of the single movement the composer was at liberty to introduce whatever contrasts he fancied. Bridge's trio is very neatly constructed in accordance with the formula ABCBA, where each letter represents a section; but this formal scheme has imposed no restraint on his invention. This is full-blooded music, with all the confidence and eagerness of youth. The quartet, too, is economical in its material, and though the writing for the piano has a Brahmsian quality there is no lack of individuality. The Sextet, a well-made work, is on the whole rather square-cut, though the rhythm of the slow movement is attractive and so is the tonal scheme of the finale. In the Quintet we meet again the combination of slow movement and scherzo – a slow movement that is open to the accusation of sentimentality though full of charm for those who do not distrust eloquence; there is a hint of Fauré here.

The 'Cello Sonata, which belongs to the same period as the second String Quartet, presents no problems; but the second Piano Trio and the Violin Sonata show that later refinement of Bridge's art which tended to cut him off from the public. The Trio, which is consistently dissonant and ends enigmatically, is more tenuous in texture than the works preceding it; there are signs of impressionist influence. But impressionism for Bridge never meant vagueness; here as in his earlier works the rhythmical background is clearly defined. Nor does dissonance imply violence: the scherzo is exceptionally delicate. In the Violin Sonata he reverts to the single movement of the earlier *Phantasies*, but the structure is much less obvious. There are frequent changes of time, and the mood is capricious. Critics of Bridge's work used at one time to comment on his orthodoxy and to stress the delight that players took in his work. The Violin Sonata is anything but orthodox, and the players must win their delight through hard labour.

The largest of Bridge's orchestral works is the suite *The Sea*, written in 1910 and published by the Carnegie Trust ten years later. Anyone who expects this to be the English counterpart of Debussy's *La Mer* will be disappointed. The Carnegie adjudicators were strangely in error in describing it as 'a notable example of what, for want of a better word, is called "atmosphere" in music'. The four movements – *Seascape*, *Sea-foam*, *Moonlight*, and *Storm* – are not 'impressions' in the conventional sense. Bridge might borrow impressionist harmony, but he was never an impressionist. The form of *The Sea* is as clear-cut as that of any of his instrumental works without a title. To Bridge, illustration for its own sake was of no interest; the problems that engaged his attention were wholly musical. It is not surprising to find that *Seafoam* includes an ingenious combination of two distinct themes. The solution of such problems was more fascinating than any attempt at scene-painting. The same is true of the tone poem *Summer*, a rich and colourful work, which admirably suggests the heavy warmth of a July afternoon. Where other composers might have been content with 'atmosphere' Bridge prefers a clear and well-defined rhythmical structure. This sense of definition in his work makes it seem odd that he should have chosen to preface the first of his *Two Poems* for orchestra with a quotation from Richard Jefferies which runs: 'Those thoughts and feelings which are not sharply defined, but have a haze of distance and beauty about them, are always the dearest.' There is no haze in Bridge's music.

His piano music, too, is free from any suggestion of vagueness or rhapsodising. In his free use of chromatic overtones he learned something from Ravel, yet there is little in common between the two composers beyond a meticulous attention to detail. The most ambitious of Bridge's piano works is the Sonata in memory of Ernest Bristow Farrar, which stands on the threshold of his later period. Here he revels in the sonority of the instrument. The music is difficult, but repays study, and the slow movement, with its charmingly delicate handling of the keyboard, is perhaps the best approach to Bridge's later style. The piano part of the second Trio, and even more of the Violin Sonata, suggests that he came to distrust sonority and preferred to concentrate on outlines. His most remarkable work in this respect is the posthumous *Phantasm* for piano and orchestra, where the writing for the solo instruments is for the most part thin in texture and often consists of a single line, doubled at the octave. All Bridge's piano music, like his chamber works, is grateful to the player. The difficulties are a legitimate part of the technique of the instrument and not obstacles that persistently defy conquest.

It is possible that Bridge would have been known to a wider public if he had been a native of a country where instrumental music takes pride of place. In the England in which he grew up the choral tradition was still strong: the most respected composers were those who had established their reputations with cantatas or oratorios at the various provincial festivals. With his incomparable technical equipment Bridge could easily have won victories in this field. But his whole career shows that he was too much an artist to put success before his own inclinations. He did, however, leave a single choral work so sincere in expression and so rich in artistry that one cannot help regretting that it stands alone. It is a setting of *A Prayer* by Thomas à Kempis, beginning: 'Grant me Thy grace, most merciful Jesus, that it may be with me, and may labour with me, and continue with me to the end.' Bridge's music shows respect for the English choral tradition but does not accept its characteristic weakness. That weakness consists in allowing the words to dictate the form. For Bridge such an error was inconceivable. Instead of an incoherent sequence of ideas he offers a texture that is economical and closely knit. The result is an alliance of design and emotion that reaches the inmost places of the heart. There is no striving after effect, no exaggeration. In its simplicity, and in its fervency, lies its appeal.

Sir Henry Wood in his autobiography speaks of his admiration for *The Sea* and mentions the numerous performances he has given of it, both at home and abroad. He adds that whenever he referred to the success of these performances Bridge would say: 'Oh, that! It's such an old work, why do you play it?' The remark throws some light on Bridge's attitude to his own development. Composers do not invariably lose interest in their earlier works; and there was certainly no reason why Bridge should despise *The Sea*. It may be that he was sensitive about that 'orthodoxy' of his earlier years. He grew up at a time when the language of romanticism was the accepted thing. *The Sea* is contemporary with Elgar's second Symphony. But by the time he reached middle age romanticism had become old-fashioned and new modes of expression were current. Perhaps Bridge felt ashamed of the outspoken eloquence of the

Piano Quintet or the moving simplicity of *A Prayer*. Or again it is possible that his absorbing interest in technical problems made him anxious to conquer new territory. Whatever the reason and whatever may be the listener's re-action to Bridge's later work, it is certain that his develop-ment was continuous. The outlines of his later compositions may be more spare, the texture more tenuous. But in the truest sense of the word he remained a romantic to the end.

His technical mastery has sometimes led to an under-estimate of his invention. Such mastery undoubtedly has its dangers, and there are places in Bridge's work where the craftsman's efficiency makes the dominant impression. But he was never what is known as an 'academic' composer, and no one who has studied his work could think that he in-dulged in mere note-spinning for its own sake. That very impulsiveness which appears over and over again in his allegro movements is the refutation of any such opinion. The basis of his invention was emotion – an emotion that found its natural expression within a framework of discip-line. It is the quality of urgent sincerity, and not merely technical adroitness, that has made his chamber music so acceptable to professional and amateur players alike.

Some mention has been made of influences in his work. They are general rather than particular. Bridge was strong enough to absorb influences without surrendering to them. It is characteristic of him that his work shows no trace of two of the most powerful forces in twentieth-century English music – the example of Elgar and the folk-song revival. Bridge, whether orthodox or unorthodox, pre-ferred to be himself. There is in his work much that reminds one of Fauré – not in its idiom but in its general develop-ment and its relation to the music of its time. Like Fauré he began as a romantic in the nineteenth-century tradition and later refined his style to such an extent that it made an appeal only to a limited circle. Like Fauré he had a classical sense of fitness and a gift for achieving clarity without apparent effort. And like Fauré he had brilliant pupils.

CHAPTER VI

Ralph Vaughan Williams, O.M.

B. 1872

SCOTT GODDARD

*

As far as common knowledge goes Vaughan Williams spent twenty-nine years, from his birth at Down Ampney in Gloucestershire in 1872 to his proceeding to the Mus.D. degree at Cambridge (1901), in schooling. Judged by standards generally accepted as being normal for creative musicians, this was a generous allowance. It suggests no grim tale of early struggle nor any brilliant one of youthful achievement. It was a thoughtful man's slow development. Whatever the cause, it provided the right mental discipline for a musician whose work was to show protean adaptability. It brought him by gradual maturity to that condition corresponding to the musician's diminished seventh, the chord from which it is possible to remove a given music immediately, imperceptibly, without violence, and as though by a natural law, into other harmonic spheres. From such a point radiate innumerable perspectives. Of them the specialist would choose, or be chosen by, one. But the eclectic artist holds the position for as long as he dare, whilst keeping as many lines of perspective open as his mind can compass. It is a hazardous position, how much so the history of the Italian Renaissance shows in the lives of Alberti and of Pico della Mirandola, and in the one that is at present considered to provide the classic warning of failure, Leonardo da Vinci. Alone among British composers working today Vaughan Williams has succeeded in keeping open all the lines of communication that lead back to his unique point of departure. Thence he explores now one perspective, now another. Vaughan Williams is unpredictable in a way no other British composer is; the next move may not be taken for granted or its nature foreseen.

*

This point of departure may conveniently, if vaguely, be placed at 1901. Vaughan Williams then appears rightly as a musician of the twentieth century. His general education had been that normally appertaining to a parson's son, public school followed by university. An interval of two years between Charterhouse and Cambridge was given to music, and he returned to the R.C.M. after Cambridge. Charles Wood, most inspiring of all Stanford's men, taught him at the university; at the R.C.M. he was under both Parry and Stanford. When he left (in 1896) it was to spend his time between Lambeth, where he was a church organist, and Berlin, studying under Max Bruch. Wherein precisely the influence of his various teachers once lay is a subject of idle speculation. The grounding with Charles Wood must have stimulated his powers of thinking musically. From Parry breadth of vision, from Stanford the proprieties of construction, texture, and movement of parts, from Bruch some hint of how to add the spice of colour and accent to a page of full score, these may possibly have been initial causes of what in his own work was to appear strongly transformed. Of the public school there are none of the usual signs, unless in an intermittent conservatism in the man. There are more of those signs that mark great minds who have learned to think daringly at the most liberal of universities. One further educational adventure was to come, a visit to Ravel eight years after the Cambridge doctorate. By then Vaughan Williams was fully launched on his career, and in 1905 had been collecting folk-tunes in Norfolk. Folk-music was his first significant enthusiasm.

The *Norfolk Rhapsody* and another short orchestral work, *In the Fen Country*, were an early result, and this particular perspective was to lead at least as far as the *Pastoral* Symphony (1922).

It will be found that Vaughan Williams is a composer whose work does not fall naturally into stylistic periods. He follows many trends of thought, uses various methods to express them, follows many philosophical and musical perspectives; and from pursuing one he returns to take up another at the dictates of an impulse known to himself alone. In general two main trends are discernible. The one has to do with humanity and nature, founded on an early attraction towards folk-music. The other is the mystical aspect, and here the perspective opens out at first to the discovery of a personal affinity with Tudor church music. The beginnings of these influences may be suggested; their subsequent developments are too complex to be exactly traced. Vaughan Williams has always remained changeable and free.

The first impressive works now begin to appear. *Towards the Unknown Region* (1907), a choral work, dignified and of a Stanfordian classicism, ends with a climax as splendid as anything Parry could have imagined. Here Walt Whitman, a poet to whom Vaughan Williams was often to have recourse, is set with a fervour as impulsive as his own. In the next choral work, *A Sea Symphony*, the musician makes closer contact with the poet's spiritual explorations reported in Whitman's direct speech. To such vernacular Vaughan Williams's music complies with unusual felicity and force. Between these works a cycle of Housman poems set for tenor, string quartet, and pianoforte appeared under the title *On Wenlock Edge*. This was just after the visit to Ravel. That there might have been any influence from this contact, or alternatively any influence for good, has been denied by Vaughan Williams's admirers, in especial by those of a younger generation who prided themselves on being self-taught. But the evidence of the music cannot be set aside.

Wenlock Edge shows no submission to French ideals but some awareness of French methods. Nor was this to be a passing phase, for thirty-four years later the scherzo of the fifth Symphony gives the same evidence. Between the two men there could have been little sympathy. Vaughan Williams is said to be antipathetic to Ravel's music. Ravel is known to have spoken with courteous interest of the Englishman as well as with some wit. ('C'est bien possible qu'il aurait profité de sa visite; mais retournant en Angleterre il rencontrait sur le quai ...' and then the name of one of those musicians, fabulous to the Frenchman, either 'Sir Parry' or 'Sir Elgar'.) *On Wenlock Edge* had little to do with Parry, nothing with Elgar. The pessimism and nostalgia of Housman's verses are reflected in a quality of music at once more acute and more supple than theirs. *On Wenlock Edge* brings drama, dark and light, into Vaughan Williams's work. The music of the singer is rooted in an already instinctive personal folk-song idiom; the instrumental music has Gallic transparency. The fusion is not complete; yet this very sense of struggle, which would have disrupted settings of Byron or Tennyson, mirrors curiously well the hapless fortunes of Housman's lads and lasses whose thoughts hurt them. A closer fusion of folkish music and refined art occurs three years later (1912) in the *Fantasia on Christmas Carols*.

In the previous year a new trend of thought appeared with a new style of expression. In this the modern semi-mystical aspirations of Whitman are abandoned; their place is taken by the metaphysical mysticism of George Herbert. The music becomes aloof and cool. Two main works here – the *Fantasia for Double Stringed Orchestra on a Theme by Thomas Tallis* (1910) and *Five Mystical Songs* (1911) – have an ethereal quality not heard before in British music. In fact no music was being written in Europe that had the translucent massiveness of the *Tallis Fantasia* or the gentle urgency of the *Mystical Songs*. If we study the *Tallis Fantasia* the design of the long single movement is seen

to be as simple as is the harmonic scheme through which
Tallis's noble third mode melody pursues its endless way.
The great chords are removed from position to related
position among a restricted series of modal harmonies;
they return inevitably and soon to their place of origin as
though impelled by gravitational force. There is about the
Fantasia a sense of intense deliberation. Its dynamics are
as restrained as its harmonies. Weight of tone more than
loudness gives emphasis. The chords are of vast proportions, often in ten or more parts extending over five
or more octaves. In the sudden reduction of these huge
chords to a phrase for solo quartet a hushed sense of
drama comes into the music. At times a single instrument
ponders over the Theme, seeking out those pentatonic
outlines that will become a hall-mark (*London Symphony*,
Job, *Flos Campi*) from now onwards. If the music sounds
modal its modality is of a modern type. For the listener
who can give himself to this music it has the force of a
revelation, the immediacy of the mystic's vision. As
string writing it is more daring, because it relies on so
much less, than Elgar's *Introduction and Allegro*; and what
Gerontius may be to the Roman Catholic this may be for
spirituality to the Protestant.

The *Mystical Songs*, settings of poems by Herbert,
continue that sentiment. The voice gives an emotional
character to the music other than that of the *Fantasia*.
What in the *Fantasia* seems the calm unfolding of a dream
of abstract beauty, in these songs becomes a more precisely
delineated vision as the defined images of words are
enunciated through the personality of a human voice.
It is, after all, a personal experience of mystical communion
that Herbert relates. The spoken word could still serve him;
it had not yet among mystics become a barrier between this
beginner and the unspeakable deeper experience. And it is
strangely moving to hear how Vaughan Williams's music,
which has its own angularities as well as its ecstasies, by
turns keeps level with Herbert's thoughts and at moments

obliterates them in an intensity of understanding from which the poet's very words seem to withhold him.

The more abstract expression of mysticism returns three years later in the lyric fantasy for violin and orchestra called *A Lark Ascending* (1914). Richard Jefferies himself, lying on the turf of the Wiltshire hills, noted down no finer vision of nature than this. The music covers a slightly wider harmonic field than in the Tallis work, and of its essence the lark's song ranges higher, is more swift and ornate. With the mystical enchantment there is a vague sense of something folkish, a mundane lilt that dissolves back into the shimmering atmosphere in which the music came into being. Eight years later appeared the opera *The Shepherds of the Delectable Mountains*, based on Bunyan's *Pilgrim's Progress*. By rights this should be considered with the other stage works later in this chapter. But its passionate intensity is of the same quality as the foregoing compositions and it also belongs among the mystical works.

The unaccompainied *Mass in G minor* seems now as daring a work as the *Tallis Fantasia*, a challenge to the Tudor composers on their own ground. Sixteenth-century English church music, at once the expression of the Tudor composer's powerful invention and an assertion of his freedom from the dogma of the schoolmen, attracted certain alert minds in the present century. Vaughan Williams had already shown the force of this attraction in the modal part-writing of the antiphons of the *Tallis Fantasia*. This manner and the method of handling chords as single entities, blocks of harmony movable intact from point to point, were carried through to the unaccompanied double-choir anthem *O praise the Lord* and thence to this *Mass*. Comparison with a Tudor work such as Byrd's five-part *Mass* tends to show that the modern method is similar and also that in the intelligent use of it certain individual conclusions could be reached.

Sancta Civitas, the vision of the Holy City, in words

from the Authorised Version and earlier bibles, prefaced by a quotation from Plato, and set for tenor and baritone soli, semi-chorus, distant chorus, and orchestra, is the logical outcome of those tendencies we have traced. There is the nostalgic humanism of Whitman, the mystical vision of Herbert; there are the musical traits of folkish melody that sometimes flow into plain chant, pentatonic melody that arises from both, consecutive motion of chords used as individual entities. And now these chords are to move in counterpoint; so that where once a line of single notes moved in relation to other such lines, here each line may be as much as three or four deep in notes, making one of a number of simultaneous, unrelated progressions of chords. This method was first used in British choral music by Holst in *The Hymn of Jesus* (1917), where it was exploited with great daring and hardihood. *Sancta Civitas*, resuming so much in Vaughan Williams's aesthetic, can be considered the central composition of all his work written up to 1926. And the wail 'Babylon is fallen', high in the soprano semi-chorus over a deep constant bass, is one of those types of gnomic exclamation which from now onwards are to haunt his music, both choral and symphonic.

Once again it can be seen that all these categories to which the various works belong are interdependent. The bewildered cry of the mourners over fallen Babylon refers back to 'Whither, unsatisfied soul?', Whitman's Adam and Eve descending from the Garden of Eden, the last movement of the *Sea Symphony*. The later is a projection of the earlier, a development of the music and an extension of the thought. Vaughan Williams seems always to have been a visionary and a seeker. It is an active quality of mind that has become a fundamental attribute of all his music. The choral writings, as much in the *Five Tudor Portraits* (1936) as in *Towards the Unknown Region* (1907), inevitably show it more clearly than the abstract wordless music; yet there also it is present. To anyone intent on understanding the symphonies a study of the choral works is of the first importance. These render articulate the abstract instrumental music, softening what at first seems austere, bringing nearer to the range of average intelligence what at first seems distant and aloof.

The Symphonies include in their span (1907–43) practically the whole of Vaughan Williams's effective creative musical life and represent all the main tendencies of his work. There is the eloquent humanism of the First, the *Sea Symphony*. In the Second, the *London*, this moves towards the folkish element, which is combined in the Third, the *Pastoral*, with the mystical quality of the Herbert songs and the Bunyan opera. That quality is supreme in the Fifth in D. There remains the Fourth in F minor, a work of peculiar significance. As *Sancta Civitas* stands in relation to the whole of the music as far as 1926, the Fourth does to that of the next nine years. It resumes the composer's aesthetic and philosophy up to that point, the year 1935.

The *Sea Symphony* (1910) is an oratorio in character (a work for soloists, chorus, and orchestra), a symphony in its design of four movements – the opening allegro, the slow movement 'on the beach at night alone', the scherzo of 'whistling winds', and the rondo-like finale, the 'vast rondure swimming in space'. At the time of its appearance it was strikingly new in idea and execution and there are still passages in it, notably in the scherzo, that retain freshness. The scherzo is the first of a series of such symphonic movements possessing a quality of swiftness plus weight peculiar to Vaughan Williams. The symphony is the poet's, not the sailor's, view of the sea, inspiration as much as experience; yet the winds that blow through the scherzo are salt. For the rest the work is remarkable for the grandeur of its melodies. Before this only Parry among the renaissance composers had been so prodigal of splendid melodic outlines.

The *London Symphony* (1914) dreams into articulate utterance by way of certain formulae, since recognised as the true mark of this composer, a Brahms-Sibelius-Kodaly pentatonic ladder of rising fourths and a succession of chords waving back and forth, such a figure as Ravel and Holst were using for differing ends at the same period. The Westminster chimes hum on the air and suddenly London wakes, the Great Town nearer to Whitman's occupational centre than to any Sancta Civitas. For all its picturesque detail the Symphony is a deeply thoughtful work. Compare it with another bright evocation, the clear picture of the surface of Edwardian London in Elgar's *Cockaigne*. Then turn to the uneasy sighs at the end of this scherzo or to the rending wail that begins the last movement. This is a different London and a musician not viewing it but pondering over it. It is a town haunted by the countryside it devours, the Nocturne (the second movement) recalls walking home along Piccadilly in the small hours of a summer's morning when, petrol fumes at their weakest, the light winds from the country blow across the Green Park where Handel's *Music for the Royal Fireworks* was first heard. The errand boys whistle tunes such as Swift might have heard while bathing in the Thames before his house in Chelsea, tunes that have a country air and a folk-song turn of phrase.

The *Pastoral* (1922) is a far less approachable work than either of the earlier symphonies. It is possibly the most exacting of the five for the reason that the music is quite unemphatic, as eventful to a Beethoven-trained ear as is the landscape of southern England to the eye of a man from the Alps. This is one of the purest, most uncompromising examples of philosophising musically. It is not *mehr Ausdruck ... als Mahlerei* but wholly the expression of emotion, and that emotion recollected in tranquillity. The music, when at length it does speak to the ear, has an intense lyric quality. Again it is in the scherzo, with its weird galumphing gait, that the essential originality of the thought is apparent. The natural horn solo at the end of the first movement and what balances that, the human voice at a like moment in the last movement, are touches of high poetry in this exquisite abstraction.

Within three years the astringent Fourth in F minor appeared and startled those who, ignoring Satan's music in the ballet *Job*, had imagined the composer finally given over to a pastoral dream. The two Symphonies, this and the *Pastoral*, seemed incompatible. That they should issue from the same brain was incredible. The mental conjunction may have been hard to find, the musical link should have been evident. Compare the two scores. It will be noticed that the syntax is the same. By effectively using this same syntax for such disparate works Vaughan Williams proved that his private language was an instrument able to express all shades of emotion and reasoning the public might want, or in the case of this trenchant Fourth in F minor might not want but would have to hear. The music has the rasp of a file more than the cutting edge of a razor, an effect produced not alone by the clash of harmonies but by their relentless grinding one against the other, and never by striking orchestration. It is still the orchestra of the *London* and of *Job*. The Symphony was finished five years before the events of which it now seems a warning vision.

During those eventful years the Fifth appeared (1943), a work as unlike the Fourth as that is unlike the Third. Diatonic and luminous, the music in motion and texture has clarity more concentrated than any of the great number of works that have come before it, works of which it seems the crowning achievement in its complete discipline of expression. The Fifth resumes much in these former works – the impassioned string writing of the *Tallis Fantasia*, the bold shifts of key in the *Mass*, the piling of line upon line for the building of a climax in *Dona Nobis*. The dedication to Sibelius 'in sincere flattery' makes history, the significance of which is not yet clear. A quotation from Bunyan, heading the Romanza (the third movement embodying material from an unfinished *Pilgrim's Progress* opera), gives a clue to the whole symphony; the Alleluias of this movement are already foreshadowed in the first and blaze out again in the last. This is a symphony of cross-references, as homogeneous as Sibelius's Seventh. Its scherzo is a notable example of the swift-sure manner; there is also a feathery lightness, almost, French, in the scoring. The scherzo seems as though it were standing off from the rest of the work, becoming separated from the scheme that binds the other movements together; but by the end it too is seen to be part of their thought.

Of the various perspectives explored by Vaughan Williams one of the earliest (it was to be the longest and to lead him farthest from his starting-point) was choral music having special reference to dramatic possibilities. The *Sea Symphony* was the first signal achievement and already by then (1909) the incidental music to *The Wasps* of Aristophanes had brought contact with the stage. The first opera was *Hugh the Drover*, and it is significant that the scene of this very English opera was a village, the tale a romance of true love triumphant, the idiom folk-song and national song. When the opera was revived at Sadler's Wells in 1937 people who had misconceived the Housman song-cycle *On Wenlock Edge* and the last movement of the *Sea Symphony* were surprised that so 'English' (undemonstrative) a composer could write love duets so warm-hearted and impulsive. The music perfectly fulfilled its functions; it was highly dramatic, it was good theatre. If only the words ...

The next libretto was from Bunyan, a one-act pastoral episode called *The Shepherds of the Delectable Mountains* based on *Pilgrim's Progress*. The four male voices of the shepherds and the pilgrim might have given the opera a still more sombre character than even the solemnity of the action portends, were it not for the ethereal music of the chamber orchestra, the voice of a bird singing the twenty-third Psalm, and the distant chorus of female voices whose repeated Alleluias end the work as the pilgrim goes on towards his Sancta Civitas. The whole minute scene is drawn with unfaltering strokes. It may appear a delicate trifle, though it is more; a careful and subtle commentary, in beautifully discreet terms of quasi-parlando recitative, interspersed with flowing song and the clearest of choral counterpoint.

Sir John in Love was produced in 1929, a Falstaff opera in four acts. Of this the composer has said, in reference to Holst's *Boar's Head*, that he hopes he has 'treated Holst with the sincerest flattery [see above, the dedication of the Fifth Symphony] not only in imitating his choice of Falstaff as the subject of an opera but in imitating his use of English folk-tunes in the texture of the music'. And he goes on to explain that his 'chief object ... has been to fit this wonderful comedy with, I trust, not unpleasant music'. Those who see in the *Merry Wives* episode a bitter truthfulness to certain brutal aspects of human nastiness will miss the vinegar in this music; whoever thinks of it as a wonderful comedy will be better served. There are exquisite things in the score. All the Windsor Forest episode (it has been parted from the opera and published alone) is of great charm, 'See the chariot at hand' one of the most ravishing of his opera choruses and all the *Greensleeves* music completely lovely. The opera is one of Vaughan Williams's cleverest, most 'literary' scores, full of topical allusions and technical kick-shaws.

In the next year (1930) there appeared the Blake ballet *Job*, the composer's most popular work in that it is the one known to the widest public. It is wholly remarkable, musically self-sufficient, altogether apt for the purposes of dancing and miming for which it is intended, a work of great originality and power. It is also the most direct introduction to Vaughan Williams's music for the general intelligent musical listener, though for that it should be heard away from the stage with, instead, Blake's illustrations to the Book of Job to which each section of this Masque for Dancing is complementary, each picture noted in the score. The work thus serves two distinct types of listener, those for whom the music is an adjunct to a story danced, those for whom it is the concomitant in sound of Blake's vision. Neither will be absolutely at one with the other's point of view, but both may be with the music. The morality of God's game with man is played out to music having qualities that can be traced to various historic sources (Tudor church music, folk-song) and to others in Vaughan Williams's own work, but which ends by becoming the expression of a personality unlike any other drawn into the orbit of the stage. The originality is in the rejection of practically every readily available stage effect that the story might have suggested – such suggestive features as Richard Strauss exploited in *The Legend of Joseph*. The surface glitter of *Joseph* has no place in *Job*, which is all fire and ice, human misery and divine power. The two elements mingle for a fleeting moment of earthly time when the Angels' song of triumph over the fall of Satan is taken up by Job's young men and women and transformed into a pastoral dance. The art of ballet has possibilities reaching beyond the actualities of physique. Few ballets before *Job* have insisted on the intellectual aspect of a danced allegory; fewer have so completely combined pure intellectualism with the heat of emotionalism and the extreme emphasis of melodrama.

In the next year (1931) the single-act opera *Riders to the Sea* was finished, a word-for-word setting of Synge's play and the most original of all Vaughan Williams's stage works. As a principle the thing is not to be intellectually entertained, this setting of a stage play through the medium of quasi-parlando recitative (the manner of the Bunyan opera but with no sustained song nor any choral effects); yet it succeeds astonishingly and becomes a conception fulfilled, an aim reached. As such it exists by a right unassailably its own. It is Vaughan Williams's finest stage work and his least known. Were the French less provincial they would see in it the reflection, perhaps the precise effect, of their own methods of understatement, the restrained approach leading spontaneously and unforcedly to the ultimate climax.

The four-act *Poisoned Kiss* (1936), a tale of a princess who

had magic and a young man who had sex appeal, is design-
edly modern. It suffers, in spite of some lively tunes and
good melodies, from its libretto, a farrago of improbable
affairs carried out, or on, in beauty parlours and florists'
shops in an atmosphere of psycho-analytic foolery (impro-
bably guyed with an eye to the accepted conventions of
'decent' affection) that has all the jejune moralising of
Gilbert with none of the rare pert humour of that resourceful librettist. One cannot but admire the intellectual vitality
of a composer who could turn from the *Benedictus*, the
Magnificat, and *Riders to the Sea* to undertake an excursion
into musical comedy. But he was badly served, except in so
far as *The Poisoned Kiss* may have enlivened his sense of
humour and so stirred him to write the *Five Tudor Portraits*.

While these operas were being written a number of impressive and beautiful choral works were appearing, in the
succession and tradition that had begun with *Willow Wood*
and reached *Sancta Civitas*. Vaughan Williams had by now
installed himself in the retired quiet of a rural surrounding in Surrey. There he had made use of the experience
gained in teaching the London Bach Choir to guide local
(to him more congenial) activities in music – to guide and
to provide material. A result of this participation was the
Benedicite (1930) with the name Leith Hill at the head of the
score; a setting for soprano solo, chorus, and orchestra of
words from the apocryphal *Song of the Three Holy Children*
and lines by the seventeenth-century poet J. Austin. Another
is the *Magnificat* (1932). These short works are of a noble
and most poetic utterance, religious music more than
church music. If they really were designed for societies in
small towns they must at moments put a strain on such resources; but the difficulties must be immensely rewarding.
With them may be mentioned a Prelude and Fugue in C
minor for organ; the former treating that grave instrument almost as cavalierly as was done to the solo part of the
Pianoforte Concerto (1936). The fugue begins as though it
were a cousin of Ravel's fugue in the *Tombeau de Couperin*,

and ends as its wise, vastly experienced grandfather. Here too belongs the Festival *Te Deum* on traditional themes (1937), one of the composer's happiest conjunctions of yesterday and today; and the *Three Choral Hymns* (1930) for tenor solo, chorus, and orchestra, another notable work for Leith Hill.

For a wider audience and on a more imperative theme *Dona nobis pacem* appeared in the year (1936) following the portentous Fourth Symphony. It is a tract for all time, implicit with the anguished struggles of humanity that would fain, but dare not, learn from the past. It grossly offended men of that day in Europe who were intent on war. This cantata for two soli (soprano and baritone), chorus, and orchestra, is formed out of three poems by Whitman (one of them a superb setting of the *Dirge for Two Veterans*), sentences by John Bright and from the scriptures. It is the most individual and impressive of all his choral works, and if no more mention is made of it here it is because words to describe it succinctly are not adequate.

In that year, as though to restore symmetry, there was published the choral suite called *Five Tudor Portraits* (for contralto and baritone, chorus and orchestra), which is charming, delicate fun mingled with coarse, fleshly jesting. This is no work for local societies; a large orchestra, a highly trained choir, and soloists of the utmost pertinacity are needed. The five movements, founded on poems by John Skelton of Diss, run the gamut of emotion from pathos in the exquisite Lament for Philip Sparrow (a remarkable use of contralto tone-colour) to brute enjoyment of the good life in the description of Elinor Rumming of Leatherhead, the brewer of strong ale. This suite shows the composer using with absolute mastery a technique that has so become second nature that it seems forgotten by him as it is by us who listen. The glove now fits the hand; under it the muscles move unseen with their own natural freedom.

In these two disparate works of 1936 are exemplified the wide aims of the musician and the completeness of the

artist. There is no aspect of life foreign to him, none beyond the reach of his art; and that art, which is the most
individual in the history of this country's music since
Purcell, has reached a width of reference and a depth of
comment never attained by musicians bred here. Such
vague suggestions are all that can be offered now. Nothing
can be said conclusively about the workings of a mind so
protean and still magnificently active.

*

[For reasons indicated in the Preface to this book, there is no consideration here of Vaughan Williams's *Sixth Symphony*, in E minor,
or of other "post-war" works by this composer.   (Editor)]

CHAPTER VII

John Ireland

B. 1879

RALPH HILL

*

JOHN IRELAND was born at Bowden, Cheshire, on August 13, 1879. He was brought up in a literary atmosphere, for his father was the editor of the *Manche ter Examiner and Times* and author of the *Book-lover's Encheiridion*, and his mother was a literary critic and author. In 1893 Ireland entered the Royal College of Music, where he remained until 1901. Like many other composers who served their musical apprenticeship under Sir Charles Stanford, Ireland began his composer's career as a follower of Brahms. In fact so strong was the influence of that great German master upon Ireland's early compositions that he destroyed or withheld practically all the works he had written up to the year 1906, when he was twenty-seven. After his studentship, Ireland entered on an exhaustive study of the music of Debussy, Ravel, and Stravinsky. From Brahms, Ireland developed a fine sense of musical architecture; from Debussy and Ravel, clarity and conciseness of style; from Stravinsky, rhythmic vitality and piquant and arresting sonorities.

Ireland is one of the most significant composers of our time. Neither an academic nor a 'highbrow' experimenter, but merely a sincere artist, he seeks to express himself to the mass of musical people rather than to select circles. His highly individual idiom is firmly rooted in the past and is therefore easily assimilated.

There is no composer of our time who has greater artistic integrity than Ireland. He puts pen to paper only when genuinely moved to write, and remains unsatisfied until his ideas have shaped themselves into the appropriate musical form. Every detail of construction is subjected to the most careful thought, and there is not a point about colour, rhythm, tempo, and dynamics that does not receive the utmost consideration. If after the work of months Ireland decides that a composition does not fulfil his ideal either in conception or in execution, he will ruthlessly scrap the result of his labours or put it away for future attention. From the smallest fragment for piano solo to extended compositions for orchestra, fine craftsmanship is always discernible. Yet, despite this, his music invariably gives the impression of spontaneity.

Ireland is very susceptible to the emotional influence of poetry and natural scenes, much in the same way that Delius was. An exquisite scene in some remote part of the countryside or the reading of a beautiful poem is enough to start musical ideas working in him. It might almost be said that Ireland's music is either nature music or the interpretation of poetic ideas. And the natural scenes and the poetry that seem to have a particularly strong attraction for Ireland are those that suggest, or are in some way connected with, pagan nature-worship. It is significant that in a broadcast talk on Stravinsky's *The Rite of Spring* Ireland said: 'I always feel that the musical sounds Stravinsky makes in this work – the musical ideas themselves – seem to have the power of calling up something from the subconscious mind; some racial memory perhaps, of things long hidden, and belonging to a remote and forgotten past.'

Ireland's spiritual home is in the Channel Islands, which have a peculiar atmosphere of their own and have many pagan associations. His contacts with the Islands date back from his earliest days, and up to the German invasion of Guernsey he was living there in comparative seclusion. Many of his works were inspired by visits to one or other of the islands: for example, *The Forgotten Rite* for orchestra, and the piano pieces *The Island Spell* and *Sarnia: an Island Sequence*.

This attraction to nature-worship and all that it implies mystically is shown again in Ireland's admiration for the work of Arthur Machen, a master at evoking strange and mysterious atmosphere and the nearest English equivalent to Maeterlinck. But Machen writes of the world of Pan, a world of magic and strange rites, peopled by fauns, satyrs, and other creatures once believed to inhabit the world of nature. Ireland is emphatic in his denial that any of his music, such as the *Legend* for orchestra and piano, which is dedicated to Arthur Machen, and the piano piece *Scarlet Ceremonies*, which is headed with a quotation from Machen's story *The White People*, is a direct interpretation of any actual scenes or events in Machen's works. But there is no doubt that certain of Machen's writings – if I may put it this way – set up a musical response and acted as a fertiliser to a train of musical ideas. However, that *Legend* evokes an atmosphere of a very striking character cannot be denied. Nevertheless, Ireland claims that practically all his titles and captions have been added *after* the music was written, to help the listener to get near the intended mood.

It is an axiom that the greatest composers of piano music have been themselves fine pianists; for example, Beethoven, Schumann, Chopin, Liszt and Brahms. The piano, indeed, is a difficult instrument to write for; it responds only to those who intimately understand its genius. Ireland is a pianist of considerable technical ability, and has made a deep study of the problems of style in writing for the piano. The piano is undoubtedly his most natural medium of musical expression. It is interesting to note that the greater part of his work is for solo piano, voice and piano, or is chamber music in which the piano has an essential part. All Ireland's piano music, from his magnificent Concerto and Sonata to the shortest piece, is written with real understanding of keyboard effect and sonority. His quick but thoughtful response to the picturesque is shown at its best in his three London Pieces (*Chelsea Reach*, *Ragamuffin*, and *Soho Forenoons*), which are the musical impressions of a Londoner who loves his London. *Chelsea Reach* is a particularly beautiful piece of writing that sets out to capture the mood of the river at Chelsea as it was in the great days of Whistler and Rossetti. The music's soft blends of tone suggest a kind of musical counterpart to a Whistler painting. Another beautiful piece that harmonically exploits an impressionistic technique is the *Island Spell*, the first of a set of three pieces entitled *Decorations*. Perhaps one of Ireland's most thoughtful and sonorous pieces in his essentially lyrical style is *April*.

Ireland has written over forty pieces of this kind, many of which are without equal in English piano music. Those pieces I have already mentioned, and others like *The Darkened Valley*, *Amberly Wild Brooks*, the three *Lyric Pieces*, *Greenways*, and the Four Preludes (particularly *The Undertone* and *Obsession*), compare favourably in their own distinctive manner with the best pieces of Schumann and Grieg.

His greatest work for piano in the purely lyrical style is *Sarnia*. Not only is the keyboard exploited with brilliant and sonorous effect, but the music of these three pieces is full of that poetry and intense feeling so characteristic of all Ireland's work. Each piece is dedicated to an islander: the first, *Le Catioroc*, to Sebire, the flute player; the second, *In a May Morning*, to Michael Rayson; the third, *Song of the Springtides*, to Mrs Mignot. *Le Catioroc*, which is the name of a part of the west coast of Guernsey where evidences of prehistoric nature-worship still remain, and the influences of pagan antiquity are still strongly felt, bears a revealing quotation from Pomponius Mela. This piece is outstanding for its melodic and harmonic expressiveness. *In a May Morning*, which is direct in expression and full of ardent personal feeling, has an apt inscription from Victor Hugo's *Les Travailleurs de la Mer*. The Song of the Springtides has the sweeping strength and abandon that the title leads us to expect. The writing offers scope for the virtuoso, but it is, nevertheless, subservient to the underlying poetic idea, which is taken from Swinburne.

Like Brahms, Ireland has little or no sense of showmanship; the effect of his music relies on its content, not on superficial decoration. The texture of his piano music is always rich and colourful, and he obtains expressive and sonorous effects with the imaginative use of arabesque. He has a fondness for close harmony, and does not avoid dissonant chords if he feels that they add depth and point to the working out of his ideas. Thus the beauty of his music is not always apparent on the surface. One of the most striking characteristics of Ireland's music in general, and his piano works in particular, is a curious mixture of lyricism and ruggedness. The latter is shown especially in his predilection for aggressive and dynamic rhythms, which are powerfully displayed in the Sonata, his most ambitious work for the piano. This remarkable work, which is so full of intensity of expression, would appear to have been generated by deeply felt experiences; nowhere are Ireland's keen melodic style and his apt and expressive use of harmonic colour shown to greater effect. I hold that this Sonata is not only the greatest written by a British composer, but one of the finest and most important since Liszt's in B minor. It ought to be in the repertoire of every virtuoso pianist, but unfortunately virtuosity and artistic discernment are rarely combined in one pianist.

Ireland's Sonatina is also music that one must know well before it delivers up its secrets. Underneath its hard and glittering surface it is full of deeply felt emotion. Compared with the powerful and profound Sonata it is thinner and more transparent in texture; while the Sonata is essentially romantic, even dramatic, in character, the first and last movements of the Sonatina are imbued with a certain ironic humour. The short slow movement has something of the queer atmosphere of a nightmare. In 1928, a year after the

Sonatina had been completed, John Ireland gave a radio performance of it. A few days later he received a letter from that keen and sensitive critic, Philip Heseltine, who said:

It is quite one of the best things you have done, and your performance came off magnificently. You are one of the very few living composers in whose work one can discern a steady development along wholly personal lines, through a number of years; and in these days when so many musicians leap from one style to its opposite extreme in two successive works in the hope of achieving a factitious semblance of originality, it is more than ever pleasing to encounter a work such as the Sonatina which, for all its very real originality and newness, is clearly the logical development of a style that was already very individual fifteen years ago, or more.

Ireland says that his aim in sonata form is the attainment of unity in diversity, without resort to mechanical and academic means. This is exactly what he accomplishes so successfully in all his works in so-called sonata form. Everything is co-ordinated into an organic whole, and one feels that every bar is the natural outcome of its predecessor. This feeling for logical construction and organic growth is apparent even in such an early work as the *Phantasy Trio*, composed in 1906, which the composer considers to be his first representative work. The music falls into a skeleton design of sonata form, though the themes of the three contrasted but continuous sections are all derived from the first section. It is a youthful and exuberant work imbued with romantic feeling. Ireland's love of sonority, conciseness, and well-knit texture is strongly in evidence in this Trio, which has been carefully conceived from the point of view of balance between the three instruments. The melodies are very striking and expressive, and the harmonic scheme is lucid and colourful.

In 1909 Ireland won Cobbett's International Competition for a Violin Sonata with his Sonata in D minor, an important work, but unduly neglected. Ireland's Violin Sonata

No 2 in A minor was finished and first performed in 1917 by Albert Sammons and William Murdoch. It created a sensation and made the composer's reputation at the age of thirty-seven. Here is an extract from a very interesting letter to Ireland from Frank Bridge after he had heard the first performance of the Sonata in 1917:

Until I send you a line or two I shall not be able to get your new work out of my head. Not that I shall ever lose the impression – that's impossible – but while the recollection is so vivid I feel I must write and tell you how overjoyed I am with the Sonata. ... Its power is tremendous. I have the greatest faith in its future. ... It is not only for the comparatively small circle of people who are interested in British music, but for the whole world, regardless of nationality. ... It is possible that you may not think this is your *best* work, but personally I am convinced it is not only a landmark in your own history but also in that of contemporary music. ... I feel proud that any one of us has produced such a work. ...

The Violin Sonata in A minor is a very beautiful and expressive work; like the Piano Trio No 2 in E (in one movement) it is emotionally coloured by the influence of the First World War.

Ireland's Piano Trio No 3, which appeared in 1938, is based on the material of a similar work written, but not published, in 1915. It was virtually a new work and represents the full maturity of the composer. Its form is characteristic of Ireland's methods in that it is condensed and there is little actual repetition of material. The romantic first movement and the terse finale possess a certain relationship in their themes. Both the finale and the very beautifully conceived scherzo are full of that rhythmic intensity, or aggressiveness, which is an important 'fingerprint' of Ireland's style. The slow movement is a lovely lyrical outpouring that might easily have been inspired by the solitude of the sea in, say, some remote spot in the Channel Islands. Unlike that of many piano trios of turgid texture, the writing for the three instruments is extraordinarily clear; every note of the strings can be heard, for the piano part is obviously contrived never to obscure their outlines.

This ability to overcome the difficult problem of combining the sonorities of the piano with string instruments is also shown in the Sonata for 'Cello and Piano. Ireland succeeds here where most composers have failed, with the result that the 'cello always stands out clearly. From the point of view of form this work is extremely interesting; the greater part of the material is derived from the opening theme for the 'cello, but these derivations are very subtly contrived, and as the various themes and motives are introduced they are to all intents and purposes quite new. If in the 'Cello Sonata few concessions are made to sensuous appeal, there is a rugged power and poetic beauty that impress us increasingly as our knowledge of the music is extended.

Ireland's latest Sonata, composed in 1943, is for clarinet and piano. It shows the composer at his full stature as a creative artist. The music is full of varied changes of mood and is a complex piece of *ensemble* writing – the clarinet and piano parts are interwoven into a texture of great subtlety. The writing for the clarinet taxes the virtuosity and musicianship of the finest players – it was composed for Frederick Thurston.

One of Ireland's two most ambitious works is his Piano Concerto, one of the finest concertos written this century. It is interesting to note the clever and successful way in which Ireland reconciles certain features of the classical form with those of the cyclic method of Liszt. The first movement is typical of Ireland's terse but eloquent style; the second, which takes the form of a dialogue between orchestra and piano, is essentially lyrical and romantically expressive; the third is very rhythmical and has a faint flavour of Stravinsky about it. The fact that Ireland insisted from the first that the trumpets should use fibre mutes (now in general use, but then confined to jazz bands) instead of the old pear-shaped brass ones, and the use of the Chinese block in the finale, has led some undiscerning critics to claim the influence of jazz. Such a claim is ridiculous, for the music is singularly free from syncopated rhythms. As one might expect, Ireland approaches concerto form from an individual angle. His aim is to break away from certain rhetorical conventions of the late nineteenth century and invent a more logical, concentrated and organic design. In this he is wholly successful. Although exploiting the percussive qualities of the instrument, the piano writing is graceful and the orchestration is conceived with the utmost care for balance and appropriate colour.

With the orchestra Ireland is not a vivid and startling colourist. His orchestral effects are always restrained and appropriate to the aesthetic idea that he has in mind. His writing for the orchestra shows the same calculation that is characteristic of his works as a whole. These characteristics are noticeable in all of his handful of orchestral works, from the early impressionistic tone poem *The Forgotten Rite*, which was composed as long ago as 1913, to his stirring and expressive *Epic March*, his last venture with the orchestra.

The Forgotten Rite is a beautiful orchestral tone poem, shapely in design, compressed and economical, delicate in colour, and written in an idiom that harmonically offers no problems to the normally experienced ear. The title has no programmatic significance. The music was written spontaneously after a visit to Jersey. It begins and ends in an atmosphere of mystery: the first twelve bars are occupied with a quiet theme for strings, then a flute introduces a motive that seems to have a special significance in the work. It is heard again, slightly varied, on the oboe against tremolo strings, and for a third time as the basis of a harp glissando which might almost suggest that the 'rite' had been consummated. There are two big climaxes, of which the second is the culminating moment of the whole work, which gradually dies away *pianissimo* with a reference to the opening phrase. The music grows organically from the initial subject-matter. The texture is sometimes full and sometimes thinned down to an unaccompanied melodic line. As with all Ireland's scores there is a complete absence of padding – every note is an essential part of the design.

In 1921 Ireland composed another tone poem entitled *Mai-Dun*, which is the ancient name (used by Thomas Hardy) for the huge prehistoric 'camp' or earthwork near Dorchester, now known as Maiden Castle. Ireland's work, with the sub-title *Symphonic Rhapsody*, was written as a result of a prolonged stay in the neighbourhood, where a remote past seems still vividly alive and active to anyone open to influences of 'the world beyond the walls', as Arthur Machen puts it. In a sense, *Mai-Dun* bears a direct relation to *The Forgotten Rite*, representing as it does the reverse side – a sense of strife, effort, and achievement on the part of man in nobler and more primitive times, when the elemental forces of nature, personified as spirits and gods, were something real and definite in relation to human personality, and the objects of recognition, worship, and sacrifice. While *The Forgotten Rite* attempts to bring in terms of music the attitude of man towards the gods, *Mai-Dun* suggests mankind's reaction to the earth and mankind itself, and to Fate.

Musically considered, the two principal themes of *Mai-Dun* represent effort and aspiration respectively. Neither is definitely repeated in the musical structure; this is freely built up into an elastic form, closing with the introduction of a motive of triumph and exultation, which forms the coda. The work is very condensed, and though it follows in its construction a modern approach to sonata form, this is secondary to the emotional sequence of ideas, with their subsidiary implications, that underlies the general design of the music, in which material, colour, and form combine to make unity a complete idea or impression of things felt. For some unaccountable reason *Mai-Dun* has been studiously neglected by orchestral organisations and therefore, as the composer once remarked, it might be more correctly entitled 'May-not-be-Done'.

Another orchestral work that is even less often played is the *Legend* for piano and orchestra, dedicated to Arthur Machen. It was composed in 1933 during a four months' sojourn in a lonely cottage situated on the Sussex Downs. Although Ireland offers no programme to his *Legend*, it is not difficult to imagine that the atmosphere of the music is connected in some way with the lonely, wind-swept upland where human company is rarely found even today. And there, maybe, only a solitary tumulus forms a memorial to some tragic, legendary figure, incidents from whose fateful story the music might well illustrate. *Legend* is a dialogue for piano and orchestra. It opens with a long passage for a solo horn, providing the melodic basis for the main structure of the work, which possesses a sombre and mysterious character. A notable incident in the music is a section for the piano based on a melody resembling the *Dies Irae*. This section is worked up to a strenuous climax; then comes a contrasted episode that at first has the character of a ghostly and unsubstantial dance. The use of orchestral resources is exceptionally economic, and the instrumentation is unusual for the absence of trumpets and for the fact that the heavier brass consists of only two tenor trombones that are used very sparingly.

Two other works complete Ireland's list of orchestral compositions: the brilliant and melodious *London Overture* (1936) and the *Concertino Pastorale* for string orchestra, which was written in 1939. The latter is a magnificently rich and ingenious piece of string writing with a slow movement, entitled *Threnody*, imbued with that tender and profound feeling so often expressed in the composer's slow movements.

The second of Ireland's two most ambitious works is *These Things Shall Be* for chorus and orchestra, which was first performed in 1937. It is a setting of verses from John Addington Symonds's *A Vista*, which looks forward to the time when Mankind will condemn for ever the stupid and unnecessary barbarity of war as a means of settling international disputes. When that time comes man will truly be able to flatter himself on his civilisation. Symonds and Ireland combine in emphasising that 'these things – they are no dreams – shall be'.

The work falls into four sections, divided by three orchestral interludes of varying length. The short orchestral introduction, which is based on a terse rhythmic motive that reappears at various subsequent points, is sinister and seems to suggest the gloom and uncertainty of the future. The chorus then enters with the question: 'What will the future bring, to happier men when we have gone? What golden days shall dawn for them, transcending all we gaze upon.'

Before the answer is given there is a vigorous orchestral interlude which symbolises human determination to create a safe and better world. Then comes the answer. 'These things shall be! A loftier race than e'er the world hath known shall rise with flame of freedom in their souls and light of science in their eyes.' This section is worked up to a fine climax – a mighty assertion of faith.

The orchestral interlude that follows is pastoral in character and suggests that the earth is the basis of everything. Finally comes a broad and stately melody full of deep feeling. It tells us that 'Nation with nation, land with land, in- armed shall lived as comrades free; in every brain and heart shall throb the pulse of one fraternity.' As the things that shall be are described, this fine tune is built up with varied orchestration to an imposing climax.

There follows a calm and reflective orchestral interlude that seems to meditate on the peace and serenity of the future, and afterwards the chorus enters whispering the question: 'What will the future bring?' The answer is confidently asserted. The music is brought to an end quietly and expressively, the last note of the chorus changing to a humming tone accompanied only by strings.

The many felicitous touches of harmony and orchestration are characteristic of Ireland's resourceful musicianship. *These Things Shall Be* is one of the composer's most inspired works, and worthy of being placed among the finest products of the English choral tradition.

Ireland's fondness for organic unity and growth is to be seen not only in his larger instrumental works but even in the songs, such as the *Five Songs to Poems by Thomas Hardy*, *We'll to the Woods no more* (a cycle of two settings from Housman, and a piano piece which 'may be performed separately, but must be considered as a completion of the two previous numbers'), *The Land of Lost Content*, *Five Songs to Sixteenth-century Poems*, and the cycle *Songs Sacred and Profane*. As a song composer Ireland is undoubtedly one of the foremost of our time. His songs number over a hundred, embrace a remarkable variety of style, and are all notable for that finished craftsmanship and delicate poetic sense which are the hall-marks of his music. I doubt if Ireland has ever set any words that are not among the best, or near best, in English lyric poetry. His choice ranges from Shakespeare and Blake to A. E. Housman, Arthur Symons, and Rupert Brooke.

Ireland possesses the three qualities that are essential to the art of great song-making: a perfect sense of metre, the ability to invent a vocal melodic line that evokes the mood of the poem, and a keen sense of harmonic colour and its dramatic possibilities. These qualities are seen at their finest in such beautiful examples as in the cycle of six songs from *A Shropshire Lad* entitled *The Land of Lost Content*, and in the separate songs *When I am dead, my dearest*; *Sea Fever*; *Rest*; the two songs of the First World War (1917) entitled *The Cost*; *The Adoration*; *The Rat*; *Spring Sorrow*; and *I have Twelve Oxen*. In these songs and in many others Ireland evokes in his music the emotional essence of the poems.

It is strange that Ireland's songs are so neglected by singers, for here is a golden treasury of lovely material for a really musical singer. Singers of the past have made themselves notorious for their laziness in learning and presenting anything new, unless it is childishly silly and obvious and promises to be popular in the vulgar sense. It is to be hoped that the singers of the future will want to be, and will have to be, better and more intelligent musicians. It will be then that John Ireland will come into his own.

I would sum up Ireland's music as one of the greatest contributions to the renaissance of English music that began with Elgar and Delius and after nearly fifty years happily shows no sign of diminishing. Ireland's music, however, is not for those who think and feel only in terms of the grandiose and the spectacular. His music appeals strongly to the sensitive, romantic listener who, while not averse on occasions to the emotional exuberance of Tchaikovsky and Wagner, knows that music in which the emotion is controlled by fastidious craftsmanship and exquisite taste can often be, through its subtle implications, more poignant or exhilarating than music that is obviously and directly sensuous.

CHAPTER VIII

Sir Arnold Bax

B. 1883

JULIAN HERBAGE

*

FIRST impressions are often deceptive. I remember that the first time I saw Arnold Bax was at a Promenade Concert in 1920. Harriet Cohen had given the first performance of his *Symphonic Variations* for piano and orchestra. In response to the applause, a figure in a tightly buttoned double-breasted suit came on to the platform. With a mixture of diffidence and embarrassment he bowed stiffly at the audience, obviously rather uncomfortable about the whole affair, which is scarcely worth describing, except that for many this is the only contact they have had with Bax, and it gives a false impression both of the man and of the artist.

The next time I saw Bax was some years later, at Lord's Cricket Ground, still in the same type of suit, but with a face more bucolic, and a nondescript pork-pie felt hat jammed down well over his eyes. As Bax was regarded as a romantic composer at this time, when romanticism was never more out of fashion, I wondered whether his appearance was a pose, or perhaps a protest against the artistic label which had been attached to him. But no, Bax was obviously at ease, and thoroughly enjoying himself, and it was only after we had been chatting for some time that I felt all of a sudden something far-away in his attitude, and noticed that his eyes were looking past the cricket-field – almost past the horizon. And that sudden vision gave me a clue to the duality of Bax's personality – the worldly Bax, shrewd observer and witty companion, and the unworldly Bax, whose spirit seems enshrined in some Irish legend.

The story goes that Bax is of Celtic extraction, but actually he comes of old Surrey stock and his ancestors were followers of Penn, the Quaker. In many ways he is a psychological revolt against his ancestry, and his complex character may largely have been built up through the clash between his conventionally English surroundings and the almost pagan striving after beauty in his spirit. At the age of six he distinctly remembers his first conscious apprehension of the ideal of beauty. He was taken to Arundel Park at sunset, and in his own words 'as we stood there an unimaginable glory of flame developed in the west so that all the wooded heights seemed on fire ... I watched speechlessly. To my childish perception this visitation was sheer all-conquering splendour and majesty, untroubled by the sense of the transitoriness of all lovely things. The hour was immortal.'

From his earliest years Bax seemed to take to music like the proverbial duck to water. As he modestly describes it, 'I cannot recall the long-lost day when I was unable to play the piano – inaccurately. It seems that I could always read printed music at the piano-stool with the same unthinking ease with which a man reads a book.' Indeed, as a youth he displayed an uncanny ability to read even the most complicated musical scores, and as a student at the Royal Academy of Music he amazed everyone by the apparent facility with which he overcame all technical difficulties. As a result, he started upon his career as a composer with such an exuberant confidence in his technical abilities that a string quartet, composed while he was still at the Academy, was pronounced so full of complexities as to be virtually unplayable. The mark of this early setback is still apparent in Bax's personality. Even now he will never conduct a performance of his own music, and is extremely reticent in venturing his opinion when present at a rehearsal. This diffidence has caused him to tolerate many unworthy performances of his works, and yet Bax's music, almost more than any other, demands the utmost clarity and balance in performance.

At the Academy Bax had fallen under the influence of Wagner and Strauss, though not to an extent that made him incapable of perceiving their musical tendencies. 'Wagner,' he wrote, 'had made music the language of passion and now Richard the second was turning the art into neurosis become vocal.' A little later Elgar was added to the list of idols, and it is perhaps Elgar's influence that has lasted longest with him. Stronger, however, than any musical influence in these impressionable years was the immense impact that the poetry of W. B. Yeats made upon him. At the age of nineteen he first read *The Wanderings of Usheen*, and in his own words 'in a moment the Celt within me stood revealed'. Bax realised the duality of his nature. 'I love life', he has said, 'I am an appreciative inhabitant of this world ... yet a part of me is not of it.' In the dream world of Celtic poetry, Bax discovered a second self, so much so, indeed, that at one time he seemed on the verge of abandoning music for literature.

It is not without significance, then, that the tone poem *In the Faëry Hills*, based on an episode from *The Wanderings of Usheen*, was the first of Bax's orchestral works to obtain recognition for the composer. Written in 1909, it still retains its freshness and charm as one of the most spontaneous of his tone poems. The poet Usheen is lured by a fairy girl to an island where revels of dancing and music never cease. Usheen is greeted by the fairy throng, who ask him to sing to them of human joys. Usheen sings to his harp, and for a while silence falls upon his hearers. 'A sadder creature never stept than this strange human bard.' But others seize his harp and fling it into a deep pool, and the poet is finally drawn into the unending revels. The Celtic idiom is very apparent in this work, particularly in the dance theme, and though the music has not the structural maturity of the later tone poems, it has a simple charm and directness that will always assure it a favourite place in Bax's orchestral output.

In the Faëry Hills is perhaps the high-water mark of Bax's early work. In the orchestral and chamber works that immediately followed the harmonic complexity became more marked and the form more exuberantly diffuse. In its original form the first Violin and Piano Sonata, composed in 1910, showed that the composer, never lacking in fertility of invention, was tending to over-estimate the capacity of both hearer and interpretative artist. If so, he was certainly in fashionable company. Schönberg's *Five Orchestral Pieces* belong to this era, and when they were first performed in London two years later 'almost everybody present seemed bewildered, if not shocked'. Bax, however, determined to learn from his critics, and drastically revised his Sonata, so that of the original composition only the first movement remains, and even so in abridged form. The next big chamber-music work, the monumental Quintet for Piano and Strings (1914–15), shows an equal tendency to complexity, and it is perhaps the criticism that this work received which determined Bax deliberately to simplify his style.

The chief problem, indeed, in Bax's musical career has not been that of self-expression – that has always been almost fatally easy for him. It has been to express himself in such a manner that the executant can clearly interpret his thoughts to the listener. Bax's form, the framework of his musical thought, has always been clear and based on a true development of classical tradition. His thematic material is on the whole unusually diatonic, but almost invariably the harmonic texture is richly wrought, and highly individual. It is this sensuous side of Bax's creative art that hinders our appreciation of the intellectual side. As listeners we have a double task – to appreciate the form and structure while absorbing the colour and harmony. Only too often, particularly if the performance is not highly balanced, this double task is too much for us, and the music is immediately classed as incoherent, noisy, or over-scored.

The first signs of this deliberate simplification are to be found in *The Garden of Fand* (1916). The composer further helped the success of the work by disclosing a definite literary programme. 'The Garden of Fand is the sea. The earlier portion of the work seeks to create the atmosphere of an enchanted Atlantic. ... Upon its surface floats a small ship. ... The little craft is borne on ... until on the crest of an immense wave, it is tossed on to the shore of Fand's miraculous island.' As in the *Faëry Hills*, 'Here is unhuman revelry ... and the voyagers are caught away into the maze of the dance.' Fand sings her song of immortal love, the dance begins anew, until finally the sea overwhelms the whole island. As the immortals laugh at the fate of the over-rash mortals, twilight falls, the sea subsides, and Fand's garden fades out of sight.

It is essential to the appreciation of much of Bax's work to understand his use of a literary programme. Bax once confessed that for him the problem of composition consisted in the translation of ideas and impressions into the language of music. The word 'translation' is important, and explains the fact that, while much of Bax's music is conceived with a 'programme' in mind, the composer insists that, when he has achieved a translation of his ideas and sensations into sound, the result should be listened to as pure music. *The Garden of Fand*, then, is not an essay at impressionism in music, like Debussy's *La Mer*, or an evocation, like Delius's *Summer Night on the River*. It is a much more complex and subtle synthesis of mood, thought, and sensation, the stirrings of those hidden forces in our inner consciousness caused through the stimulation of our outward perception.

Ernest Newman has brilliantly pilloried those musical highbrows who boggle at music being connected in any way with a 'programme'. 'Bax,' he wrote, 'I am glad to see is at last mustering up courage enough to admit that some of his later work is programmatic. More composers would be glad to make the same simple admission had they not been scared stiff by the superficial aestheticians who insist on the necessity of music being "pure", the implication being that any music that has the remotest connection with "literature" is necessarily impure, and therefore ineligible for admission into the musical heaven. The result of the activities of this self-appointed Vigilance Committee for Musical Morals has been to turn most composers into musical hypocrites. They have indulged in secret in this delightful dalliance with "literature", and then denied in public that they ever knew the naughty lady by sight; while as for ever having called at the house ...'

Perhaps a better description for *The Garden of Fand* and Bax's other tone poems of this period, namely *Tintagel* (1917) and the sombrely beautiful *November Woods* (1917), would be 'mood-evocations'. *Tintagel*, for instance, epitomises Bax's reaction to nature and legend, the first of which, to the composer's poetic imagination, so often evokes the second. The scene is the castle-crowned cliff of Tintagel in Cornwall, with the wide distances of the Atlantic capped by a summer's sky. From this vision of nature are evoked the legends of its past, of King Arthur, King Mark, Tristram and Iseult, and during this evocation a musician may discern a fragment of a theme from Wagner's *Tristan*. Impression and emotion have been translated into music. But it is the mood that is always the predominant feature of the music, a mood sometimes strong and spacious, sometimes tender and idyllic, often ferocious and sinister. Yet if we analyse the work carefully, we find that its musical construction is quite as close as any symphony. As the late M. D. Calvocoressi expressed it: 'His dramatic and poetic fancy is at work simultaneously with his purely musical imagination'.

The inherently symphonic nature of such work is shown even more clearly in the Symphonic Variations for Piano and Orchestra (1917) in which, though no definite programme is disclosed, each variation bears a separate title, such as *Nocturne*, *Strife*, *The Temple*, and so on. The translation into symphonic thought, has indeed, been complete, and the work can be enjoyed as 'pure' music even by a member of Mr Newman's Vigilance Committee.

Even in that marvellously brilliant and prolific year of 1917 there were still critics of Bax's incoherence of harmony and diffuseness of style. In the following year the composer took up the challenge of these modern Beckmessers. Just as Prokofiev confounded those critics who accused him of complexity with the production of his *Symphonie classique*, so Bax met the same criticism with a similar retort. His First String Quartet in G major (1918) is a model of simplicity, clarity, and conciseness. It is indeed an ideal work for the music-lover to embark on his exploration of Bax's music. It has the vigour and sparkle of a Haydn quartet, together with the naïve charm of Dvořák's national dances. Like most of Bax's later works it is in three movements: an *allegro semplice*, a lyrical *lento*, and a lively *rondo*, in the course of which occurs a beautiful melody that shows how essentially Bax has absorbed the poetic curve of Irish folksong.

For the next year or two Bax confined himself mainly to chamber-music works, as if in a deliberate attempt to deny himself the luxuriance of orchestral colouring. Hitherto his harmony had often been luscious for its own sake. He had used harmony as a sort of chromatic façade to his inherently diatonic structure. From this period a change came over his use of harmony. The chromatic became woven into a polyphonic texture, so that polyphonic harmony gradually emerged that is both individual and peculiarly characteristic in all his later works. At the same time the harmonic basis tended to be more austere and uncompromising, and spiritually the mood of much of his music developed a more grim and dispassionate outlook, though the harder and more rugged outline involved no sacrifice in intrinsic beauty. This development can be studied most clearly in the Sonata for Viola and Piano (1921), where the exuberant virtuosity of the earlier chamber works has matured into a structure of powerful yet mellow loveliness. Few composers have made better use of the sombre beauty of the viola, and few indeed have overcome so successfully its limitations in expressive range. The Viola Sonata is constructed with such balance of form and technical variety of treatment that, though the work is deliberately cast in one mood, yet the mood never wearies. No other British composer has blended together so skilfully the qualities of concise musical thought and mystical contemplation as Bax has in this great work.

From his early years Bax had shown an interest in choral music. His preoccupation with the 'translation' of literary ideas into musical forms had probably caused him to neglect this field for a while, and it was not until the year 1921 that he turned to choral music again. It is possible he felt that he had reached a point in his development as a composer when a further and intense study of the methods and practices of the great polyphonic composers was essential to the widening of his art. Certainly this study was subsequently to have an effect on his entire output, of equal importance to the simplification of style begun in the First String Quartet. Bax absorbed the whole spirit of polyphony with the same essential thoroughness with which he had earlier made the Celtic folk-idiom his own. The motet *Mater ora Filium* (1921) is a true evocation, in both mood and musical style, of the golden age of polyphonic music. There is nothing of the 'period piece' here, or of the highly spiced old-world pastiches that the post-war Parisians were then serving up to a jaded world in such large synthetic quantities. Both technically and spiritually Bax is so much in tune with his subject that one is scarcely conscious of the personal harmonic idiom, so naturally does it arise out of the skilfully handled counterpoint.

With the achievement of *Mater ora Filium* on the one hand, and the Viola Sonata on the other, Bax seems to have realised that he had reaped the full harvest of his self-imposed discipline, and now, in the fullness of his musical powers, he embarked on his career as a symphonist. In some ways Bax's seven symphonies tower above the rest of his output, and they are undoubtedly the works on which future generations will assess his musical reputation. Though his more recent orchestral compositions have included several tone poems, including the beautiful and much-neglected *The Tale the Pine Trees Knew* (1931), yet it is in his symphonies that Bax's creative talent and technical accomplishment are exploited at their fullest. Unfortunately they are not easily accessible to most music-lovers at the moment. Only one of them, the third (1928–9), is recorded, while their technical complexity and the large orchestra they require have made performances of them a comparatively rare event.

In this connection one is tempted to think of Sibelius, whose seven symphonies at first made little headway in this country. But Sibelius was helped by the gramophone. Recordings made it possible for music-lovers to know and admire his symphonies by means of constant re-hearing. When a work is issued in recorded form one does not have to depend on the conservative attitude of concert promoters, who consider they have 'done a composer proud' if they give a single performance of a difficult new work. A notable exception to such conservatism is Serge Koussevitsky, who, when Bostonians gave a cool reception to Sibelius's Fourth Symphony, announced to the assembled audience that he intended to repeat the work in all his future programmes until they got to know and like it. The symphonies of Bax could well be afforded the same treatment, for their difficulties, to both performers and audiences, are at least as great.

Bax's symphonies are certainly not for those who desire only a shallow attractiveness from music. They demand from the listener the same clear intellect and austere sense of lyrical beauty that the composer himself possesses. Bax rarely indulges in mere repetition as a process of symphonic development; when he repeats at all, it is always with some variation of harmony or orchestral colour. The mind must be constantly on the alert for any implication of underlying ideas in order to be prepared for their later development. Bax himself thinks quickly and spontaneously, and expects the same quality from his listener. His symphonies cover a wide and rapid emotional range, from the menacingly cruel to the lyrically beautiful, and each mood is conceived with the same dispassionate intensity.

His use of orchestral colour is unusual. It is probably the last sign of his uncurbed virtuosity that he delights in the extreme ranges of the less-used instruments, such as the low notes of the bass clarinet. On this account, and on account of the frequent luxurious exuberance of his orchestral texture, his critics sometimes accuse him of being a 'muddy' orchestrator who overloads his score. Such criticism reminds me of the fact that when I first saw Sickert's pictures, I thought his colour was muddy too. It was only when I had fathomed the balance and mood of the colouring that I realised how wide was its range, and how perfectly it expressed the intentions of the painter. With Bax, however, the problem is even more difficult, as a realisation of the composer's intentions depends to a great extent on the actual performance, and few performances of a Bax symphony, at least in my hearing, have approached perfection.

There are certain superficial points of resemblance between all the symphonies: their three-movement form, for instance, the employment of a lyrical, sometimes elegiac epilogue from the Third Symphony onwards, the importance of the introductions and the frequent use of 'motto' phrases. As Robin Hull has said: 'The newcomer to the symphonies may be struck less quickly by their points of difference than by rough similarities arising from Bax's highly personal style'. More frequent hearing will convince us that they are all essentially different, and each seems set on solving some new spiritual problem. The mood of the First Symphony (1921–2) is personal, bitter, and challenging. Its powerful and explosive conflict could not be resolved within the bounds of a single work, and it is left for the Second Symphony (1924–5) to pursue the battle into the innermost depths of the soul, and for the Third Symphony (1928–9) to achieve in its beautiful epilogue a peaceful resolution to the bitter and troubled spirit. In the Fourth Symphony (1930–1) new paths are sought, and for the first time an external programme is allowed to make a fleeting appearance. The composer himself admits that the beginning of the first movement represents to him a rough sea at flood-tide on a sunny day – compare this opening, indeed, with the beginning of *Tintagel* – and much of this work, written in Donegal and Inverness-shire, is nature music. After the bitter and uncompromising introspection of the first three symphonies, the fourth is unashamedly extrovert.

In the Fifth Symphony (1931–2) Bax returns to his earlier problems, but with renewed vigour of thought and command of resource, gained through the emergence from his introspective mood. In this great work Bax's dual nature seems to strike a perfect balance, and the conciseness of the musical thought is equalled by the vigour and lyrical beauty of the expression. For once the epilogue ends with a sense of triumph, which proclaims both spiritual and intellectual victory. In its power, imagination, and maturity, it is perhaps the greatest of the seven symphonies.

Bax the musician seems to gain something of an ascendancy over Bax the poet in the Sixth Symphony (1934), of which the chief feature is the interesting and unusual structure, particularly of the finale. This movement, headed 'Introduction – Scherzo and Trio – Epilogue', is based on a short phrase heard at the beginning of the introduction, and the vigorous treatment of the scherzo, followed by the ecstatic tranquillity of the epilogue, produce a musical *tour de force* that even Bax himself has rarely surpassed. This preoccupation with musical problems is indeed significant of much of Bax's most recent output, and adds a mellowness that enhances the mature philosophy of the Seventh Symphony (1938–9), the last the composer has yet given us.

The Seventh Symphony in many ways seems to belong to a different world from its predecessors. Though the conflict of its first movement is deep and massive, it seems more impersonal, and the second movement leads us into the twilight of things far away. It has a middle section marked *In legendary mood*, a memory of some Nordic ballad of far-off days, and the whole seems to be set in some ageless world where conflict has been resolved by the sheer passing of time. The third movement is a *Theme, Variations and Epilogue*. It has about it the atmosphere of an apotheosis, of striving ended, peace and tranquillity. This epilogue is indeed strangely ultimate and final.

It seems natural to turn from Bax's symphonies to his concertos, even though the concerto is a form of which many symphonists have fought shy. Schubert is, of course, the classic example of a composer with nine symphonies to his credit who has written no concertos. Mahler and Bruckner are two further symphonic writers who have added nothing to the concerto repertoire, and in our own day both Sibelius and Shostakovich have written only one concerto each. The different treatment necessary for symphonic and concerto form is one that only the greatest classic composers have been able successfully to solve. Bax, however, is too much a musician to try to by-pass the concerto problem. He has dealt with it in several ways. His two major works for piano and orchestra, the *Symphonic Variations* and *Winter Legends* (1930), both offer a different solution, though, fundamentally, both have a common factor in that the piano is never allowed to dominate the organic development. *Winter Legends*, indeed, is an elaborate symphonic poem, which, though it has no definite programme, tells of

> Legends that once were told or sung
> In many a smoky fire-side nook
> Of Iceland, in the ancient day,
> By wandering saga-man or scald.

It is in the 'Cello Concerto (1932) that Bax first treats the solo instrumentalist as a virtuoso, and with his genius for orchestral technique has written a work wherein the soloist is always the principal orator. When Gaspar Cassadó gave the first performance of this work he confessed that he was amazed how easily the 'cello line came through the brilliantly orchestrated score – an example of Bax's inherent musicianship, and a crushing reply to those who accuse him of muddy orchestration. The Violin Concerto (1937) goes even farther in the exploitation of the soloist as a virtuoso. Its first movement cleverly avoids the 'time factor' inherent in symphonic form, a factor for which the static virtuosity of true concerto has little use. The composer describes this movement as Overture, Ballad, and Scherzo, the Ballad taking the place of a second subject, and the Scherzo (which makes mock of the Overture and Ballad) being the development section. This Concerto is one of the most immediately engaging of Bax's major works, and it is indeed tragic that the early death of Eda Kersey deprived us of its first and most sympathetic exponent.

Though other orchestral works, such as the *Overture, Elegy and Rondo* (1929) and the (slightly Straussian) *Overture to a Picaresque Comedy* (1930), deserve more than a mere mention, too little has yet been said about the more recent chamber-music works. These by their variety and musical interest have given Bax a position unique among British composers in this field. The first 'Cello Sonata (1923) has much of the personal drama of the First and Second Symphonies, of which it is a contemporary. It is a spacious work, with a heroic first movement, an idyllic and sensuous second movement, and a finale wherein the cruelly warring elements eventually become transformed into a peaceful epilogue. In thorough contrast is the Oboe Quintet, written in the same year. This charming and unpretentious work, dedicated to Leon Goossens, is cast in Arcadian mood throughout, and has a spontaneous attraction quite its own. The Second String Quartet (1924) again reverts more to the mood of the symphonies. Its ruthless and uncompromising style is not easy to assimilate, and its contrapuntal complexity demands both a finished performance and attentive listening.

Of the later chamber-music works, several are for a large ensemble, such as the Concertos for flute, harp, oboe and strings (1934) and for bassoon, harp, and string sextet (1936). Perhaps the most successful of these is the Nonett (1931), a concise, colourful, and immediately attractive work that can well bear comparison with Ravel's Septet. Mention, too, must be made of Bax's exploitation of the harp in chamber-music *ensembles*, particularly the Sonata for Harp and Viola (1928), a technical *tour de force* that only an accomplished composer like Bax could have even attempted. But from the imposing list of some thirty chamber-music works, it becomes invidious to select any more for special mention.

As a composer for the piano Bax has been unduly neglected. In many ways the four sonatas provide a contribution to the literature of that instrument as important as do the symphonies to the orchestral repertoire. Harriet Cohen, their chief exponent, to whom three of them are dedicated, has given me the following description of them. 'Of the four sonatas, the first three have one particular element in common in that they all are marked by an epic-romantic atmosphere. The first, in F sharp minor, was written in the Ukraine in the summer of 1910, and contains features obviously derived from Russian landscape and character. The sonata is in one long movement, and may be said to be the descendant – formally – of Liszt's celebrated Sonata in B minor. The earlier part of the development section was certainly suggested by the almost illimitable distances of the Russian plain, and the finale of the whole work (composed ten years later than the rest of the sonata) was conceived in a mood of almost aggressive triumph, the first subject of the sonata reappearing in a march with each phrase interrupted by a suggestion of the multi-rhythmed jangles of Slavonic church bells during the Easter Festival.

'No. 2 in G (also in one movement) is again an epic conception, this time taking the form of a contest between a legendary hero and the powers of darkness. It has been described as "The Battle with the Loathly Worm". There must be something lurid and sinister about this work, for when it first appeared and was often being played, Arnold Bax was on one occasion taken aside by a Danish mystic and very seriously warned that he must be extremely careful, as he was temporarily possessed by a devil. Bax told him that he had just written a work (the first symphony) which he feared the Dane would think still more deeply concerned with Demonology: to which he replied that he hoped it would never be performed. Bax said this was an uncanny experience, and made a deep – if unenduring – impression upon him. As a matter of fact the sonata ends with the victory of St George (or whoever the hero may have been) and in a mood of complete tranquillity.

'The third sonata in G sharp minor is cast in the conventional three movements. The first is again epic in character, and was once strangely used by Marie Rambert as the basis of a ballet upon the subject of the Death of Cuchullain. Bax did not think this experiment a success. The second movement is an idyll, calm and broad in design, certainly a Celtic folk-song (of his own invention) in full flower. The last is a dark-hued toccata or perpetuum mobile.

'The fourth sonata, in G, composed quite a quarter of a century after the first, is almost a reactionary work in that it is purely classical in design and proportion, and even in content, in spite of the very modern harmony in the final rondo. The second movement is a kind of exotic dream in which one of the longest pedal-points ever used acts as a species of opiate upon the imagination. We imagine that it comes as a relief to the hearer when the tension is at last resolved, as though he could once again breathe freely. This movement is one of Bax's favourites amongst his music for solo piano.

'As for the score or so of short piano pieces, three of

them, the *Vodka Shop*, *Gopak*, and *May Night in Ukraine*, derive from impressions made upon the composer during his visit to Russia in 1910. There are several English nature pictures, such as *Apple-blossom Time*, *Country Tune*, *On a May Evening*, *The Maiden with a Daffodil*, and *Hill Tune*, though the last is more Irish than English. Two of these short works, *A Mountain Mood* and *Lullaby*, are in variation form. *A Mountain Mood* is perhaps the most remarkable piece of pianoforte music since Debussy, whilst the passacaglia *Winter Waters* is a magnificent tone poem in miniature. *What the Minstrel Told* is again a heroic legend, and *The Princesses' Rose Garden* a love poem, a nostalgic dream. Finally *Burlesque* and *Toccata* are knockabout, virtuoso pieces, the second exceedingly difficult to play.' Even Harriet Cohen's list makes no mention of the charming and characteristic music for two pianos – the two miniature tone poems *Moy Mell* and *The Poisoned Fountain*, and the delightful Norwegian dance (with a Celtic lilt), *Hardanger*.

Only one field of music has Bax neglected – he has as yet written no opera. In his handling of a chorus in such works as *St Patrick's Breastplate* (1923-4) and *The Morning Watch* (1935) he displays a sure dramatic touch. His lyric vein is unquestioned, as is witnessed by such beautiful songs as *The White Peace*, *Cradle Song*, and *The Rann of Exile*. Turning to film music for the first time he has given us the vitally dramatic *Malta, G.C.* Dare we hope that the poetry of a Yeats or Synge may now fire his Celtic imagination to produce in operatic form a work such as Synge's *Riders to the Sea*?

*

[See note at end of Chapter on Vaughan Williams. Much the same could have been added here. (Editor.)]

CHAPTER IX

Eugene Goossens

B. 1893

ROBIN HULL

*

EUGENE GOOSSENS, the renowned conductor of the Cincinnati Symphony Orchestra, bridges the gap between Bliss and Moeran in that generation of British composers born during the last decade of the nineteenth century. Scion of a musicianly family, his early repute as violinist and pianist was rivalled from his eighteenth year by an astonishing skill in composition. Goossens's first works, although freezingly clever, reflected over-much the cosmopolitan fashions of a period when ballets such as Ravel's *Daphnis and Chloé* and Stravinsky's *Rite of Spring* were still enthralling novelties. His mature compositions, many of which are rewarding to approach, combine real if variable individuality with a logical and colourful style. Ranging from symphony to song, and revealing an extraordinary mastery of technical resource, their most characteristic pages make clear that Goossens is a romantic at heart. Admittedly he can refine emotion almost to the point of classical purity, and intensify it until the romantic element becomes engulfed in a flood of rhetoric, but the larger part of his output achieves a fine variety between these extremes. Although, even in Goossens's fifty-second year, no up-to-date recordings for gramophone were available, he has composed much that there is a fair chance of hearing in the concert hall. A swifter approach, naturally, is to play for oneself some of his simpler music, or to search out friends willing to embark upon a combined voyage of discovery.

Kaleidoscope, a set of twelve short pieces for piano, makes an excellent starting-point. These polished and witty epigrams, though free in movement around their key-centre and consequently full of accidentals, are less difficult than they look. That is true of many works by Goossens. The best plan with *Kaleidoscope* is to work backwards from the final piece, *Good-Night*, to *A Merry Party* and thence to *Promenade*, after which further choice can be left to individual taste. This opening sequence ensures a serviceable introduction to Goossen's style of harmony. *Promenade*, especially, will familiarise the eye and ear with his fluid chromaticism. It is vitally important to tackle that feature at an early stage if one wants to make any real headway. Again, the beautifully pastoral melody of *Folk-Tune*, the first of *Two Studies for Piano*, simplifies the task of appreciating the luxuriant harmony used for its setting. Here Goossens builds a rich structure mainly upon consecutive sevenths, with stimulating clashes between chords in contrary motion, but his bass line is firmly rooted in the key of D despite its flexible movement by semitone. The ornate scherzo which follows offers a dazzling entertainment to the listener, but players, unless exceptionally able, are advised to return to it after mastering the engagingly fanciful pages of *Four Conceits*. Of these, *Dance Memories* is the most quickly accessible to listener and player alike. *The Gargoyle* and *The Marionette Show* are brilliant grotesques, while *A Walking Tune* is whimsical without falling into affectation. Goossens's vividly picturesque *Nature Poems*, entitled *Awakening*, *Pastoral* and *Bacchanal*, demand such a high degree of virtuosity from the pianist that performances are rare, but any chance to hear a skilled interpretation ought not to be missed.

Goossens's experience as violinist, which included membership of the Philharmonic String Quartet, serves him particularly well when writing for small numbers of combined instruments. The popular yet still characteristic

Two Sketches for String Quartet, *By the Tarn* and *Jack o' Lantern*, offer an attractive opening for study of his work in this field. Certainly the deft caprice of *Jack o' Lantern* is more quickly fascinating, but *By the Tarn* cuts deeper with its finely contemplative mood. It is an easy step from these Sketches to *Five Impressions of a Holiday* for piano, flute (or violin) and 'cello, which have likewise held a firm place in the repertoire. The *Impressions*, although an earlier composition, are sufficiently mature in style and sentiment to remain typical of Goossens's flair for depicting pastoral scenes. Those he evokes here, notably in the limpid music of *By the Rivers*, are distinguished by evidence of a poetic feeling absent from some of his bizarre fancies.

The works mentioned above should be regarded, of course, merely as a prelude to exploration of the two main groups into which Goossens's 'household' music falls. As romance is the key-note of the larger group, one could scarcely find a more appropriate lead than the expressive *Romance* for violin and piano transcribed by the composer from his second opera, *Don Juan de Mañara*. The violin melody is warm, lyrical, and more straightforward than the piano part, which needs light treatment if an effect of thickness is to be avoided. This piece makes a helpful preliminary to the short but much finer *Lyric Poem* for the same instruments, of which a version with orchestral accompaniment (lately clarified in revision) is less well known. The *Lyric Poem* shows Goossens's thought in a tauter, more concentrated design, his invention touching a higher level of imagination, without any loss of that spontaneity which is a striking feature of the *Romance*. Listeners intent upon still bolder objectives will find a good deal to reward them in the two Sonatas for Violin and Piano written about twelve years apart. No doubt these significant works would have reached a wider public by now but for complexities of piano-writing which could have been pruned more easily from the first Sonata than its successor. Here, likewise in the *Nature Poems* for piano,

Goossens has reaped the natural if regrettable consequence of taking as a norm his exceptional capabilities at the keyboard. Musically, Sonata No. 1 is impressive alike for vigorous and idyllic eloquence. The meditative beauty of the slow movement is relatively so free from the distraction of virtuosity that it may well be studied before the first or third. Goossens's Second Violin Sonata is not only clearer in texture but more compactly organised as regards material. The combination of warmer feeling with greater distinction of ideas makes for much readier acquaintance, and in general this Sonata, which may be expected to prove the more enduring of the two, should be given precedence by the listener. There is a romantic spirit, too, throughout the Second String Quartet, of which the originality and expert craftsmanship place it high among the quartets of recent years. The fact that the slow movement is based upon the well-known folk-song, *Searching for Lambs*, provides a landmark convenient to remember. Any difficulties which may be met with in the music as a whole are due chiefly to the merit of concise writing, and will certainly recede as intimacy with Goossens's pithy subject-matter increases. The virile breadth of the first movement, the wistful poetry of the second, and the mood of spirited burlesque in the third, reach their epitome during a succinct and, indeed, deeply moving Epilogue, which contains some of the most imaginatively wrought pages to be found anywhere among Goossens's compositions.

The second and smaller group of 'household' music, in which romance becomes subservient to classical discipline, is less typical of Goossens today. Of these works, the Concertino for String Octet (or double String Orchestra) remains the one most likely to be heard. Devised on lines rather similar to a seventeenth-century concerto in the Italian style, with keen interplay between two bodies of strings, the Concertino shows firm individuality of style and material despite an antiquarian veneer. The athletic opening and concluding sections, which flank a graceful interlude, sustain a powerful 'drive' deriving from ideas of truly forcible invention, and it is the working-out of these ideas that gives so striking an interest to Goossens's skilful texture. In view of the fact that he writes exceptionally well for strings, it seems puzzling that the First String Quartet, the Piano Quintet, and the Sextet for three violins, viola, and two 'cellos have suffered so depressing an eclipse. Granted that the Second String Quartet is entitled to precedence, its well-knit and very likeable forerunner still deserves recognition. It may be that the Piano Quintet, whose single movement is conceived with fine sweep and strength, and the intricate yet logically realised Sextet both fall into that category of works which will always be found more fascinating to players than to audiences, but neither composition ought to be kept so resolutely on the shelf. The same remark applies in more urgent degree to Goossens's *Silence, a Fragment for Chorus and Orchestra* (text by Walter de la Mare), of which the inventive subtlety and ingeniously woven part-writing are so accomplished as to excite regret that the composer has contributed no more in this medium. The executive and appreciative demands of his songs (apart from one or two operatic numbers) are too highly specialised to warrant more than passing mention of two groups, the six songs from *Chamber Music* (James Joyce) and four settings of poems by Mrs Bettie Holmes, among which *Gentle lady, do not sing sad songs* and *O cool is the valley now* in the *Chamber Music* set are the least exacting.

The main emphasis has been placed upon Goossens's 'household' music because this heading covers his best compositions up till now. His works for orchestra include alternative versions of some already discussed – *Kaleidoscope* (Suite), *Four Conceits*, the *Lyric Poem* (solo violin and orchestra), and the *Concertino*. A transcription of the meditation on *Searching for Lambs* in the Second String Quartet has been made for string orchestra. The melody used for the piano solo, *Folk-Tune*, reappears in *From*

Bredon in the Cotswolds, the second of *Three Pictures* for solo
flute, strings, and percussion (or flute and piano), with
less revision of harmony than might be expected after
twelve years. *From the Belfry of Bruges* and *From a balcony in
Montparnasse*, which complete this series, strike one as
passing impressions but ably drawn. Goossens's orchestration of *Cadet Rousselle*, variations on a French folk-song
harmonised by Bax, Bridge, Ireland and himself, makes a
good introduction to the range of instrumental colour at
his command. A vivid glimpse of what he can do with
more substantial forces is given by the light-hearted *Tam
O'Shanter*, a brief but brilliant scherzo, which offers a
reliable stepping-stone to the *Sinfonietta* in three movements. This splendid work, won from Goossens's richest
vein, is welded into convincing unity by logical and
strongly incentive treatment of a cyclic 'motto' theme.
More elaborate use of a 'motto' scheme proves surprisingly
ineffective in Symphony No. 1. There Goossens relies
overmuch upon purely technical skill to forward the music,
though conductor and orchestra are royally entertained. A
second Symphony is announced[1] for the Jubilee of the
Cincinnati Symphony Orchestra. Further performances of
the *Phantasy* Concerto for piano and orchestra will allow
listeners a better chance to judge whether this recent work
is more clearly defined in style than the gracious but rather
impersonal Oboe Concerto written by the composer for
his brother Leon.

It says much for Goossens's two operas *Judith* (one act)
and *Don Juan de Mañara* (four acts), with libretti by Arnold
Bennett, that each aroused interest despite initial productions that were scarcely ideal. A clue to their respective
styles can be found in orchestral extracts such as the ballet
music from *Judith* and the Intermezzo linking the third and
fourth acts of *Don Juan*. The latter work, especially, is
remarkable for Goossens's largely successful attempt to
solve by novel means the problem of flexible alliance

[1] In 1945. (Editor).

between words and music. Some idea of his method may be gathered from concert versions of numbers, among which *Don Juan's Serenade* and *Ines' Song* are notable. Although Bennett's libretti are inclined to pull against the musical flow, Goossens does much to counter this tendency by his first-hand experience of what is practicable for the operatic stage. *Judith* and *Don Juan* are long overdue for fresh and fuller appraisement. Their rightful place is within the orbit of the new régime promised at Covent Garden.

CHAPTER X

William Walton

B. 1902

COLIN MASON

*

WILLIAM WALTON belongs to what may be called the middle generation of English composers. Though he showed early talent, he was not a prodigy, nor were his early years devoted exclusively to music. He was, however, a choirboy at Oxford Cathedral, where he learned something about choral singing and wrote a good deal of ambitious choral music, which he no longer acknowledges. Subsequently he had a little tuition from Sir Hugh Allen, but has been practically self-taught except for this.

His music was not long in acquiring a convincing professionalism (not to be confused with technical facility, though he had that too), with all the slickness of post-1918 smartness. Then, as now, Walton was a man of the moment, the fashionable composer of the intelligentsia. His intellectual development proceeded in the same way as most of his contemporaries', and his music reflected it, and was inevitably fashionable. When the reaction came, Walton, affected by it, could equally sincerely write the Viola Concerto and later still, the Violin Concerto, reflecting the changed outlook of each decade. (For this reason Walton's music has always seemed rather too impersonal, even at its most sincere, to live comfortably with. It has a cool, if not cold, prickliness which repels real familiarity and affection, though it excites much more than admiration.)

Probably no composer has ever reached artistic consciousness in a sillier age than Walton in the nineteen-twenties. No serious contemporary musical style visibly existed which could have helped him to find himself, and he was almost overwhelmed by the prevailing superficial imitations of serious thought. The fact that he was not is some indication of the strength of his personality, and his musical originality. (It is worth noting that he has no important exact contemporary except Rubbra, who matured rather later and escaped this period of superficiality.) Walton's early association with the Sitwellian group had a good deal to do with the compositions he began to produce, full of their deliberate, violent perversity or some other form of extremism. His music differed only from their poetry in that it was immaturely sincere, not simply a grotesque mask to disguise an insignificant thought.

However, as the same bravado had been assumed almost everywhere by artists who did not quite know what they wanted, Walton found favour, particularly with the International Society for Contemporary Music, which had not escaped the disease. So, for two works which we can now see are unimportant, he was hailed as an important composer. They were *Façade* and the String Quartet. Certainly they were original, but not much more distinguished than any young-mannish compositions of the period. *Façade* was overwhelmingly popular, partly no doubt because of the association with Edith Sitwell, but mainly because of the prevalence of the perverse highbrowness which indulged in the low (having gone beyond the primitive earnestness of the romantics). Now the original *Façade* has almost been forgotten, and there remain two orchestral suites taken from it. But these are of little more importance; although of their type they are outstandingly good, they are neither distinctive Walton nor interesting music. The desire for laughter in the concert hall is only a naughty whim, which will soon pass, for music is not meant to make

rude jokes consciously as in *Façade*, any more than unconsciously as in Rossini's *William Tell Overture*. Parody
must be always as vulgar as what it parodies, just as the
'wrong-note lyricism' of Prokofiev's *Third Piano Concerto*
is as vulgar as the street tunes it distorts. When sanity is
re-established, *Façade* will be recognised as no better
Walton than the *Musical Joke* is good Mozart.

Walton shared the indecision of the period and therefore wrote at the same time a work completely different in
idiom and spirit, the String Quartet. The importance of
this is hardly more than that of *Façade*, its agonised earnestness and its fugal finale having as little mature inward
seriousness and less outward charm. Just as much as
Façade, it was a fashionable work, without real distinction or
personality. They are only better than most art of the period
because immaturity is an excusable fault, whereas in-
sincerity is not.

The next important work in Walton's development was
the *Portsmouth Point* overture, which was selected by the
I.S.C.M. and has since been performed more often than
any of his other works. In it he paints a clattering represen-
tation of a print by Rowlandson, though the audible
legibility is rather less than the visual, on the score (which
is as crowded as the picture). The boisterous gaiety of the
overture, no less slick than the more recent *Scapino*, in the
same mood, is less convincing than that of the later work.
Though there is an occasional glimpse of Walton, it is
still very much a work of the nineteen-twenties.

It was only after this that Walton began to emerge as a
composer who could think for himself. The first work
showing this independence was the *Sinfonia Concertante*
for piano and orchestra, which despite its name is really a
concerto. The quality of the music is still hard, especially
in the finale, but some of the sharp heartlessness of *Portsmouth Point* has been taken out, by the reconciliation of
the horizontal logic with the vertical. In the slow movement particularly, Walton has become almost romantic,

gratifying the ear with more sensuous ornamentation than he has previously written. Harmony here is not just incidental to the contrapuntal progression. The harmony is most important, and the counterpoint has its corners rounded off to fit, without becoming any less independent. There are in the music all the devices of augmentation and diminution and imitation, but these should be regarded as part of the essential technique of every composer, not as a miraculous gift with which God has equipped Walton, to be admired for their own sake. The best and sincerest contrapuntist is the man who can sustain the melodic self-sufficiency of each part without neglecting any harmonic implications.

This is what Walton succeeds in doing in the first two movements of the *Sinfonia Concertante*. The softer lines, sinuous and flexible, leave *Portsmouth Point* behind and look forward to the Viola Concerto. In the finale he replaces brittleness with lyricism, but even here there are almost sentimental interludes of romantically rich harmony, clinging more firmly to the tonality of the moment than Walton's usual harmony.

After touching the edge of romanticism here, Walton was not long in becoming completely soaked in it. The result of this spiritual change was the Viola Concerto, which is still his most successful and perhaps his best work. The Concerto, though not avowedly a Sinfonia Concertante, approaches nearer to the spirit of such a work than the earlier one for piano and orchestra. This is partly because the viola tone is more easily concealed by the orchestra and partly because the music seems more symphonically logical. It is the most grateful of Walton's music, rather richly chromatic in idiom, but at the same time having a better-defined tonality than any previous work; it leans strongly towards A, sometimes major, sometimes minor, in spite of the array of accidentals on the score and the continual use of what are senselessly known as false relations. These are a feature of Walton's music, which he uses frequently in long successions of thirds and sixths, or sometimes in successions of complete triads, giving his music a strangely picturesque colour, as indescribable as it is intangible.

Formally, the Concerto breaks away from convention, without eccentricity, by having no slow movement proper, but suggests the mood one looks for there, in the two out-side movements, particularly the first. The middle move-ment is a combination of the usual styles of scherzo and finale.

In the first movement, Walton creates a rather melan-choly lyrical beauty, like a dance, tinged with a subtle sort of exultance. It combines harmonic richness (a rich con-sonance it may be noted) with an elusive rhythmic and melodic curve. Ethereal is a high claim for any music, but it is the epithet this music seems to call for. The scherzo is nearer to the earth, but has less definite outlines than the name usually implies. The one-in-a-bar effect is avoided not by cross rhythms, but by skilfully managed internal cross accents, and the occasional insertion of a five-four bar to disturb the equilibrium. The music is on a much lower plane than the other two movements, to which it really acts as a relaxation of intensity.

The finale is probably the best movement of the Con-certo, setting its mood of disquiet from the beginning by the melodic and rhythmic shape of its first figure. The ascending major ninths, split into two perfect fifths, and the rhythmic succession of three crotchets followed by a triplet, give it an uncertain tread. It is rather bare music, but violently emotional, bringing Walton's heart nearer to his sleeve than we have yet seen it. The limping rhythm of the opening is never lost for long, and the upward fifths are later expanded into gigantic steps, always falling to the triplet. By way of a coda, Walton reverts to the mood of the first movement, with a very sensuously beautiful episode. But even from this the uncertainty never vanishes, for in the last bar of A minor chords the C sharp of the solo viola is still present, pianissimo, like a vague but persistent echo.

This is quite Walton's most beautiful work, and perhaps the most convincing. He has never since recaptured its certainty of mood (the uncertainty being, of course, an integral part of its certainty) and expression, except in *Belshazzar's Feast*, which has its dramatic programme to solve the problem of what to express, if not how to express it. Walton has the technique to express what he wants perfectly, but he seems, like many of his contemporaries, to be puzzled to know what he wants. It is this, rather than anything to do with technique, which creates the problems and causes the obscurity of much modern music.

Walton's first mature attempt at a choral work was *Belshazzar's Feast*, gigantically laid out for chorus and modern orchestra. This is a long narrative poem adapted by Osbert Sitwell from the Old Testament, beginning with the vehement prophecy of Isaiah:

> *Thy sons thou shalt beget,*
> *They shall be taken away,*
> *And be eunuchs*
> *In the palace of the King of Babylon.*
> *Howl ye, howl ye, therefore:*
> *For the day of the Lord is at hand!*

Walton expresses this with brutally violent harmony in an abrupt rhythmic pattern. He heightens the intensity by exactly opposite means to those of classical composers, by interposing occasional consonances in the middle of the harsh progressions, tempering the cruelty of the prophecy with a foretaste of pity for them at its fulfilment.

This is followed after a short orchestral passage by a lament sung by the chorus, *By the waters of Babylon we sat down and wept*, which has often been praised as Walton's finest music. The magical change from the first mood to this, effected neither by a long transition, nor by a distinct pause, takes place it seems inevitably, though we wonder afterwards how it was done. The passionate sorrow of the captives is expressed here as finely as the brutality of the prophecy, the repetition of words being used not in the classical ornamental way, but to give the impression of their echoing cries, lamenting for Jerusalem.

From this point the intensity rises until the dramatic moment of Belshazzar's death, after which Walton gradually changes it into an exultant hymn, with some passages almost of the beauty of the prisoner's lament, and a massive, Handelian Alleluia.

The extraordinary rightness, musically and dramatically, of *Belshazzar's Feast* makes it one of the most vivid and powerful of all choral works, at any rate modern ones. Its nearness to perfection as a cantata equals that of *Petrushka* as a ballet. Walton was, of course, helped by the magnificent text, of which the climax is:

> *In that night was Belshazzar the King slain,*
> *And his kingdom divided.*

Repetition is entirely eliminated, and this terrific climax is over in a second on the exultant shout 'slain'. Walton presents the drama with the bold and artistic simplicity of the Old Testament, without any artificial elaboration, thus giving the work its tremendous vitality and dramatic intensity.

The grimness of *Belshazzar's Feast* is faintly echoed in the Symphony, his first important work after it, despite the four-year interval between them. To this grimness is added a flavour of the melancholy of the Viola Concerto, intensified into tragedy, though this mood exists only in the first movement of the Symphony. Walton is reported to have said recently that if any classification were to be done, he would rather be classed with Elgar than with Vaughan Williams. There are few affinities with either to be found in his music, least with Elgar, but there is a distinct similarity between this symphony and Vaughan Williams's F minor Symphony, both in mood and idiom. They both paint with harsh outlines and colours a rather chaotic scene, full of surging impetuousness violently expressed. And it is notable that both took a step nearer than usual to classical ideas of tonality, Vaughan Williams sacrificing his modality for a declared F minor, and Walton his atonality, or at least ambiguous tonality, for a definite B flat. He even calls it B flat minor, but the mediant seems hardly strongly enough defined for this, and has no place in the concluding chords of their first or last movements. Nevertheless, it is nearer to a definite key than he had previously been.

For the first time, too, echoes of another symphonist became audible in Walton. The constant repetition of one figure, not typical of either Walton, is a definite mannerism of Sibelius, particularly used, as here, in the strings. And the wood-wind scoring, where long, winding tunes and figures appear like separate strands in the texture, gives the effect, as often in Sibelius, of a thin shaft of light in a gloomy room, momentarily appearing, vanishing, and reappearing in a different place.

The Symphony first presents three motives: a rhythmic figure which dominates the whole movement; a tune which bends between B flat and D flat; and a descending minor seventh (which subsequently becomes sometimes major and sometimes diminished). The whole movement is really based on these three motives, for the principal themes of the second subject are very similar, in their willowy B flat minorness, to the tune of the first subject, and are accompanied by the rhythmic figure in the form of a diminished seventh. And the other element of the second subject bears a very seventh-ish relationship to the bare figure announced before. Walton builds up around this material a movement of very great intensity, and unity, which he is artist enough to manage without monotony or overstatement. The movement has in fact an almost orthodox symphonic form, filled with the expansive conciseness of a Beethoven movement.

In the scherzo, seriousness gives way to malice, an unusual mood for musical expression, but one which Walton creates, with tight-lipped venom and speed. The rhythm, like that of the middle movement of the Viola Concerto, is frequently upset by the insertion of a jagged five-four bar into its regular three-four. The impression of malice is helped by accents on the wrong beats, continual false relations, unfinished phrases and the occasional sudden omission of a bar, for no reason at all, it seems. Very near the end there is an unaccountable hole of five bars. Walton uses all the tricks of exotic orchestration; strings *sul tasto* (playing a ludicrous diminished seventh), *spiccato punta d'arco*, *sul ponticello*, horns constantly changing from open to closed notes, and blown hard. All this gives the effect of a pent-up hiss escaping where it can, viciously.

The third movement reverts to melancholy, set from the beginning in a theme played by the flute over a C sharp pedal, falling itself frequently to C sharp. The scoring, though apparently full, is light in texture, allowing the nostalgic wood-wind conversations to be plaintively heard. They continue to give out fragmentary sighs, until Walton leads us gradually into a huge *ff* climax, but are recaptured again as the movement ends like a breath on a solitary C sharp once more.

The fourth movement was written some time after the rest of the Symphony, and topical criticism in 1935 pretended to find that Walton's inspiration had petered out, and that the fugal finale was a slightly lame finish. But if one hears the four movements of the Symphony it is obvious that the movement fits into its proper place in the whole conception as if it had been originally part of it. This fugue is not a mere feat of technical virtuosity, an *enfant terrible* fugue of the type so much admired by nineteen-twenty intellectuals. Its value, like that of the previous movements, is its emotional content, which is more balanced, but no less sincere. The test is: 'Does it seem inevitable?', and the answer is, 'Yes'.

Frank Howes draws attention to 'the organic connection of the finale with the rest of the Symphony', quoting a fragment thematically related to various themes in the previous movements. Thematic similarity, however, is surely much less important than what he calls 'the superficial testimony of the ear'. It is the spiritual unity that matters, without which any formal similarity is of no importance. And of spiritual unity only the ear can be conscious. The thematic relationship is superficial, and indeed is hardly definite enough in shape to be observed at all.

The fugue here is not what Bach would have understood by the word. It is prefaced by a long section of angular anticipation of the subject, in a contrapuntal prelude of great violence, a mood which is sustained and augmented as the fugue subject appears and reappears, clothed with fiercer counterpoint. This suddenly but only momentarily vanishes, while a new theme makes a subdued entry, and then returns with a violent crash of brass. In another section horns and violins expound a theme which, with its accompaniment, is of almost classical contours, agitation being substituted for violence, until the original subject returns, bringing with it the forceful energy of the *maestoso* prelude to conclude the Symphony.

The Symphony marks a climax in Walton's development as a serious composer. Development is not, of course, meant to imply progress, musically, though here it does philosophically or spiritually. The exultation of *Belshazzar's Feast* is brutal, almost pagan, and is drawn with pitiless objectivity by Walton, who seems to share none of the struggles of his characters, despite the convincing realism with which he expresses them. The Viola Concerto exemplifies a more sympathetic appreciation and expression of some subtler emotional values, but one still feels that Walton is little affected by this wistful melancholy. Before, he would not have presented such a mood; now he does, but so impersonally that there still remains a touch of coldness about it. It brings a vague picture of a film director instructing his heroine to try to look a little sad and pensive. But in the Symphony the impersonal director seems to have given way to the creator, concerned with a problem of personal expression, moulding the material of his own experience into an artistic form. The impulse is no longer the *desire* to express for others, but the *necessity* to express for himself. The difference is like that between consummate acting and overwhelming reality.

There was a big gap between this and Walton's next large-scale work, the Violin Concerto, which, however, instead of sustaining or further developing the spiritual advances of the Symphony, was retrogression to the plane of the Viola Concerto. In effect, the actor had returned, with Walton guiding but not sharing the emotional interest of the work. Technically, too, there are many similarities to be found with the Viola Concerto, particularly in the first movements. Both are marked *andante*, both have the same distinctive harmonico-contrapuntal figuration and sinuousness. And though the Violin Concerto is in four-four time, its triplets give it almost the flowing effect of the nine-eight time of the Viola Concerto. In mood, both begin at least with a gloomy but not quite tragic discontentment. But whereas the first work sustains this, the Violin Concerto colours it with interludes sometimes of ferocity, sometimes of untroubled tranquillity.

The second movement here, too, is a scherzo, with two big beats in a bar, but each beat made up of irregular rhythms, three, five, or six per beat. The trio sweeps along in the same way, though the internal rhythms are less complicated, and the whole thing is more regular, with an almost four-four clarity of outline. This is transformed into twelve-eight, where in consecutive thirds Walton reverts to his false-relations technique of constantly changing inflections, and leads us back to the scherzo. In the finale we seem to be witnessing a struggle between Walton the demon in the three-four and Walton the poet in six-four and even twelve-four. One wonders, after

several alternations of these rhythms and their corresponding moods, just how Walton will resolve it satisfactorily.
The several elements of the movement and of the Concerto as a whole simply cannot be reconciled, so which
shall eventually remain? Walton's own uncertainty is
shown in the conclusion, which is in four-four, following
one of the poetical episodes. First a *pianissimo* echo of the
demon; a pause, followed by another echo, this time of
both moods; a crashing chord of B Major, and a unison B.

If one can make such a distinction, one might say that
the work ends there, but is not concluded there. Somehow,
despite its decisive finality technically, it seems to leave
something unsaid, and to leave a sense of waste of much of
the fine music that is in the finale.

Not only in this spiritual indecision and reversion to the
cool objectivity of his earlier music, but in some ways
technically, too, this Concerto seems to mark a retrogression. Walton has advanced from peppery frivolity to
harsh seriousness, and from there to more gracious and
sensuous seriousness, with a corresponding increase in
sincerity (or maturity). This advance was marked by a
gradual rejection of harsh dissonance for more romantic
dissonance and for more consonance. The consonance is
not classical, however, because chords are used in new
progressions, giving them new colours and an unstable
tonality according to classical ideals. This technique really
is an extension of the chromaticism of the nineteenth century, and it seems a sane idiom, with as many possibilities
for the future as modal and diatonic idioms have provided for the past. The upsetting of tonality is unimportant,
for in the Viola Concerto, where the technique is best
shown, the tonal centre, A, is quite distinct and even
A minor can be felt more than major. As long as
one can define a tonic somehow, the classical major or
minor scales can be rejected. It is the ability to create a
sense of cadence upon which tonality depends, and Walton's idiom certainly has this ability, whereas much music

from Debussy onwards depends on its rhythmic shape or dynamic effects to create a point of rest or finality.

The danger of such a highly chromatic idiom is that it may produce ephemeral, exotic hothouse plants. More vulgarity is descended from chromaticism than from any other musical idiom or device. Perhaps Walton is afraid of this and has veered away from it in the Violin Concerto towards a more sternly puritanical speech, with the effigy of Spohr before him. But a great enough man should be able to avoid the merely exotic and create something vital and new. That Walton is great enough is proved by the Viola Concerto. The chromatic consonance of this, rich harmonically as it is, is far more valuable musically than the grinding diatonic thickness of self-denying ascetics. The greatest Beethoven will usually be found to be the most sensuously beautiful Beethoven, because he realised that the philosophic importance of music depends entirely on its aural appeal to the senses.

The balance of the sensual and intellectual appeal of his music without vulgarity or anachronism is the problem that Walton has not quite solved in the Violin Concerto, now four years old, and has not attempted to solve in *Scapino*, his only important work since. This is just an improvement of *Portsmouth Point*. The work that next appears is sure to be interesting, and a critical work in Walton's development, for by it will be estimated his future importance. What we look for to confirm his greatness is a work, if not of the dimensions, at least of the sincerity and sureness, of the Symphony.

*

[See the notes at the end of the Chapters on Vaughan Williams and Bax. (Editor)]

CHAPTER XI

Sir Arthur Bliss

B. 1891

ALEC ROBERTSON

*

THE first thing a reasonable man wants to know about a composer is whether he can write a tune: for, as one of the composers discussed in this volume has said, 'Melody is not only the most important element in music but an all-embracing one. Harmony without melody is only an aural tickling, and rhythm without melody is not even rhythm – it is only metre, and can have at the most a vaguely mumbo-jumbo appeal with no true musical significance'.

It is true, of course, that people differ widely in their recognition of melody. For many there is a great gulf fixed between a Gregorian chant and, let us say, a tune by Gounod: and as great a gulf between 'classical' and contemporary music. The readers of this book, however, can be presumed to be open-minded explorers, free of foolish generalisations which history has so often made to look silly. They will be free, therefore, of the usual charges brought, by the ill-informed, against the composers of today.

Let us, in case there are any lingering doubts, start our exploration of the Bliss musical country in the cinema. For the H. G. Wells film *The Shape of Things to Come* Bliss has written music which shows that he thoroughly understands what is required for the purpose, music obviously tuneful, descriptive and direct in its appeal.

The two most attractive numbers of the Suite he has made out of the music are *Ballet for Children* and *March*.

The Ballet is a very tuneful affair. The children are robust creatures who bounce about with the greatest exuberance and their dance is lusciously orchestrated. This enjoyable piece sounds like Luigini up to date. The March, a really good one, suggests the tramping of a thousand feet. It is urgent, exciting and highly coloured. Only a poor spirit could fail to be stirred by the fine swing of the Elgarian tune and the clusters of descending trumpet notes.

This occasional music is not, of course, the real essential Bliss with whom we have now to come to terms, but, composed, as it was, as late as 1935, it is a useful reminder that he can write a popular kind of music if the situation demands it and that he may well do so again.

Since the aim of this book is to be helpful in a practical way I propose now to deal with all of Bliss's more important compositions that are recorded – and are therefore available to everyone; then to recommend some works to performers; and finally to list, briefly, other works that should not be missed when advertised to be broadcast or given in concert hall. But, first of all, let us take a look at Bliss's musical progress and see what sort of a composer we may expect to meet in his representative works.

He has gone through two clearly defined phases. After the war of 1914, in which he served in the Royal Fusiliers and then in the Grenadier Guards, he revolted against a form of romanticism that seemed false in the light of the disillusionment that came upon the returning soldier. Two works he composed in 1918–19 became well known – *Madame Noy*, for voice and six instruments, and *Rout*, for voice and ten instruments; in between these came a *Rhapsody* for soprano, tenor, two wind instruments, string quartet, and bass. In both these last compositions the voices are treated as instruments and only vocalise.

Madame Noy is described as a 'witchery'. If you like the description you will like the music. I don't. *Rout* (subsequently orchestrated) is a joyous piece, which delighted the young and scandalised the elderly, who called it a riot. The *Rhapsody* was in sharp contrast to these works; quiet poetical music, much more representative of Bliss's future writing.

In addition there was a set of five programme pieces for strings and wind called *Conversations*. Of these the first, 'The Committee Meeting' – a meeting with a monotonously insistent chairman (viola) and a furiously resentful committee – still seems to me one of the wittiest small things in music. I cherish an early and long out-of-print recording of it.

In 1922 the Gloucester Festival, in response to a commission, received the *Colour Symphony*. Bliss was still concerned with extra-musical associations, and his exuberant imagination, though controlled, as Eric Blom has said, by a trained instinct, revelled in the descriptive possibilities suggested by the titles of the four movements, Purple, Red, Blue, Green. But in a later revision of the symphony the detailed programme has significantly gone from the score, the movement headings alone remaining. Songs and piano pieces were the composer's chief preoccupation until 1926, when the first phase of his creative activity came to an end and he turned increasingly, though not exclusively, to classical ideals – in other words, to what is vaguely called 'absolute' music.

It would, however, be quite wrong to regard this first phase as a sort of naughty-boy period and see in it merely a young composer aping Stravinsky and Ravel.

Bliss still enjoys setting himself problems of form – each new work is, for him, an adventure – and he has retained every bit of the inherent vitality, one of his most valuable and attractive qualities, that used to shock the reactionary. His always mobile inner parts have become increasingly supple and subtle, and his well-marked melodic outlines have a rare distinction.

Though at times some of his harmonies may exacerbate the conservative, the works I am going to write about contain many pages of lovely sound that bear testimony to an unusually acute ear.

Bliss, it may as well be said at once, makes no concessions. The popular note found in his film music finds no place in his major works. In the true, and not the debased social sense, his music is aristocratic. Physically it is entirely healthy and sane, mentally it is distinguished without being aloof, spiritually it is undenominational. It displays unvaryingly fine craftsmanship, a wit that has mellowed with the years, and – the most surprising thing, and in English music a most welcome one – a note of almost Mediterranean passion and liveliness.

Like Elgar, of whom Bliss's figuration and richness of texture – but these only – often remind one, Bliss very rarely takes a turn on the village green. He has only once quoted a folk-tune, *Conolly's Jig* in the *Oboe Quintet*.

Where now do we go from here? The answer to that question must depend upon the reader's predilections. If he is, as I think all lovers of music should be, reasonably eclectic in his tastes, the question will be one of mere choice and convenience. But if he considers himself allergic to chamber music, then he must turn to the one large and purely orchestral work recorded[1], *Music for Strings* (1935).

The title is significant and indicates the composer's change of direction since writing the *Colour Symphony*. *Music for Strings* imposes no restrictions as to form or content. In actual fact the work follows sound English tradition and was generally felt to be the most considerable thing of its kind since Elgar's *Introduction and Allegro* for the same medium.

The strings are the usual orchestral body. To secure variety the composer occasionally divides each part, giving the players different instead of the same melodic lines to play, and thus increases his richness of texture. In the first movement, at one point, each group plays in two parts, ten parts in all. For special effects of contrast the composer forms solo groups out of the leaders of the various desks. At the opening of the second movement a

[1] Now out of print. (Editor).

solo violin and solo 'cello are accompanied by the remaining strings divided. Another effect is secured by
first violins playing a tune against the remaining strings
pizzicato – and so forth. This constant variation of texture
is something to look out for. You might try the last
movement first – no particular sanctity attaches to playing
the work straight through in due order – and you will, I
believe, be exhilarated by its tuneful brilliance and verve.
In the first movement Bliss changes his topics rather
abruptly: but as the music becomes familiar everything
falls into place, and even at a first hearing the passages of
massive chords and of great sweeps of tone are thrilling.

Do not expect a contemplative slow movement, still
less one of purple passages. You will get a rather bitter-
sweet and passionate rhapsody.

The only other recorded work by Bliss involving the
orchestra is the *Piano Concerto*. It was commissioned by the
British Council for the New York World Fair and first
performed in Carnegie Hall on 10 January, 1939, by the
New York Philharmonic Orchestra, conducted by Sir
Adrian Boult, with Solomon as soloist, and it is dedicated
to the people of the U.S.A.

This is a piano concerto in a big way. The critic may
find some inconsistencies of style, some of the music hard
and too highly-coloured. For myself I say, away with such
criticisms. This is not music for eunuchs. Personally I
rejoice in the bold use of the brass: hieratic, dynamic,
dramatic. (It is an occasion for the piling up of adjectives!)
I like the full-bloodedness of the opening, a pyrotechnic
swirl of octaves up and down the keyboard after a brief
call to action by the orchestra. The directions give a good
idea of the virile contents. In the first movement, *Allegro
con brio – marziale.* In the last movement, *Maestoso – con
ardore*, and (has English music ever been so marked
before?) *con somma passione.*

There is some affinity here with Elgar's Second Symphony, but Elgar celebrated the over-fed sumptuousness

of the Edwardian era and could not conceal his awareness of the hollowness of it all. No note of disillusionment sounds in Bliss's Concerto: and what he celebrates is the glowing vitality of a young and great nation.

But there is more than ceremonial splendour in the work. In the ardent last movement there is a lovely 'cello solo delicately accompanied by the solo piano, and the quiet opening of the very expressive slow movement is magical as well as wholly classical in conception.

'Classical' is a term which in text-books excludes romantic: but classical music does not come out of a refrigerator. Romanticism can be found in the music of every period. There is plenty of it in this Concerto, and much more in the chamber music to which we now come.

I recommend the reader to tackle Bliss's three recorded chamber-music works in the following order: *Clarinet Quintet* (1930), *String Quartet* (1941), *Viola Sonata* (1932). It has been pointed out that as Mozart had his Stadler, and Brahms his Mühlfeld – two famous clarinettists of their day – so, in our day, Bliss has his Frederick Thurston: and I entirely agree that his Quintet is in the direct succession with the two lovely works by Mozart and Brahms.

In these days the clarinet is sometimes made to utter odd sounds, but its true nature is warm-hearted and romantic. The opening bars of the first movement, apparently announcing a fugue, may cause the listener to wonder what he is in for, but these bars are merely a short introductory meditation preceding a gracefully lyrical tune without any of the wide, rather angular, leaps that are typical of so much modern melody. Another thing in this work that makes for easy listening is a frequent use of sequences (the repetition, satisfying to the ear when used with discretion, of a melodic pattern at a higher or a lower pitch in the same part).

The first movement has a full measure of Bliss's pulsating vitality; every instrument sings of the joy of living. As in all his music, one must concentrate on horizontal as well as vertical listening so as to savour the beauty and interest of the inner parts. The scherzo and last movement are full of high spirits and good humour, and there is lovely rich sound in the slow movement, if again a certain lack of repose.

Only those who insist in wallowing exclusively in the Tchaikovskian brand of romanticism could fail to find the String Quartet, composed in 1941, equally delightful and rewarding to hear. Like the Quintet it speaks the sane melodic and harmonic language of today, and its workmanship is as fine. Sometimes, indeed, instead of handing out a lily Bliss seems to give you a smack in the face. This is done not from any desire to be rude but simply because the composer is using the direct and forceful language that, at the moment, comes natural to him. And any reasonable person should find these rare shocks stimulating.

The music, well stocked with themes, creates its own form and is always easy to follow so far as its main lines go: but, because the contrast of a wind instrument with the strings is lacking, repeated hearings are necessary to appreciate fully the eager conversation of the inner parts. The writing is, in technical language, extremely contrapuntal. The strong and melodically widely ranging first movement, full of brilliance and vigour, is followed by an allegretto which, after an amiable start, lands on unpredictable notes and traces unexpected curves, but is provided with an enchanting chromatic episode to soothe the ear. Bliss has never written a better slow movement. This is noble, finely wrought music with a particularly lovely closing page – and he is a master of lovely endings. In the last movement – which is scherzo-minded – Bliss, not for the first time, flouts some chamber-music conventions, but with such zest and speed that by the time you have decided he has overstepped the bounds he is well into another passage that quite certainly is chamber music! This Puck-like, extraordinarily vivacious movement has one very attractive tune placed just exactly where it is needed.

The *Viola Sonata* is dedicated in admiration to Lionel Tertis, prince of viola players. Last on our list, it is not an easy work to get to grips with, but it is very well worth a good wrestling match. The melodic lines are clear, the dissonances beautifully calculated, and the composer appeals to us by line and force; a fluid and continuous interplay of lines, which comes perhaps from Bliss's declared interest in plastic art, and a force that gives energy (without brutality) to the progress of the music.

If the opening movement is austere the great passionate climax of the slow movement – the highest emotional peak of the work – should convince the listener that the composer has a heart and not a book of theories in his breast. After a brilliant Furiant in the style made familiar by Dvořák, Bliss provides one of his novelties of form and ends with a movement called Coda – a coda not to the Furiant but to the whole work and based on the themes of the previous movements.

Now we come to music for the performer of moderate ability – that is to say most of us. We are badly catered for by contemporary composers and Bliss has little to offer us. His piano pieces belong to his earlier days, when he was often inclined to write too many notes and nearly always treated the piano not as a singing but as a percussion instrument.

A series of pieces called *Masks* is strong and effective stuff in the hands of a skilled player. Moderately skilled pianists could perhaps make something of the little Pastoral on a ground. Then there is the rather gritty Polonaise from the Suite. You can hear it on the spare side of the Clarinet Quintet recording. My own feeling is that it takes a Pole to write a Polonaise.

There are some charming songs. *The Buckle*, the third of the *Three Romantic Songs*, has an immediately attractive tune and always makes a hit. The three songs to words by W. H. Davies – *Leisure*, the last one, in particular – are worth looking at. Then, to words by Siegfried Sassoon, there is a touching little song, suitably simple, called *A Child's Prayer*. If you know a clarinet player, try the *Two Nursery Rhymes*, which are for voice and clarinet. They are delightful. I personally don't care for Bliss's settings of Chinese poems. Like all Western attempts of the kind they are about as near to China as one of the Chinese restaurants in Soho. Bliss's last-published songs to words by American poets are, in my view, his best. He avoids altogether the whimsies that date and prejudice many of the songs up to 1926.

There remain two works of which you can get some idea at the piano, the Pastoral *Lie strewn the white flocks*, and the Symphony *Morning Heroes*. The *Pastoral* (1928) is scored for chorus, mezzo-soprano solo, solo flute, drum, and strings: and the poems are selected from the works of Ben Jonson, John Fletcher, Poliziano, Theocritus, and Robert Nichols. Bliss has excellent literary taste and I think he means to suggest by this rubbing shoulders of different centuries that human emotions remain the same in every age.

This little work, as charming in its different way as Handel's *L'Allegro*, is frequently performed. Bliss's native vigour sparkles in the *Song of the Reapers* and the *Hymn to Pan*, but he shows surprising delicacy in the Naiads music and the succeeding Pan and Echo (not a conventional Echo), and above all in the exquisite *Pigeons' Song* (mezzo-soprano solo with flute obbligato). The last number, *The Shepherd's Night Song*, gives him a chance, which he seizes, to write one of his loveliest endings.

You will enjoy playing over this Pastoral at the piano: but *Morning Heroes* (1930) is a more difficult proposition. Dedicated to his brother and all other comrades killed in battle, Bliss's music is necessarily reserved for great national occasions. The words chosen again range the centuries.

The Symphony has five movements. In the first movement 'Hector's Farewell to Andromache' (from the *Iliad* is spoken by the orator to orchestral accompaniment. *The City Arming*, the next movement (Walt Whitman), is a very exciting scherzo. Then comes *Vigil* (the slow movement) in which the lonely Chinese wife of Li Tai-Po's eighth-century poem is brought into close relationship with the American soldier in a poem from Whitman's *Drum Taps*. This imaginative conception, carried out with great restraint and beauty, is moving even when read at the piano from the vocal score. For the next movement, again in two parts, Bliss returns to the *Iliad*. Achilles goes forth to battle and – another imaginative touch – there is a roll-call of the Heroes. The first part of the final movement, *Spring Offensive* (Wilfrid Owen), is spoken by the orator to an intermittent roll of drums, but in the last section, *Dawn on the Somme* (Robert Nichols), chorus and orchestra rise to a great climax of splendid sound and exalted emotion. The music then fades down to a soft and sombre chord.

I regard this work as the touchstone of Bliss's high qualities as a composer. Inspired by intense personal emotion, it shows no trace of either sentimentality or jingoism. The music has the moving restraint, the inward strength and integrity, of great art and, like the words, speaks with a universal tongue.

One thing only militates against the complete success of the Symphony, and that is the use of the speaking voice to orchestral accompaniment. In the first movement the marriage is not altogether a happy one.

Don't fail to hear in the theatre the Ballet *Checkmate*, or in the concert hall the suite made from it. There is a quite playable piano transcription of the score. And, in addition to works already mentioned, do not miss the Introduction and Allegro for Orchestra, the *Mêlée Fantasque*, the *Hymn to Apollo*, and the Oboe Quintet. Bliss's most recent works are music to the ballet *Miracle in the Gorbals*, produced in 1944 by the Sadler's Wells Ballet, and *Phœnix March*, written to commemorate the liberation of Paris.

CHAPTER XII

Lord Berners

1883–1950

J. A. WESTRUP

*

LORD BERNERS has been called the English Satie; he has also been described as an amateur. These labels may be convenient for quick characterisation, but they can also be misleading. Erik Satie (1866–1925) is regarded by some French critics as the precursor of Debussy; by others he is repudiated as an imitator. He studied music seriously at the Schola Cantorum in Paris, but he made his reputation as the composer of some quaint trifles, distinguished both by eccentricity of style and by an extravagant mode of presentation. The titles, the directions to the performer, even the printing were dictated by a freakish humour. Lord Berners has also a strong inclination to humour. He enjoys parody and has no objection to a witty title: the third of his *Valses Bourgeoises* for piano duet is headed 'Strauss, Strauss, et Straus', and the illustrated cover mimics the fashions of our grandfathers. But he is far from being a mere playboy in the world of sound. His art is disciplined, and even when it seems most novel pays its tribute to tradition. To call him an amateur is correct in the sense that he has not made music his profession. He has been diplomat, artist, and novelist. But if the term implies that he does not know his job as a composer it is not well chosen. There is in much of his earlier music, in particular, a strong element of improvisation; but there is no bungling.

Berners's early essays in composition suggest the influence

of impressionism. Yet there is nothing vague or merely atmospheric about this music. The expression is clear-cut, the form is definite. So much is obvious in the *Three Little Funeral Marches* and the *Fragments Psychologiques*. The first of these sets of piano pieces provides music suitable for the demise of a statesman, a canary, and a rich aunt respectively. Here we have not only economy of means and a curiously direct expression, but also an example of that vein of satire which is not infrequent in Berners's compositions. The first funeral suggests empty pomposity, the last gives rise to savage glee; and if we turn to the second of the *Fragments Psychologiques* – *Le Rire* – we shall find details very similar to those in the memorial to the rich aunt. Berners tends to work in patterns cut to a small scale, and some of these recur more than once in different works or in different sections of the same work. *Le Poisson d'or* is a good instance of impressionistic harmony set in a very regular frame. The mood of this piece is also characteristic. It is not, like Debussy's *Poissons d'or*, a mere picture in sound. The music is preceded by a prose poem, written by the composer, which presents the joyless existence of the solitary goldfish in his bowl, and the music has the same air of satirical melancholy.

Satire also finds scope in Berners's songs, whether in English, French or German. His setting of Heine's *Du bist wie eine Blume* not only parodies the sentimental turns of expression characteristic of the romantic *Lied*, it also introduces a disturbing element in the shape of intermittent grunts. Heine's poem is said to have been originally addressed to a white pig, and the composer has taken the opportunity to provide what he considers a fitting background. Such rude pictorialism is, however, rare in Berners's work. He has no need of it in his setting of three poems by G. Jean-Aubry, where he relies rather on a deliberate imitation of the French style of song-writing. Here the satirical approach finds justification in the irony of the words. But nowhere is the composer's art of caricature more apt than in his thumb-nail sketch of *Theodore the Pirate King* (words by John Masefield). Only performance by a sympathetic singer could show how irresistibly the music translates the words:

> *But Theodore, though dripping gore,*
> *Was always courteous to the Ladies.*

It is like a successful parlour trick. Once again there is the element of improvisation. One can imagine the composer doing it impromptu for the amusement of friends; but few impromptus would show so certain a touch. By comparison the imitation of folk-song heartiness in the *Dialogue between Tom Filuter and his Man*, though amusing enough, is less convincing.

Berners's talent for parody is very happily illustrated in the orchestral *Fantaisie Espagnole*. There are three movements – *Prelude, Fandango, and Pasodoble* – which follow each other without a break. Here the Spanish idiom, which is familiar to us not only from the work of Spanish composers but also from the concoctions of foreigners, is held up to our inspection as something so easy to achieve by following a recipe that its success becomes laughable. Yet the result is not mere caricature. The composer pokes fun at all the Spanish capriccios that ever were, and yet takes an obvious delight in playing with the idiom himself. Every detail of monotonous reiteration, every little conceit of orchestration is brought into the picture, and the whole thing has an exuberant vitality. It is a common thing for a parodist to aim his shafts at something with which he himself has an unconscious sympathy. This seems to be the case here. Berners's predilection for neat little patterns has led him naturally to choose for caricature an idiom in which neat patterning is a commonplace. The same is probably true of the setting of *Du bist wie eine Blume*. The evident delight in the accents of German song betrays a Romantic impulse. Paradoxical though it might appear, Berners is a Romantic at heart. This is evident from the sentimental

Adagio in the ballet *Luna Park*. Indeed the whole of *Luna Park* is a repertory of romantic idioms, from Schumann to Strauss; and there is more than a passing nod to Delibes.

Romantic composers are not generally successful in handling large structures, and it is not surprising that Berners has not attempted to do so. The single exception – the orchestral Fugue in C minor – is exactly what one might expect. Traditional devices, such as inversion, augmentation, and a major third at the end, duly make their appearance, and there is plenty of ingenuity and vivacity in the part-writing. But the work gives the impression of being a series of episodes rather than an organic whole. Instead of the growth of an idea there is rather a succession of formulas. It must have been obvious to anyone who studied Berners's early adventures in composition that ballet was his ideal medium, and this has proved to be so. In ballet it is no disadvantage for music to be short-breathed; and an insistence on formal patterns can become a virtue. In *Luna Park* Berners had a subject that suited him admirably. The story deals with an exhibition of freaks – a man with three heads, a three-legged juggler, a one-legged ballerina, and a man with six arms. We see them first performing their several antics. Then, when the show is over, four perfectly normal human beings emerge from behind the curtain. They decide to leave the circus and go out into the world. When the second performance takes place, the showman discovers to his horror that merely the extra heads and limbs are left, while the juggler's billiard balls revolve in a slot by themselves. The music matches the fantastic story. It has wit and charm and offers no obstacles to listeners whose limited acquaintance with modern music is apt to make them suspicious. It was, in fact, written for one of C. B. Cochran's revues.

The Triumph of Neptune, written for Diaghilev, is a more ambitious work but not substantially different in method. This 'English Pantomime' is based on scenery and costumes sold for toy-theatre productions at Benjamin Pollock's shop. The characters range from the Fairy Queen to news-paper boys; fantasy, harlequinade, and nautical jollity are all there. The result is a series of genre pieces which at times re-mind one of the capricious alternations in Schumann's *Carnaval*. In range of imagination and variety of expression this is Berners's most successful work – so successful that a suite has been extracted from it for concert performance. No doubt it is difficult, as so often in Berners's work, to know where sincerity ends and parody begins. But in the theatre no one worries very much about questions of that kind; there is a sufficient delight to be found in the aptness of the musical patterns to the ballet. And if the listener finds himself enjoying the lingering end of the *Farewell* when he ought, perhaps, to smile knowingly at the luscious progres-sions, no one is any the worse.

In *A Wedding Bouquet*, written for Sadler's Wells, Berners showed his versatility by designing the costumes and decor as well as writing the music. This ballet, not inappropriately in view of its title, is fully choral. The words, by Gertrude Stein, are full of chattering, inconsequent repetitions, in which sound counts for more than intelligibility. Here is a sample chosen at random:

> *Arthur Julia Arthur Julia Arthur*
> *this would make a dog uneasy dog uneasy*
> *Guy would it be possible to believe it of three*
> *Guy would it be possible*
> *Guy would it be possible*
> *All of them having come to the door*
> *this is now scene four*
> *this is now scene four.*

These word-patterns are the exact counterpart of the sound patterns to which Berners is so faithful in his music. The little repetitions, the artificial symmetry, are devices already familiar in his work. This unanimity between librettist and composer might have been expected to produce a master-piece. No doubt *A Wedding Bouquet* is a masterpiece of its kind. But to the listener who is not, so to speak, a convert the total effect, in its persistent brightness and sophisticated simplicity, is as wearisome as smart conversation.

Berners is, in fact, essentially an instrumental composer. His one attempt at opera – a one-act setting of Mérimée's *Le Carrosse du Saint-Sacrement* – fails to come to life because the music is so obstinately harnessed to the text. A less conscientious composer might have made a success of the work by paying less scrupulous attention to Mérimée's prose. As it is, the best pages are those in which the singers are silent. Elsewhere one is confronted with whole tracts of what is virtually accompanied recitative. A good production and first-rate acting might make the piece convincing, but its success would owe comparatively little to the music. A particular difficulty in this work is the fact that it offers little opportunity for that vein of parody to which Berners so naturally turns in his instrumental works. It is often a weakness in impersonators that they have no striking personality of their own or else are shy of revealing it. In Berners's work in general, as in Stravinsky's, there are mannerisms which are immediately recognisable, but little that can be called individual style.

Berners has a habit, most pronounced in his earlier work, of decorating his melodies and harmonies with chromaticisms of the kind that the ordinary listener calls 'wrong notes'. But there is not the faintest suspicion of atonality in his work. On the contrary his harmony is rooted, as I have suggested, in the romantic tradition, whatever superficial excrescences it may have acquired from the twentieth century. The influence of Stravinsky, who took an interest in his first efforts and to whom *Le Poisson d'or* is dedicated, is actually slight. Nor is there in his orchestration any of the daring experimentation which characterises Stravinsky's work. The instrumentation of the Fugue in C minor is sometimes pungent, but there is nothing 'dangerous' in it and little that is unexpected; and the strings, as so often in English music, are the foundation of the score.

CHAPTER XIII

Constant Lambert

B. 1905

HUBERT FOSS

*

THE tradition of English music has always led us to think of a composer as a provider of music, as a worker in the field rather than a thinker in the study. Purcell made music where it was wanted, and his capacity for making music in every extant field that lay around the court and church of the Restoration has not yet brought the variety of his genius as a composer under public notice. The discovery of Purcell's works offers an interesting new task for a sea-faring nation of Empire-builders.

Constant Lambert has a wide following today as a maker of music, that is as a conductor, particularly of ballet. But the honour of discovering him as a composer is payable to no Englishman, but to Serge Diaghilev, who, when Lambert was bordering on twenty-one, commissioned him to write a piece for his famous Russian Ballet. No other English composer shared the honour before Diaghilev died. And so Lambert stands isolated, with his *Romeo and Juliet*, which was produced at Monte Carlo in May 1926, and his second ballet, *Pomona*, which Nijinska staged at Buenos Aires in September 1927.

Nearly everything that Lambert has written has been published, but that does not mean that his music is easy of access. Two of his larger works – the Piano Concerto and *Summer's Last Will and Testament* – have not together had more than twenty performances. *Music for Orchestra* is occasionally given. But mostly, despite their rhythmic vitality, Lambert's scores lead the sedentary life of books on shelves. The printed scores yield only a poor modicum of their secrets, and only a shadow of their intensity. Thus it may be said that a writer who deals with Lambert's music is dealing with a comparatively unknown quantity, and addressing ears and eyes that are unfamiliar with the material under discussion. Except for one work – *The Rio Grande*.

It is an interesting example of Lambert's eclecticism. *The Rio Grande* is a setting of a poem by Sacheverell Sitwell for piano solo, chorus, alto solo, and an orchestra of brass, strings, and percussion (no wood-wind). The forces asked for (two cornets, as well as two trumpets, and five percussion players, for example) would appear to make it an exclusive work, suitable only for special occasions. In fact, the opposite happened. *Rio Grande* was taken up by Sir Hamilton Harty, with the Hallé Orchestra, he himself playing the piano part to the composer's conducting. It was repeated, and recorded; it went the rounds of the choral societies and the public schools and has now been recorded again.

So much for eclecticism: it is thought to be a sign-manual of the small audience. Yet the policy of the Sadler's Wells Ballet, of which Constant Lambert was musical director from its start, has always been eclectic, with a mounting audience that filled the theatre even during the menace from flying-bombs. The Charing Cross Road, as we in this country call 'Tin Pan Alley', has sometimes failed because it worked to a formula – because it knew nothing and thought nothing, in other words, of eclecticism.

The reference to 'popular music' is deliberately introduced, for Lambert is a devotee of first-class popular music. He likes Chabrier, he admires Sousa, he revels in the repertoire of the old ballet: indeed he conducts 'light music' as a scholar and a live man should. His criticism (in *Music Ho!*) of Duke Ellington is masterly in its penetration. And there are few 'swing-fans', however enthusiastic, who could keep pace with him on their own subject. *The Rio Grande* is a study in jazz rhythms, with much of the nostalgia as well as the energy of Negro folk-music. Lambert is much affected by exotic and Negro cultures, and writes *con amore* in the idiom that that culture distils. There is something more than English in this music, a sense of the South and the flaming sun. His feet are on the English soil, his mind floats away, now with Sacheverell Sitwell to the South, now with Li Po to China, now with Thomas Nashe to Elizabethan London – to many worlds unrelated to London's pavements.

The Rio Grande won popular success, and I believe that the success was due less to its introduction of a jazz idiom into a world of high-brow respectability (though that of course helped) than to its intensity of feeling, which transcends the common slang of its idiom. It is a haunting piece. At about the same period, Lambert was making other experiments in rhythms, mathematical patterns of a kind to make the professional dance-boys jealous, if they bothered even to look at them. The results were the Piano Sonata and the Piano Concerto.

These two works are more remote from daily experience. They have nothing of narrative about them; they tell no story, but only divulge thoughts. *Rio Grande* is, Lambert once explained to me, Hollywood to the other two works, which resemble the French films or Cavalcante's. In *Rio Grande* the composer was 'joining in the fun'; in the Sonata and Concerto he was examining a modern city in cross-section, ruthlessly analysing its hard, brittle, pitiless qualities with a critical and almost menacing eye. *Rio Grande* is as pleasant as the other two works are truthfully uncompromising. You and I are on the dissecting slide, under a microscope, and the result of the investigation is exactly as delightful as our own bitterest thoughts of ourselves in the small hours of the morning. There is great strength here, and the strength is that of a fellow-sufferer in an ill-cast world; without fear, but with no less sad feelings than we groundlings have ourselves.

The *Piano Concerto* and *Music for Orchestra* are at the opposite ends of orchestral texture. The *Concerto* uses only nine players (flute, three clarinets, trumpet, trombone, 'cello, bass and percussion), while *Music for Orchestra* demands triple wood-wind, four horns, three trumpets, three trombones, tuba and strings. Each is a study in musical texture, a side of composition to which Lambert devotes endless pains as well as accurate and imaginative skill. He is full of odd contrasts in texture, ranging from bare two-part writing, or fugal writing of an almost acid simplicity, to a heavy, chordal, damask-like writing for choir and orchestra.

But 'heavy' is hardly the word, for Lambert's music has no trace of solemnity or pomposity. The fresh air blows through it and keeps it fresh and clean. On the whole, he is melodic rather than harmonic – indeed, unconventionally so. He is compact of humour, and there is a chuckle to be heard always, save in his movements of deepest gloom.

Here is another contrast in Lambert's music – the sparkle and ebullience of his rhythms (few composers can write really rapid music as well as he), and the despair of his sadder moments.

This elegiac nostalgia pervades the whole of Lambert's work, and has at times a poignancy that is almost unbearable. The haunting spectacle of death and decay is there, the *lacrimae rerum* of a soul saddened by what he cannot avoid seeing. A particular example is the male-voice chorus, with tenor and baritone solos and strings, set to the Dirge from *Cymbeline*, 'Fear no more the heat of the sun', which may be taken as centrally representative of Lambert's nostalgic style. It is impossible not to think as one reads it of Bernard van Dieren, or of 'Peter Warlock', the first acting through the second in his influence on Lambert's thought. A less direct but no less poignant example is the *Intermède* from the Piano Concerto, that whole work indeed being dedicated 'to the memory of Philip Heseltine'. Here the rhythmic and threnodic styles are mixed in development. The *Nocturne* in the Piano Sonata, the early *Elegiac Blues*, and the later *Aubade Héroïque* have the same quality – the last is a remembrance of that dawn in Holland when Lambert, a visiting conductor there, witnessed the parachute invasion at The Hague by the Germans. Clearest of all can this nostalgia be seen in *Summer's Last Will and Testament*, of which more will be said below.

No one could read Lambert's book *Music Ho!* without discovering that he has not only a wide knowledge of painting but a strong pictorial sense himself. Son of a painter, brother of a well-known sculptor, lifelong student of the ballet – little else could be expected of one so placed. But here again comes a contrast, for Lambert has indeed the picturesque eye, yet his music is not in the least pictorial, but on the contrary absolutely self-contained and concerned with nothing but its own pattern. He rejoices in quaint titles for his short pieces, taking them often from the old dances – Coranto, Brawles, Siciliana, Sarabande. Anyone less archaistic or antiquarian than Lambert it would be hard to find; what he takes from the spirit of the past, he transforms into the idiom of the present, that idiom so personally and unmistakably his own. A good case in point is the ballet *Horoscope*. It was conceived symphonically, yet as a ballet. The absoluteness of the music is seen in the fact that one movement is a palindrome – that is, it may be read backwards or forwards. Yet the stage picture is needed for completeness of realisation, and it is not without significance that the printed cover is adorned with a design by Edmund Dulac, the whole cover being Lambert's own invention. Indeed, all his covers are designed by himself, though executed by others.

The most considerable work in Lambert's list is the choral work, *Summer's Last Will and Testament*. It consists of five poems from the 'pleasant comedy' of that name by Thomas Nashe, with an *Intrata* and a *Rondo Burlesca* for orchestra only – a large orchestra of triple wood-wind, two extra cornets, two harps and three percussion players, with brass and strings as usual. Nashe was an associate of Marlowe, a contemporary and admirer of Shakespeare. He had that special characteristic of poetic yet satirical realism which marked the Elizabethan drama, and his play is a panorama of the plague which recurred in summer every year around 1592. Nashe writes: 'Forsooth, because the Plague reigns in most places in this latter end of Summer, Summer must come in sick'. Lambert takes Nashe's words very literally and paints the picture with a ghastly brilliance of colour. There is something of El Greco, something of Doré, something of Rubens and Goya, of Berlioz and Le Fanu and Poe, in this music, reproducing as it does the laughter, the poetry, the tragedy, the realism of Nashe's vital words. The riotous drinking chorus, the Rondo called *King Pest*, the *Madrigal*, all lead up to the *Sarabande* when, in the famous lines,

> *Queens have died young and fair;*
> *Dust hath closed Helen's eye:*
> *I am sick – I must die.*
> *Lord, have mercy on us!*

Nashe tells of the horrors of the plague. Lambert does not spare us. With his mind stretched to its fullest resources, he expresses here the Elizabethan age in the reality of all its splendour and all its dirt.

Music for Orchestra is Lambert's most extended piece for the concert hall, the conditions of the ballet having imposed upon him the need (and so the habit) of writing much in a small space. It is a study in symphonic development, a work of tremendous energy and of powerful abstract thought. There are some charming songs, slight in texture but of marked originality, and the *Merchant Navy Suite* is a reminder of Lambert's only incursion (up to 1944) into the world of films.

Printed words can haltingly describe music; they cannot, at their best, do more. I can tell you of Lambert's astonishing instinct for matters of today and tomorrow, his almost prophetic 'in-touch-ness' with life as it really is. How that comes out in his music, Lambert alone can tell you in the music itself. Nor can I hope even to sketch in a rough outline how intensely musical these works are. They have no connection with conventional idioms or commonplace phrases; they come not from the habits of tradition but from a nearer kind of burning passionate perception of sound. Here is music that stands on its own, alone in its idiom, personal in its thought and vocabulary, the expression of an intense individualism. Above all, it has the quality of being musical – a phrase which I hope will be understood even if it cannot be defined.

CHAPTER XIV

E. J. Moeran

B. 1894

J. A. WESTRUP

*

AMONG the influences that help to shape a composer's work must be counted heredity and environment. The evidences of environment are generally more striking. It is difficult to imagine Sibelius's music having been written anywhere but in Finland, while the background of the English provincial festival helps to explain the early trend and slow development of Elgar's work. The effect of heredity is not so easy to assess, but sometimes the signs are definite enough. Anyone coming to Moeran's music for the first time could hardly fail to be struck by a recurrent character in his themes which is unmistakably Irish. Such a character might be assumed. In the case of Bax it is the result of residence in Ireland and a curiously sympathetic understanding of her traditions and culture. With Moeran we may safely attribute it to Irish ancestry, even though his birth and upbringing were English. The attraction that Ireland has for him may be guessed from the fact that the greater part of his Symphony in G minor was written, in his own words, 'among the mountains and seaboard of Co. Kerry'. He adds that the work 'may be said to owe its inspiration to the natural surroundings in which it was planned and written'. Not all the symphony, however, was the product of the Irish scene. 'The material of the second movement was conceived around the sand-dunes and marshes of East Norfolk.' Here, then, in Moeran's biggest and most ambitious work we have the record of two different influences, and of these the second is not the less important. His origins may be Irish, but Norfolk has been his home. He has himself collected the folk-songs to which his melodic idiom is so much indebted, and a fragment of one of them not only forms the basis of the orchestral piece *Lonely Waters* but is intended to be sung in a 'clear and natural manner' at the end.

This quotation of an actual folk-tune is unusual in Moeran's work. He does not, like some other composers, rely on traditional material for his melodies: he makes his own. But he has so soaked himself in folk-song that his tunes seem to become impregnated with its idioms; and as in folk-song the same phrase is liable to turn up in dozens of different melodies, so in Moeran's music the same melodic progressions are apt to reappear in different surroundings. It is obvious that these reappearances are unconscious. There is in Moeran a fund of simple lyricism which is too sincere to become mannered. He is one of the comparatively few composers who use the idioms of folk-song not artificially but as if it were their native language. It would have been difficult for anyone so constituted to escape altogether the influence of Vaughan Williams. *Lonely Waters* is, in fact, dedicated to him. But the influence is not marked in that work; it occurs more clearly in the earlier *In the Mountain Country* for orchestra and in the group of Housman songs entitled *Ludlow Town*.

This influence is one of several to which Moeran has been subject in his development as a composer. It is evident from some of his songs – for instance the settings of *Seven Poems of James Joyce* – as well as from the Piano Trio in D major that he has been susceptible to the wayward charm of Delius. The slow movement of the trio irresistibly recalls *Brigg Fair*. It was in memory of Delius that Moeran wrote his *Nocturne* for baritone solo, chorus, and orchestra, though the idiom here is far from being a slavish imitation. Delius and the Elizabethans seem to join hands in *Whythorne's*

Shadow, an orchestral piece based on a part-song of 1571. The Elizabethan influence is obvious in the choral suite *Phyllida and Corydon*, and admiration for Elizabethan rhythms has left its mark on the final Passacaglia of the Sonata for two violins. In his Irish mood Moeran sets one thinking of Bax. But more enduring is the influence of John Ireland, with whom he worked after the 1914–18 war. It was from Ireland that he acquired the habit of decorating his work with clumps of dissonant chords, while the diatonic foundation remains unchanged. He uses this method to excess in his Violin Sonata in E minor, and there are other tricks of style which can be traced to the same source. In his later work, however, this influence has declined, and the Symphony in G minor shows that he has learned something from Sibelius.

This catalogue might be regarded as an indictment. It is not intended to be anything of the kind. An artist finds himself not by self-conscious attempts at originality but by learning from others; and this process is likely to take some time with a composer like Moeran, who was largely self-taught. In the eighteenth century no one would have been surprised to find a musician using the current speech of his time; but in this highly critical age people are apt to be supercilious if a composer's work reveals that he is aware of his contemporaries. There is no good reason for adopting this attitude with Moeran, whose music, except in *Phyllida and Corydon*, is never guilty of conscious imitation. From the first there has been evident a personality with something to say, even when the manner of saying it seemed reminiscent; and a study of Moeran's works in the order of their composition shows a progressive freedom in expressing that personality. It is also significant that with all his impulsiveness Moeran is extremely self-critical. A large quantity of early work has been discarded, and the comparatively modest output of the last twenty years shows a determination to take the work of creation seriously. I should imagine that Moeran works slowly and does not readily compose to order. His *Overture to a Masque*, written during the war in response to a commission from E.N.S.A., is lively and neatly scored, and these qualities might make it popular. But it has no strongly marked individuality and little of the lyrical inspiration which is characteristic of Moeran's work in general.

It is this lyrical vein which makes him so successful a song-writer and so readily approachable by the ordinary listener. Song is his natural speech. He has an enviable gift of finding a melodic curve and a rhythm to suit a poet's text. This is clear enough in the early Housman settings and is just as marked in the more subtle treatment of Joyce. It is also very happily illustrated in the *Songs of Springtime* for unaccompanied chorus. Here Moeran has not hesitated to set such familiar poems as *Under the Greenwood Tree* and *Sigh no more, Ladies*, but he does it with a freshness and spontaneity that prove immediately attractive. The rhythmical freedom of *Sigh no more, Ladies* is particularly happy. So is the delicate pathos of *Fair daffodils, we weep to see*. Choral singers, who are notoriously conservative, will find this set of part-songs the best introduction to Moeran. They will not find them all easy; some of the progressions are likely to tax the skill of the best-trained choirs. But the music does offer a reward for the labour spent on it, and does give the singers something that they can sing with pleasure to themselves and to others. *Phyllida and Corydon*, the second set of part-songs, is not quite so successful. It contains delightful things like *Come, be my valentine*, whose nonchalance recalls the lilting rhythms of the earlier set; but it suffers a little from a mixture of styles. The deliberate imitations of Elizabethan idioms which occur here and there have a self-conscious air, particularly as they are set side by side with a rather precious chromaticism.

The lyrical vein is not confined to Moeran's vocal works; it overflows into his instrumental music. It is one of the attractive qualities of his Violin Concerto that it turns its back on empty virtuosity and allows the solo instrument to sing. In the Symphony, too, one cannot help noticing how readily the composer abandons the strenuous opening of the first movement and allows his invention to run in channels which instantly recall the tranquil mood of *Lonely Waters*. By a natural reaction against this prevailing lyricism – or perhaps as a subconscious protest against it – we find also violent outbursts and climaxes which are sometimes excessive for their context. Even *Lonely Waters,* which is in the main reflective music, rises to triple *forte*, with a blow on the cymbals; and the exceptionally concise slow movement of the String Quartet, which is equally reflective, is whipped up to a passionate climax before it has reached the end of the second page. These contrasts are particularly noticeable in the Symphony, where there is a good deal of savage protestation. The mood of the lyrical B major section in the first movement is shattered as abruptly as the luscious D major episode is in the first movement of Tchaikovsky's Sixth Symphony. In both cases we may guess at the same psychological explanation: the dreamer is impatient with his own dreams and must prove himself a man of action.

A lyrical invention often finds difficulties with construction. A good tune is so self-sufficient that it does not lend itself easily to development, and the composer finds himself compelled either to manufacture continuity out of unsuitable material or else to go on inventing something new. A lyrical composer is best suited by smaller forms, or if he attempts larger forms is most successful in rhapsody, where contrast is more important than coherence. Moeran's early work illustrates this principle. The slow movement of the String Quartet owes its effectiveness to the fact that there is no artificial attempt at development. It consists almost entirely of a single melodic idea set in a simpler frame. In the other movements one is aware of the carpentry which has joined the sections together, and the same is true of the Piano Trio and Violin Sonata. In Moeran's output for orchestra there is no large-scale work until the Symphony, which was written

during 1934–7. It is probable that he was aware of the
difficulties of writing a work of this kind, since he had been
commissioned to compose a symphony for the Hallé Orchestra as early as 1926 but did not feel able to accept the
commission. Of his earlier orchestral works, *In the Mountain
Country* and *Lonely Waters* are short impressions (the former
an unpretentious but well-knit piece), *Whythorne's Shadow* is
wholly lyrical in conception and structure, and *Farrago* is a
suite on rather similar lines to Warlock's *Capriol*, though
not, like *Capriol*, based on borrowed material. There are
also, characteristically, two Rhapsodies (the first dedicated
to John Ireland), in which there is an agreeable sequence
of tunes but little coherence between them.

The Symphony is a landmark in his career, not merely
for what it attempts but for what it achieves. In the first
movement Moeran has faced squarely the problems set by
his own inclination to lyricism. The opening theme, though
mildly tinged with the flavour of folk-song and cast in a
symmetrical mould, is not merely a song tune with little
possibility of development. For one thing, though its style
is not unvocal its range marks it as instrumental in conception. For another, it is seen to be composed of segments
which lend themselves to manipulation later on. It is this
concentration on thematic fragments which shows that the
composer is capable of thinking symphonically. In fact
there is only one complete statement of this theme, and
that is at the beginning. A restatement begins but breaks up
almost immediately into one of its component parts. In the
course of the development the opening bars are heard in
augmentation, but that is all. The climax before the recapi-
tulation is based on a mere fragment of the theme. The re-
capitulation itself is fragmentary, the theme being tele-
scoped and presented as a reminiscence rather than a repetition. In spite of this closely-knit development of his opening
material the composer cannot entirely forget his passion
for lyrical utterance. Hence the tranquil and reflective B
major section, which has the effect of a contrasting episode

after the insistent opening and inevitably gives the movement a rhapsodic character. Moeran has not denied himself
in this movement. He has realised the importance of logic,
but he is also willing to allow himself to be diverted from
his argument. We find this tendency again in the finale,
where there seems to be an excess of material. Moeran has
sometimes been criticised for not knowing what to reject.
The criticism is valid, but may be modified by suggesting
that he does not really want to reject. A desire to create beyond the immediate needs of a particular movement seems
to be one of his natural impulses.

That impulse is resisted in the slow movement, where
everything grows out of four pregnant themes, presented
in succession at the opening. These themes are mere scraps
of melody, not insignificant in themselves but certainly
more significant for what they promise. Here particularly
Moeran has profited from the example of Sibelius, who excels in the art of encouraging germ themes to grow into a
fully developed structure. There is some harsh assertiveness
in this movement, but it is all relevant to the subject.
Moeran has also followed Sibelius in creating out of formal
patterns a background of sound against which the thematic
material is set in relief. These pattern backgrounds appear
also in the first and last movements, but there they seem to
be more artificially designed. The scherzo, like the slow
movement, is economical in material and there is some
effective dovetailing. It is for the most part light and flut-
tering – 'a spring-like contrast,' says the composer, 'to the
wintry proceedings of the slow movement.' Here there is
not only a strong resemblance to Sibelius's methods in
general but also a specific resemblance to the scherzo of his
Fourth Symphony. Moeran's scherzo, like Sibelius's, begins
with a sustained melody for oboe above a persistent quaver
background on the strings in two parts. In both there is a
change from 3/4 to 2/4 time; in both there is an effective
use of sustained chords for brass, with a crescendo (trumpets and trombones in Sibelius, horns in Moeran); in both

the initial theme emerges from a *fortissimo* at the end of the movement and is, in Moeran's words, 'snuffed out'.

After the Symphony Moeran reverted to works on a less ambitious scale, in which he could follow his natural gifts without so severe a concentration on the problems which symphonic writing imposes. His Rhapsody in F sharp for piano and orchestra is in some sense a confession of his own preferences, though it is actually not more rhapsodic in style than the Violin Concerto, published in the same year. The two works make an interesting contrast. In the Concerto, as we have seen, the emphasis is on lyricism; there is a warm-hearted Irish flavour in this music. The Rhapsody, on the other hand, is direct and bold in expression and thematically less distinguished than some of Moeran's other works. It is made up largely of rhythmical patterns, and the writing for the solo instrument is on the whole conventional. Of the two works the Concerto is certainly more characteristic of the composer, and its evident sympathy with the nature of the violin gives it an endearing quality which triumphs over any logical weaknesses.

The basis of Moeran's harmony has always been diatonic, with a modal flavour suggested by the melodic contours of folk-song. In the earliest works, such as *In the Mountain Country*, this diatonic basis is clearly and plainly marked. Later on it became overgrown with a luxuriant chromaticism, to which he sometimes yielded too willingly. The third stage, of which the symphony is a representative, shows no less skill in handling chromaticism but also a clear realisation that there is nothing to be ashamed of in the simplest diatonic treatment. The composer has learned by this time that originality does not consist in avoiding what is familiar, but in using available material in the most effective way. In all his work he has concentrated mainly on harmonic, as opposed to contrapuntal, treatment. This is true even of those part-songs where homage is paid to the Elizabethans. Moeran may introduce polyphonic passages in his works, but he seems to do so less from conviction than from a sense of duty. Perhaps it was a realisation of this that induced him to concentrate on simple part-writing in the String Trio and the Sonata for Two Violins. The second of these works was the severer test of skill, and the result is rather what one might expect from a composer of Moeran's tendencies. He is obviously happiest when he can use one of the violins as a harmonic support for the other. Where he is committed to two independent lines his invention flags, and the Passacaglia which forms the last movement is decidedly arid.

Writing after the first performance of Moeran's Symphony a critic said that it was a work 'of such exceptional earnestness and unusual incidental qualities that the very effort it had entailed must enrich and deepen the composer's future work'. That might seem an odd thing to say of a man who was already forty-three. But Moeran began the serious study of composition comparatively late, and his development, though continuous, has not been rapid. The point is that that development is still going on. In everything that he writes one is aware of a mind that is not content to stand still. Moeran is a composer who takes stock of himself and adds to his stature. It is this open-mindedness, this looking forward, that helps to give all his music, even when it is most in earnest, a youthful freshness. To him music is primarily a vehicle for the emotions. He is more inclined to express himself than to reason. It may be that here we have a further evidence of the Irish strain in him: the Irishman is never strongly committed to logic. But, as the Symphony proves, Moeran is too good a musician to neglect the claims of form, with which indeed he has wrestled in a number of works. Hence the 'exceptional earnestness and the unusual incidental qualities' of which our critic speaks. The incidentals in any work by Moeran can be fascinating, even when the shape of the work as a whole invites criticism. It is the expectation of such incidentals that makes the performance of a new work by him something to look forward to.

Such music wins affection. It reveals a personality at once

frank and friendly. You can guess from Moeran's work that he must be a companionable man. This is also music that is characteristically English, in spite of the Irish strain. This characteristic is not due merely to the influence of folk-song, which is not sufficient in itself to give a national flavour. It is rather that Moeran's work, like that of so many of his contemporaries, has qualities that we expect to find in the English temperament – a certain robustness of speech and a willing surrender to sentiment, together with that earnestness that we have already remarked in the Symphony. It would not be likely to win much appreciation on the Continent; but it has made, and will make, friends at home, particularly among those to whom poetry and imagination are precious.

CHAPTER XV

Mixed Gallery

EDWARD LOCKSPEISER

*

Joseph Holbrooke – B. 1875
Cyril Scott – B. 1879
Sir Granville Bantock – B. 1868
H. Balfour Gardiner – 1877–1950
Sir George Dyson – B. 1883
Sir John McEwen – 1868–1948
George Butterworth – 1885–1916
Herbert Howells – B. 1892

Julius Harrison – B. 1888
Ivor Gurney – 1890–1937
Roger Quilter – B. 1877
Thomas Dunhill – 1877–1946
Benjamin Dale – 1885–1943
Rutland Boughton – B. 1878
Sir Hamilton Harty – 1879–1941
Bernard van Dieren – 1884–1936

*

AT this juncture, after a series of one-man shows, my orders are to escort the reader on a tour of a mixed gallery. Let me say at the start that I cannot promise more than a rather mixed pleasure. In the first place, the composers under review in this chapter, from Sir John McEwen to van Dieren, are brought together not from any suggestion of an affinity between them, but simply because none of them has a place sufficiently important in the main stream of English music to warrant a full-length study. At any rate, so it seems to us now. Former generations would no doubt have thought otherwise, for the period from the beginning of the century down to the present day has seen the whole face of English music change more than once. At one time Bantock was a composer of the rank of Elgar; at another Holbrooke was a 'revolutionary' or Cyril Scott as disconcertingly modern as Schönberg is today. It is only recently, in fact, that values in modern English music have become stabilised, that we have at least established some sort of hierarchy. At last we can say that the spade-work of criticism has been done: the features are familiar and we may now approach a little closer to see the detail. Even so, there are many provinces of recent English music still unexplored, many composers whose work has not received assessment. Some of these are the subject of this essay. The tour, then, is of a gallery of minor composers, some of them unfortunately forgotten, some of them fortunately so, and others not yet discovered.

*

Controversy in the past has put JOSEPH HOLBROOKE (b. 1875) in each one of these categories. His name is spelt Josef on many of his scores, and Hannen Swaffer once called him 'the Cockney Wagner'. He early developed a Celtic strain, which he seems to have derived from his mother, a Scotswoman, and in his early twenties he was sponsored by the German conductor, August Manns, who produced his tone poem *The Raven* (inspired by Edgar Allan Poe) at the Crystal Palace. Wagner, the Celtic twilight, the Crystal Palace – the garishness of the period is obvious enough, and soon Holbrooke had completed another tone poem, *The Viking*, produced by his friend Granville Bantock. Then came his *Variations on Three Blind Mice*, once popular at the Proms, and from now on his name is seldom absent from the main festivals and symphony concerts. Poe was again the inspiration for *The Bells*, produced by Richter, and Herbert Trench provided the text for a curious work called *Apollo and the Seaman*. This was to be produced by Beecham. Holbrooke accompanied him to Paris, where they made a long search for the indispensable player of a bass-sarrusophone. At the performance at Queen's Hall, William Wallace worked a magic-lantern throwing the poem of Trench, verse by verse, on a screen.

All this provided publicity, and Holbrooke's new patron, T. E. Ellis (Lord Howard de Walden), led him to opera. Within four years he had written *Dylan*, the second part of a trilogy. The subject was Ellis's poem *The Caldron of Annwn*, and the three operas, *The Children of Don*, *Dylan* and *Bronwen* were eventually conducted by Nikisch, Beecham, and Weingartner. The predominant influence in England was at that time (1912) Richard Strauss, particularly in his realistic works such as *The Domestic Symphony*. It was said, however, that some of Holbrooke's music was not derivative but prophetic of Strauss. It may well have been so; but it was prophetic of sham Strauss, with no power of characterisation, with only a semblance of orchestral ingenuity and with Strauss's gaudy magnificence turned into shoddy.

Holbrooke has written in all forms except the forms of religious music, and for many different instrumental combinations. His string quartets are given odd titles – *Pickwick Club*, for instance, and *Byron*; another is called *Belgium and Russia*. There are also several chamber works for wind instruments, including a Quintet for clarinet and strings which has outlived the others and is considered one of his best works. Some of his smaller works, such as the songs or the piano pieces, have their merits, but they are often too spoilt by his taste for the outlandish. In his Prelude and Fugue for organ he employs chromatic pedal runs to be played by both feet. Some of his songs, such as those on words of Chesterton, are raucous. The music of Holbrooke, which once had its attractions, has nowadays at best a period value. A 'Cockney Wagner'? Well, yes – but as we see his music from this distance of time it suggests a less acceptable offspring of such a union.

*

CYRIL SCOTT (b. 1879) is more interesting. As a boy he was sent to study composition in Germany with Ivan Knorr, his fellow-students being Percy Granger, Norman O'Neill and Roger Quilter. Knorr had strong Russian sympathies in music and Scott's admiration for the Russians, noticeable in his later work, would seem to derive from Knorr, himself the author of a book on Tchaikoviky. The main influence on Scott at this time, however, came from Stefan George, one of the outstanding poets of our time, who sponsored the performance of his First Symphony at Darmstadt and introduced him to the poetry of Ernest Dowson. Scott has stated that Stefan George made of him 'an artist and not merely a musician'. Later, in Liverpool, he formed a friendship with Charles Bonnier, Professor of French at the University and a friend of Mallarmé, and at the age of twenty-one he was actively devoting himself to poetry.

It must have been shortly before the production of Debussy's opera *Pelléas and Mélisande* in Paris in 1902 that Scott's overture to the same play of Maeterlinck was first performed at Frankfort. The fact is worth noting, since both musicians had developed largely through the stimulus of literature; and indeed, at one time, Scott was regarded in England as an English counterpart of Debussy. It is difficult, now, to see where the resemblance lies. Quite apart from the fact that not even his staunchest admirers would compare him in stature to Debussy, Scott's music is altogether more rhapsodic and more exotic. It has seldom an element of suggestion. Moreover, Stefan George's literary circle, with which Scott was soon to become acquainted in Berlin, led him into channels far removed from the world of Debussy. A new influence on Scott at this time was the art of Melchior Lechter, a stained-glass window designer and a mystic, and before long he was beginning to take a deep interest in occultism, oriental philosophy, and mysticism.

Here is the type of inspiration that is at the source of his well-known piano piece *Lotus Land* and is evident in so many of his later works. But Scott seems to be essentially a pictorial mystic; the inner, more devout mysticism escapes him. Dispensing with key-signatures and bar-lines, he now develops a much more modern style, of which the main examples are the Sonata for Violin and Piano and the Piano Sonata written between 1908 and 1910. Several smaller works followed, and in 1913 his overture to *Princesse*

Maleine, another play of Maeterlinck, was given in Vienna.
By this time Scott's music was enjoying a certain reputation
in Central Europe, at all events a higher reputation than in
England. In London Kreisler had taken part in a performance at the old St James's Hall of his Piano Quartet, and
at the British Musical Festival organised by Sir Thomas
Beecham in 1915 Scott played the solo part in his Piano
Concerto. His next big work was an opera, *The Alchemist*,
produced at Essen in 1925. At the Norwich Festival of 1936
his choral work *Let us now praise famous men* was heard, and
the following year the Leeds Festival produced his setting
of Keats's *La Belle Dame sans Merci*.

Gifted with melodic invention, an original sense of harmony, and a natural instinct for the orchestra, Scott had in
him the main requirements for a good composer. He has
also been able to keep his mind open to varied and stimulating influences in literature and philosophy. His outlook is
cosmopolitan, his interests are universal. But he has somehow been unable to achieve that integration of an artistic
personality which would have made his music more compelling and perhaps less neglected than it is. Unfortunately his
wide interests, instead of having been assimilated, seem to
have led to preciosity and excessive stylisation. At the same
time there is often a showy, commonplace streak in his
music – almost the counterpart of poster-art – which clashes
badly with the literary or mystical inspiration of his works
and mars his original and vital talent.

*

SIR GRANVILLE BANTOCK (b. 1868) first came into
prominence with the overture to his cantata *The Fire-
worshippers*. We are again in the period of the fantastic
Crystal Palace at Sydenham in the 'nineties. The scene of
Bantock's cantata, given in its entirety shortly afterwards,
was ancient Persia, its plot inspired by Moore's poem *Lalla
Rookh*, describing the loves of a Mussulman Emir's daughter. This fascination of the Orient – at first a purely fictitious

vision of the Orient – has remained with Bantock almost to the present day. His operas include *The Pearl of Iran*, his choral works the colossal settings of FitzGerald's *Omar Khayyám*, and his orchestral works two symphonic poems entitled *Processional* and *Jaga-Naut* inspired by Southey's *Curse of Kehama*. These were originally intended to form part of a series of twenty-four symphonic poems on this subject, an idea that was soon abandoned if only because, as Grove's *Dictionary* naïvely suggests, 'the whole twenty-four works could not have been given consecutively at a single concert'! Bantock has also been attracted by Greek subjects, Scottish folk-music, and Celtic legends. His *Hebridean Symphony*, first heard at Glasgow in 1916, was written largely as a result of the researches in Hebridean folk-music made by Mrs Kennedy Fraser, whom he later chose as librettist for his opera *The Seal-Woman*, produced at the Birmingham Repertory Theatre in 1924. Seventeen years earlier Bantock had been appointed Professor of Music at the University of Birmingham, and it was during his early years there that his *Omar Khayyám* was produced at one of the festivals, together with *The Apostles* by Elgar (his predecessor at Birmingham), and Holbrooke's *The Bells*. It has been said, and not unjustly, that Bantock's oriental works were all made in Birmingham. His smaller, more intimate examples, however, such as the Chinese songs, have found more favour with the public today and look like maintaining themselves in the singer's repertory. A deservedly well-known work of his is the overture *Pierrot of the Minute*. Equally popular are some of his part-songs, especially those for male-voice choir, which, besides those on texts from the Chinese, include settings of Browning, Tennyson, Burns and Blake.

*

Much smaller, though not less significant, is the output of HENRY BALFOUR GARDINER (1877–1950). Like Cyril Scott, he was a pupil of Ivan Knorr in Germany without, however, coming under the numerous foreign influences that affected Scott's development. Gardiner's style is not always clearly defined, but its main features are unmistakably English. He is a fastidious composer, writing comparatively little and aiming at perfection in each of his works. His *Shepherd Fennel's Dance*, based on an episode in *The Three Strangers* from Thomas Hardy's *Wessex Tales*, is an exhilarating orchestral work, producing the same effect today as it did on its first performance at a Promenade Concert in 1911. Through the music of Vaughan Williams we have since acquired a different musical conception of Hardy; and it is a test of this early work of Gardiner that, despite the conception to which Vaughan Williams has now accustomed us, it has been able to maintain its appeal uninterruptedly. His *Overture to a Comedy* is a splendid English work – spirited, vigorous, and excellently scored. The best known of his larger works is a ballad for choir and orchestra, *News from Whydah*, on a poem by Masefield.

*

SIR GEORGE DYSON (b. 1883) has developed as a composer only in comparatively recent years. He has long been a music-master at public schools and is now director of the Royal College of Music in London. Dyson's earlier works are seldom played, but in 1928, while at Winchester, he produced a cantata *In Honour of the City*, followed shortly by *The Canterbury Pilgrims*, which rapidly became popular. Earlier Dyson had written *The New Music*, an admirable analysis of the modern technique in composition. Yet the style of his own music remained essentially conservative and little affected by the problems he so ably discussed. Four new oratorios were produced between 1933 and 1939, and at the age of fifty-four he published his first Symphony and shortly afterwards a Violin Concerto. The inspiration in these works is neither original nor compelling, but they reveal a highly disciplined technique and the hand of an honest craftsman.

*

SIR JOHN MCEWEN (1868–1948) was director of the Royal Academy of Music from 1926 to 1936. A much more prolific composer than Dyson, he wrote several symphonies besides fourteen string quartets, many of them unpublished. Much of his music has a distinct Scottish flavour. His ballad for orchestra, *Grey Galloway*, shows him as a more ornate composer than Dyson, while the eighth, known as the *Biscay* Quartet, one of his better-known works, purports to describe the windswept Biscay shore, the sand-dunes, and the joviality of the oyster-gatherers. The ninth Quartet, written during the 1914–18 war, consists of a single movement in the form of a threnody, opening with a sombre passage suggesting a funeral march and leading eventually to a tranquil close based on a Scottish folk-tune. Other quartets of McEwen are of a lighter character, such as the seventh, consisting of seven picturesque pieces, and the eleventh, in the form of a dance suite. His last Quartet in B minor, written in 1927, brought to an end this cycle of chamber works, which also includes five Sonatas for piano and violin.

*

While Holbrooke, Scott, and Bantock have been inclined in one form or another to extravagance, Dyson and McEwen represent the more conservative elements in English music. Somewhere between these two groups lies the essentially traditional music of GEORGE BUTTERWORTH (1885–1916). A friend of Vaughan Williams and Cecil Sharp, he was profoundly affected by English folk-music. Under this influence he was able to illustrate the poems of A.E.Housman, creating a distinctively English type of song, lyrical but never gushing, sensitive but not over-refined. Housman has since inspired several modern composers, but Butterworth was the first to find his equivalent in music. The cycle from *A Shropshire Lad* has become a classic of modern English music, and so has his rhapsody for orchestra of the same title, using a theme from one of the songs and first performed at Leeds in 1913. Folk-music was again the inspiration of his orchestral idyll *The Banks of Green*

Willows, given in London the following year. A third orchestral work, *The Cherry Tree*, another song cycle, *Love blows as the wind blows*, on poems by W. E. Henley, together with a few part-songs, form the entire output of this poetically inspired composer who, had he lived longer, might have achieved for modern English poetry what the French composers have achieved for Verlaine and the Symbolists. Having thus achieved distinction as a composer, Butterworth enlisted in the army at the outbreak of the First World War and, at thirty-one, was killed at Pozières in a gallant action for which he was posthumously awarded the Military Cross.

*

Another traditionalist, HERBERT HOWELLS (b. 1892), a pupil of Stanford, was similarly attracted by folk-music. This, however, has by no means been the only influence in Howells's music. He has held various posts as organist and is one of the prominent modern composers of religious music. Another aspect of his music is seen in his orchestral work *Puck's Minuet*, written in a light humorous style, kept deliberately superficial with no trace of irony. There are also the works inspired by associations with his native Gloucestershire, such as the Piano Quartet, to some extent the Phantasy String Quartet, and particularly the later String Quartet bearing the actual title *In Gloucestershire*. A more concentrated example of his chamber music is his Rhapsodic Quintet for Clarinet and Strings. Themes of folk-song origin are introduced in his music, though never obtrusively, and he sometimes makes use of the modes. What is especially remarkable, however, in Howells's music is his command of form. He can combine lyricism with architectural strength and at the same time he has written delightful movements in a winsome mood, such as the second movement of his E minor *Piano and Violin Sonata*. A recent work of Howells is the *Concerto* for string orchestra. In 1936 he succeeded Holst as director of music at St Paul's Girls' School, and then became organist at St John's College, Cambridge.

*

The music of both Butterworth and Howells leads us logically to a consideration of the strange, isolated figure of IVOR GURNEY (1890–1937). In passing, some reference, however inadequate, should be made to the numerous songs, written in a light illustrative genre, of ROGER QUILTER (1877–1946); to his *Children's Overture* based on tunes of nursery rhymes; to the light opera *Tantivy Towers* by THOMAS DUNHILL (b. 1877) on a libretto by A. P. Herbert and not far removed from the style of Sullivan; to the *Suite for Viola and Piano* and the early *Piano Sonata* in D minor by BENJAMIN DALE (1885–1943); to the *Violin Concerto* and symphonic poems by the conductor, SIR HAMILTON HARTY (1879–1941); and to the opera *The Immortal Hour* by RUTLAND BOUGHTON (b. 1878), first produced at Glastonbury, which has enjoyed a great vogue. None of these composers is a figure of national importance, but each has his separate followings in much the same way as certain authors have a special public. Of more general appeal is the music of JULIUS HARRISON (b. 1888), whose *Rhapsody for Violin and Orchestra – Bredon Hill* eloquently emphasises his inspiration by the Worcestershire and Shropshire countryside, and perhaps also by its supreme poet, A. E. Housman. These influences are present, if less intensely, in his justly popular and in places almost bucolic *Worcestershire Suite*, a much earlier work.

The songs of Ivor Gurney might have been given a gallery to themselves – a small private gallery perhaps, for, although they display a rare fusion of poetry and music, they are not songs ever likely to make a wide appeal. They are for poets as much as for musicians, which is not surprising, since Gurney was no less gifted a poet than a composer. Born at Gloucester, he was a chorister in the cathedral as a boy and, according to Marion Scott (to whom we owe a most sensitive appreciation of Gurney's character), 'his education may be said to have begun with the beauty he saw around him – the cathedral, the lovely countryside, the hills, the Severn River'. In 1911 he won a

scholarship and went to the Royal College of Music in
London to study with Stanford. Both Stanford and Parry,
then director of the College, believed that Ivor Gurney had
the stuff of genius in him. An illuminating account of his
first appearance at the R.C.M. is given by Harry Plunket
Greene. Gurney was waiting outside to take the *viva voce*
examination. In the meantime, 'Parry was greatly excited
over Gurney's MS. composition and was pointing out to
his colleagues the similarity in idiom and even in handwriting to Schubert, when Gurney was called. As he
walked into the room Parry said in an awestruck whisper:
"By God! It *is* Schubert".'

In his early twenties this Gloucestershire lad was plan-
ning a cycle of operas on the plays of W. B. Yeats and Synge's
Riders to the Sea. Another project was a music-drama on the
subject of Simon de Montfort. But these did not progress
beyond the ambitious plans of youth. Songs were his real
love. At that time, according to Plunket Greene, he was
'totally unselfconscious, untidy to a degree, lost in the
clouds. ... His MSS. were in a permanent state of hopeless
confusion, a second fiddle part of a string quartet tucked
away with the trombones of an overture, or maybe not
written out at all. He would talk of Schubert by the hour
and might have been his reincarnation.'

The war came and Gurney was soon in the Gloucestershire Regiment with which, in 1917, he was to face the
Passchendaele gas. His first book of poems, *Severn and
Somme*, had been published earlier that year. But the
Passchendaele offensive had dangerously undermined the
sensitive artist. Invalided out of the army in the last weeks
of the war, he returned in 1919 to the College to study with
Vaughan Williams and in the following three years produced some of his best work. Then, in 1922, his mental
balance collapsed. Delusional insanity developed and the
remaining tragic years of his life were spent in a mental
hospital.

Gurney's songs are not commentaries on the poems or

illustrations of them. What he attempted to discover was the music from which poetry is born, the music which, however nebulously, must have existed in the poet's mind. This is indeed the highest conception of the song-writer, realised in our age only a few times. Gurney may not have been fortunate enough to succeed more than partially in his quest; and one does not have to look very closely at his songs to be aware of his faults. Even these, though, are interesting. Chief among them is that pent-up anxiety 'to say it all out in one word' which, according to Walter de la Mare, was his poetic ideal and, judging from some of his tense modulations, seems to have sometimes been his musical ideal. There is often clumsiness in the piano-writing, too monotonous an insistence on pattern, or a lack of finish in the way he handles a phrase. But I do not wish to insist on these blemishes; those who knew Gurney have maintained, and understandably, that he could not have been Gurney without them.

His mind is best seen by his variety of mood and also by his variety of treatment. The beauty of his native Gloucestershire inspired his best work, and in France, in 1917, he wrote *Severn Meadows*, the only setting of his own words. Other poets demanded a different approach. The setting of W. B. Yeats's *Cathleen ni Houlihan* is in a narrative style, while *The Folly of Being Comforted*, another poem of Yeats, is essentially a declaimed song. He was essentially the musician of the Georgian poets. His two song cycles *Ludlow and Teme* and *The Western Playland*, the former for tenor, the latter for baritone, both with string quartet and piano, contain some of the loveliest settings of A. E. Housman's poems and show his talents at their highest. John Doyle's *Hawk and Buckle* inspires a rough-hewn folk-song style, John Ledwidge's *Desire in Spring* an atmospheric setting, and John Davidson's *The Boat is Chafing* a beautiful piece of realistic imagery. All of which shows that Gurney was certainly not content merely to be a stylist, even if he had had the required technique. Listening to his songs for the first time one is perhaps disconcerted by an harmonic mushiness – he was especially fond of the now much-abused chords of the seventh and ninth – or by a texture in the accompaniment suddenly too anxious and too urgent. Yet when he does find tranquillity how complete is the effect! Everyone may find in Gurney's songs the phrase or phrases to remember him by. Is there one with which we might appropriately leave him here? Surely, his lovely version of the closing lines of Edward Shanks's 'The Singer',

> *And still from the sweet and rounded mouth*
> *The delicate songs arise,*
> *Like floating bubbles whose colours are*
> *The coloured melodies.*

*

Much more remote than Gurney is the enigmatic figure of BERNARD VAN DIEREN (1884–1936). Born in Holland of Dutch and Irish parents, he settled in London at an early age where, in the 'twenties and 'thirties, he attracted a small band of ardent admirers. He was an esoteric composer, embracing many different styles, accomplishing extraordinary feats of technical virtuosity, extremely complex, highly sophisticated and artistic. In fact, one might almost say that there was too much of the artist in him. He was one of those rare examples of a composer in whom the artist almost stifles the musician. His idealism was such that no sort of practical issue ever seemed to affect the size or scope of his works, with the result that many of them are so complex that they can never hope to receive more than an occasional hearing. At his death only a relatively small number of his works had been published. His collection of essays, *Down among the Dead Men*, reveals a provoking and highly individual sense of values.[1]

Unquestionably van Dieren had in him the elements of an exceptional, perhaps even a great, composer. Simplicity,

[1] As does his unpublished and unpublishable short biography of Wagner. (Editor.)

however, did not seem to him to be a virtue in itself. There is something uncanny in a work like the *Diafonia* for baritone solo and seventeen solo instruments, employing the most intricate counterpoint. The same complexity of texture is noticeable in the accompaniments of many of his songs, or in his Variations for piano. His fourth and fifth String Quartets are written for unorthodox combinations. A comic opera, *The Tailor* (Robert Nichols), calls for a chamber orchestra only, while his setting of de Quincey's *Murder as one of the Fine Arts* is for baritone solo, male-voice quartet, and piano. These are certainly not the works of a composer who was interested in courting success.

His published works, consisting chiefly of songs, some of the piano pieces, and several chamber works, are generally less elaborate. What immediately strikes one is the diversity of style. He set poems in English, French, and German, sometimes in a manner suggesting Schönberg, sometimes Delius, of whom he was a great admirer, and there are some enchanting pages not far removed from Schumann. Often he deliberately resorts to stylisation for the sake of parody; or he may suddenly change from one style to another for the sake of comedy. Yet there is never anything affected in van Dieren; he does not attitudinise. He was ready to take beauty where he found it and proclaim it to the world.

Despite the recondite nature of so much of his music, there are many pages to make one regret that his vast output has been so neglected. The opening of his setting of Shelley's 'Come, I will sing you some slow, sleepy tune' (from 'The Cenci') is a moving recitative making its full effect of mingled grandeur and nostalgia. Then there is the cradle song *Balow*, showing with what delicacy he could write for voice. No less successful is the setting of Landor's *She, alas, I love in vain* – a dream of a song that might have been written by some master of the Romantic era who had strayed into our age by mistake. Pages such as these leave us wondering what van Dieren might have been had he possessed some sense of practical values in composition as well as such rare, idealistic visions.

CHAPTER XVI

Edmund Rubbra

B. 1901

ARTHUR HUTCHINGS

*

LET us postulate a sincere and interesting young composer who is at present getting known to the concert-going public. Let us call him Potternudge, so that no caps will fit even with the most perverse twisting. We first knew Potternudge as a concerto pianist whom Sir Henry gave us the chance to hear many years back at a Saturday-evening Prom. Soon afterwards he scored some Restoration dances which we enjoyed at the ballet; he did his work so neatly that they recorded this suite from *The Nasty Old Man*; today we often hear it played by the Eastern Regional Orchestra, and it is even blown by Grinder's Works Band. There is a piano duet arrangement and a good recording available. Next Prom out came the composer with a symphony, parts were Arthur Blissy, and none the worse for that; parts were sweet-sad and Englysshe, and in the finale Potternudge introduced *Everybody's doing it* as second counter-subject in a fugue. So the public liked the symphony, and the critics, though not sure whether they had found a man of symphonic dimensions – a man likely to write an Immortal Nine – praised the scoring and the competence and thought that the grumpy bits we didn't like 'showed a serious vein beneath a general cynicism'. At any rate this composer was to be watched. His next work was a jolly piece for two pianos and brass, written for his wife and himself; we saw them play it, and a nice couple they seemed. They had broadcast together and played at the National Gallery, and the unusual combination of brass and two pianos was sufficiently stimulating to help some of the rather 'difficult' writing to get past us. He wrote some songs for his wife and we found we could play these at home.

I believe that to be a fair account of our first acquaintance with a wise young musician, and if I were writing about him, I should recommend the reader to buy the songs and the records and then to look out for larger works. Unfortunately I cannot recommend any such approach to the composer whom I believe to be already the greatest among the younger set in this country, and also the 'darkest horse'. I am aware of the largeness of this claim, but I know that my opinion is that of a great number – possibly the majority – of those musicians to whose work this book pays tribute. Rubbra is first and foremost a symphonist; he has devoted the first years of his musical life to the perfection of a medium in which he needs room to move; where such room is denied, we cannot yet find his representative style, and if there are readers whose friends have told them that they received a tremendous musical experience at first hearing Rubbra's third or fourth Symphony, I can only beg them to wait till they have opportunity of the same experience, and not to seek out other works by the same composer which happen to be more accessible, until they can examine them in the light of his large-scale orchestral writing.

Rubbra has written no music for films, is not a member of any technical or performing 'set', does not immediately reveal the influences of a school of writing or the stamp of any other great musical personality: though a fine pianist, it took the Army to make him appear as a performer, and he has written no small accessible sheets for the piano. (The second Sonata for Violin and Piano is a fine work, and might be regarded as an exception to these remarks, since it has brought Rubbra's characteristics as a composer to the notice of several home musicians.) Moreover, there are no gramophone records of this one of his works to be bought. Yet I believe that, but for the outbreak of war, the last two Rubbra symphonies, and the fifth (now under completion) would have established the composer's reputation as our first consistent symphonist, with a new style showing roots growing firmly in the classics, yet entirely innocent either of neo-classical pastiche or of sophisticated nationalism.

Shortly after the first performance of Rubbra's Third Symphony (in the second year of the late war), one of the most distinguished of the older teachers and composers, a musician to whom honour is done elsewhere in this book, wrote a congratulatory letter using the following words: 'Now and again there comes a work with the power to make one fall in love with music all over again. In such a mood I found myself when listening to your symphony'. Now the significance of those words lies in the fact that they came from a professional musician and composer; such a correspondent should be among the first to have a jaded palate, proof against stimulants and novelties that might tickle the semi-musical or please a passing fashion. But let us remember that it was Wagner of all people who found refreshment in the pure music of Palestrina and Mozart, and it is doubtful if any semi-musical æsthete could draw refreshment from such sources. It seems strange to use Palestrina as a stalking-horse for Rubbra, but I propose to do so.

There may be many who, from religious or æsthetic motives, like to hear Palestrina's perfect musical clothing to the liturgy. But no man can pretend to know Palestrina's musical personality till he has first learned to love the basic things of music from which Palestrina made his stuff. To do that one must first love each interval, each melodic leap, be it only of a third, fourth, or fifth, made the more exciting because on each side of it the melody moves by step. One must love the span of each phrase, sing it, and feel its recalcitrance to any regular 'beat'; finally one must feel it as a 'point' countering other vocal points. Similarly, where plain chords occur, though they have now become the small change of music, one must enjoy them in Palestrina for their primary colour, for their vocal 'placing', be it for tenors and basses, with the root high or low in the bass registers, or for the upper voices; one must see these chords made rich by contrast with the surrounding contrapuntal texture. In other words, only a musical nature, be it long taught, self-taught or still young in its quest for musical experiences, can know Palestrina. One would do wrong to tell a merely literary or graphic sensibility that it could fully approach Palestrina without specifically musical training.

Rubbra makes the same demand. His is the homeliest, the least difficult, the least 'phoney' of modern textures; indeed, those who seek musical novelty may be disappointed in Rubbra, though his originalities are as wonderful as those of any modern symphonist. As the letter quoted above testifies, he has the power to give musical natures a new interest in the basic things of music; to illustrate this, I have quoted the openings of his last two completed Symphonies, the third and fourth. The change of mood, or

Ex. 1

mode, at the point 'A' in Ex. 1 is made forceful since there is no restless change of plain harmony before; and at that point the melody, which has hitherto moved entirely by step, takes a simple leap of a major third. The rhythm is sinuous and interesting (the bass moves *pizzicato* in quavers, and is omitted from the quotation) because the parts pace one another. Precisely comparable is Ex. 2, the opening of Rubbra's Fourth Symphony, where the two commonest of

chords, the tonic major chord and the dominant seventh,
are given a new context. Note also that the intervals used
in the melody are those of the common chord. 'Restraint'
is a word one hesitates to apply to Rubbra's ardent muse,
but the quotations illustrate the principle behind an economy which, if deliberate and even austere in Rubbra's
'prentice days, is now part of his highly personal style.
Each shift of rhythm or key has an emotional power impossible in the texture of a Bright Boy who follows 'Les
Six' and includes augmented fifths or minor ninths in his
opening gambit. Symphonies are not made of nervous,
shifting material.

Lest it be thought that the openings quoted were 'lucky
dips', the openings of the second movements of the same
symphonies are quoted at Ex. 3 and 4, and the reader may

examine for himself Rubbra's delight in the same materials
– the intervals of the common chord, followed by conjunct
movement, and a rhythmic figure (Ex. 3) beginning on an
off-beat so that its entry in another part will be effective and
beget movement.

Now there were a number of symphonies produced between the two wars full of lovely harmonies and orchestral
effects. Yet, in Johnsonian phrase, 'the interest retired' after
they had played for a few minutes, largely because they
lacked the vigour which comes from cross-rhythm, or
counterpoint. Often they were symphonic poems, which
would have been acceptable had they not been pulled out to
such inordinate length. Rubbra's job was to forge a symphonic technique wherein his contrapuntal gift could find

expression in other parts than that section traditionally
known as 'development' – often a dull part put in from a
sense of duty. This was a new and dangerous departure, since
the essence of symphony lies in large contrast, analogous to
the reactions of characters and scenes in drama. Thus even
Rubbra's first and second Symphonies show the composer
at great labour not to overcrowd his canvas, to write con-
trapuntally but in large, gracious periods which will allow
certain moments to stand out as high spots. This was difficult when his nature drove him to contrapuntal intensity
early in a movement. Ex. 5 may serve to show what discipline is required to prepare a high spot or even one of the
smaller high spots. The wonderful change of key shown
there could hardly have had such force had it not followed
the very simple step-wise melody shown at Ex. 4.

So much for the trees of Rubbra's wood. They are not
cactuses which immediately appeal to our curiosity. Their
beauty is evident only as we see them in the whole scene to
which they are functional. Perhaps I have now justified my
reference to Palestrina, though, so far as the latest examples
of large-scale writing are concerned, I do not think that
criticism justified which speaks of Rubbra's movements as
vast motets. True, he vindicates anew the precepts of older

masters (e.g. that a 'point' shall not begin on an accented syllable), and his themes often *sing*, but I feel that he has now forged a technique by which he may become the first English composer to write a consistent series of essays in symphonic form – and the third and fourth are not essays but achievements.

Elsewhere I have made a comparison between the art of the symphonist and that of the dramatic poet, and I must ask pardon for using the analogy once more. We look in all great movements for that glowing rhapsody which we call lyricism. In a sonnet or short poem, language can afford the concentrated richness of lyricism throughout; but this is impossible and ludicrous in a three-hour drama. Shakespeare therefore uses the medium of blank verse which, however tensely and carefully spun, has to carry conversation, argument, narration of things past, and situations of no immediate emotional poignancy; there come the high points, the moments of eloquence, the times of repose wherein we see into the hero's soul, are made to feel pity, anger, or horror; here the 'drumming decasyllabon' glows into lyricism as a filament glows when it is heavily charged. These memorable moments in a play are effective only from their rising from a texture of good level workmanship. So with the symphonist; he is not concerned, as is Hugo Wolf in a song, to express the poignancy of one moment, and he will make a poor work if he tries to string together a series of lyrical outbursts or orchestral effects. He must be, at any point, moving to climax or making contrast from high tension, but his colourful moments must grow from the drama, from the interplay of themes, or the apotheosis of organised material. What is quoted, even in the small snippets here, shows the kind of openings from which long movements are made.

This art did not come easily to Rubbra; for that matter it did not come easily to Beethoven or any other thinker in long periods. The remark passed by a critic after hearing Rubbra's first symphony is not so silly as it sounds: 'This is a symphony and no mistake.' The classical symphonist had used short, pregnant motives. Rubbra's job was to bend his own sinuous lines to his symphonic conception, and one of his greatest difficulties lay in scoring. With short figurations and simple texture, one can use the orchestra in the luminous, decorative way of Rimsky-Korsakov; but to underline first one, then another strand of polyphonic texture is to come up against the problem of balance at every point in a movement. I do not think that, even now, Rubbra finds it easy to bring off the orchestration conceived in his mind's ear while writing his 'short score'. Let us consider one instance of this.

In the first movement of the third symphony, just along with one of those fine delayed changes of key mentioned above, Rubbra introduces a new and exciting 'conjunct movement' tune, beginning with five iterations of the note E. (See Ex. 6.) At rehearsal, some of the composer's friends felt that the detached bowing of the fiddles did not make this phrase clear enough above the general orchestral sound. Another composer would have written accents or the word *martellato*, or even added a trumpet. Rubbra doggedly disregarded their advice. To have strengthened the upper line here would have upset his general purpose in a *crescendo* passage, and 'crescendo' with Rubbra means more than an increase of tone. The 'Rubbra crescendo' of tension, of contrapuntal additions struggling over a repeated rhythm such as that seen on the bass C of our example, has become a regular feature of his symphonic style. In this particular place, he plans, some twenty bars later, to reach a bursting-point, at which, with a huge swerving change of key, his first theme shall return in full orchestral dress.

In this symphonic writing, then, the best, most characteristic of Rubbra's music is to be found; one is therefore guarded in giving the opinion that his writing for choirs takes second place. He has the very technique that should make a fine choral writer, and such he is, especially in the second set of Spenser sonnets. It has to be remembered,

(inner parts omitted)

however, that most of his writing for the voice precedes his full development as a symphonist, and that he has regarded certain of his orchestral instruments as voices with a tremendous range. In some of the vocal works one feels that his linear writing is lovely enough, but that the precise vocal effect of any passing texture has been conceived ideally. It is therefore with the deepest interest that one anticipates the completion of his fifth (choral) symphony.

[The comments made after the chapters on Vaughan Williams, Bax and Walton apply, *mutatis mutandis,* also to what has been written about Rubbra. Ed.]

CHAPTER XVII

Benjamin Britten

B. 1913

SCOTT GODDARD

*

BENJAMIN BRITTEN, born at Lowestoft in Suffolk, had his general education at Gresham's School, Holt, in Norfolk. For as much as it may be worth, in his music (the extent of the influence can be gauged in the opera *Peter Grimes* based on Crabbe's Aldeburgh poem) he is East Anglian. Before he left school in 1928 his young talent had been encouraged by Frank Bridge, his first and most helpful teacher. Bridge quickly realised what was there; he was soon generously describing Britten's gifts by a larger title than mere talent. At the Royal College whither Britten went in 1930 he was under John Ireland and Arthur Benjamin. Bridge was not so much a great teacher as an inspiring guide. The amount of inspiration a boy of Britten's precocious ability needed from a teacher was probably small. But guidance of the kind Bridge could give through his craftsman's knowledge of technique was of the utmost value.

Little is known of Britten's music written in childhood, except that it was extensive. The *Simple Symphony* for strings or string quartet (published 1934) is 'entirely based on material from works which the composer wrote between the ages of nine and twelve', among them a Third Suite for piano and a Pianoforte Sonata numbered nine. All this music, in the fragments making the *Simple Symphony*, has charm, expertness and, in the slow movement, a warm thoughtfulness which in an older composer would suggest long experience; it is earlier than the first published works, the *Sinfonietta* for single wood-wind, horn, and strings, and the *Phantasy Quartet* for oboe and strings (both 1932). It should be noted that the *Sinfonietta* contains a set of variations, while the Quartet is in essence a succession of variations with copious linking material between them, — formalism lightened by the play of fantasy.

Variation writing, which with the use of patterns reiterated as accompaniment and background is one of the two methods most often employed by Britten, can be either the obsession of a mind naturally inclined to technical prowess or the means by which a young mind learns to move from point to point in a work of art. In the former case this kind of sectional manipulation of material remains the sole activity of the musician; he never develops into a symphonic thinker, for the reason that the art of development, as distinct from repetition and embellishment, is not understood by him. In the latter case variation writing, which is, or used to be, the first exercise set by a teacher, is a means to an end; it is gradually shed as that end, the fully developed method of the symphonic writer, is approached. Britten appears to have started variation writing at the usual age and has continued it fairly far on in his career. Much of his most characteristic work is in this style and manifestly the attraction is still strong.

In 1934 appeared what was immediately acknowledged to be an astonishingly mature work for a man of twenty-one, a setting for unaccompanied men's, women's, and boys' voices of a number of carols, displayed in a series of variations and called *A Boy was born*. It is one of the least performed of Britten's works; at a time when the naturally incurious mind of the public is bedevilled by the way the latest work is so rapidly superseded by one yet later, such forgetfulness is perhaps understandable. It is none the less regrettable; for *A boy was born* is one of Britten's finest works. Apart from its technical facility, which is immense, the music has deep feeling, dignity, and an exquisite youthful gaiety. It is, of course, difficult to perform and that may be a reason for its neglect. But it must be known by anyone attempting to assess Britten's work, where it has great significance. It is still variation technique, but a remarkable example of it.

At the Norwich Festival in 1936 *Our Hunting Fathers* amused the sophisticated, scandalised those among the gentry who caught Auden's words, and left musicians dazzled at so much talent, uneasy that it should be expended on so arid a subject, not knowing whether to consider Britten's daring style as the outcome of courage or fool-hardiness. As soon as the *Variations on a Theme of Frank Bridge* appeared in the same year opinion stabilised, and it was said that Britten was as much artist as pamphleteer. In the meantime *Our Hunting Fathers* made an impression of class-consciousness. There was undoubtedly that in the words, not all by Auden nor of the keen quality that poet's work had already shown, but in the whole libretto devised by him; this was bitter satire and the music was overshadowed by it. The same satirical treatment is in other works, though the cycle of songs *On this Island* (words by Auden) dating from the same year, and the 1939 *Ballad for Heroes*, which is Auden's and Randall Swingler's testimony to the International Brigade in the Spanish Civil War, have more than satire; in the former a high visionary quality (which Britten equals in at least one of the songs, the *Nocturne*), and in the latter there is every excuse for the acrid flavour the music takes from the words and, as well, a prophetic quality the music gives them. *Our Hunting Fathers*, therefore, has its own special significance among Britten's works because it connects him with what was then the forward-looking group of artists in England. Still more is it important as regards the work of the poet Auden. With him Britten became identified at this time, the next important influence after Frank Bridge. It will have been between this time and the beginning of the recent war that there was broadcast a script by Auden giving the historical and, more than that, the emotional character of the country

along the Roman Wall. Britten's music for this was un-
forgettable, one of the first of his many very expert scores
for radio. At this time also he was providing incidental
music for plays by Auden and Isherwood, and for documentary films. It was a time of brisk investigation in the
direction of dramatic commentary; one aspect is to be seen
in the *Soirées Musicales* entitled 'five movements from
Rossini', the distance fluctuating in proportion to the frequency with which Britten dresses Rossini in his clothes or
leaves the obese old gallant nude.

The *Variations on a Theme of Frank Bridge* for strings have
all the exciting facility of *A Boy was born*, with a sensitive
musicianship which had been lacking in the intermediate
works. This is a work of extremely capable craftsmanship,
daring but wholly justified. The variation technique is of
the utmost freedom; it takes, for instance, some ingenuity
and not a little faith to discover the provenance of the fifth
of the set. As a tribute from pupil to master the work is
notable partly as a study in contrasted varieties of outlook
(the theme from Bridge's *Three Idylls* (No. 2) transmogrified
out of all knowledge or likeness and made to serve ends
more sardonic and satiric than its creator would have imagined or himself employed); and even more as a contemporary document. For in its slightly bitter flavour (the
March with its echo of an absurd goose-step and the *Wiener
Walz*, which is perhaps not intended to guy affection as
much as it does) there is mirrored a state of mind peculiar
to the younger and more sensitive creative artists of that
day. Most remarkable and personal of all these movements
is the Chant, most cunning the final Fugue. In the Adagio
and the Funeral March there is the hint of another influence,
new in Britten, that of Mahler. This is the Mahler of the
Sixth and Seventh Symphonies, of the introduction to the
second part of the Eighth, of parts of the Ninth. The connection Britten has with this music is one of feeling more
than of technique, the same conflict of romantic emotion
with observation directed from an acute angle; with Mahler

emotion wins, with Britten that is not yet the case. The influence from Mahler has not yet fully worked itself out of his system or delivered itself of its full effect.

The next considerable works are a Pianoforte Concerto (1938) and a Violin Concerto (1939). Each shows technical ability, ingenuity that seems inexhaustible in fresh methods of manipulating material. In neither work is that material particularly distinguished: memory retains less of these than of some previous and many later works. Yet neither concerto is negligible; the very adventurousness of the thought saves them, though by a short head. For with that adventuresome quality there goes an acceptance of outworn conventions such as the waltz twisted into a grin and jerked as though it were danced by marionettes, a method which now sounds old-fashioned, for all that the presentation employs the latest instrumental tricks. The concertos interest the mind more than they move the emotions. This may be caused by the metaphysical character of the music, written at a time when the social passion of the reforming writers (Auden, MacNeice, and Day Lewis among their poets, Isherwood among their dramatists and novelists) was a strong influence. It is as though the vehemence of this group had entered into the two Britten concertos. It was a valuable influence, but more so for his completer artistic expression was the return to a deeper individual poetry (the feeling there is in *A Boy was born*) which was now to come.

The first signs of this personal poetic quality, which has transformed Britten the brilliant pamphleteer into a notable creative artist, are to be heard in the setting of poems by Rimbaud in the original French, for solo voice (soprano or tenor) and string orchestra, called *Les Illuminations*. Here the artifice is highly refined and if, as has been suggested, the immediate urge came from hearing Milhaud's *Pan et Syrinx*, there is a further refinement on the model. There is still a hint of vociferation, for instance in the first song; and the cycle begins with a fanfare. But the manifesto element goes, leaving nothing but pure poetry in the last song.

From then onwards poetic music appears in work after work. In the next year (1940) there is the *Diversions* for piano (left hand) and orchestra written for Paul Wittgenstein, a *tour de force* of skill and another piece of expert variation writing, a work of great technical interest and, as far as study of the score can show, much beauty, some of it rather acrid (there is a typical Britten March and two explosive Toccatas). The work was written to commission in America, whither Britten had gone and where he was to remain for three years. The capability to write occasional music, commissioned work, and to work to a time schedule is not the least admirable quality of this composer; he seems always able to deliver a score to time.

More impressive among the music produced during the American visit is the *Sinfonia da Requiem* for full orchestra. The Italian title is significant. Britten is the least national of composers and directs his work to whatever quarter of the world will receive it. Also in this work the fundamental principle of construction is a succession of reiterated patterns, either rhythmic or melodic; and it is possible that Italian operatic aria accompaniments from the last century, probably those of Verdi, were the initial incentive. The *Sinfonia da Requiem* is in Britten's most poetic and visionary vein, music of a very moving quality. It has been said to protest too much, and there is undoubtedly a trace of the old vociferation in the first movement (*Lachrymosa*) as there is gall in the second (*Dies Iræ*). But the very nature of the work allows, if it does not in fact demand, dramatic emphasis, and beneath that there is deep feeling. It is, after all, music for those of one mind with its own particular situation. Such listeners would be closely touched by the beauty of the last movement, the *Requiem* opening with a wailing chorus of flutes over a repeated pattern on harps and bass clarinet from which, with admirable economy, is developed a movement which reconciles the claims of the brain with the desires of the heart.

In the same year appeared a setting for tenor and

pianoforte of *Seven Sonnets of Michelangelo* set to the Italian text. Britten cannot be described as instantly sensitive to the rhythm of words. In *Les Illuminations* there are signs that the melodic idea was of prime importance, and when that conflicted with the scansion of a line the music led. In the *Seven Sonnets* there are further traces of this habit. The cycle has an energising quality of directness, many moments of an appealing beauty, and is another example of Britten's pattern-making (in the accompaniments). As a means of unifying songs this has its uses; but the risk of the obvious is very large. One at least of the songs, the final *Spirto ben nato*, which is a near relative of Ravel's *Le paon*, is a masterpiece for which may be prophesied longer life than the rest.

In 1941 appeared the amusing and vinegarish *Scottish Ballad* for two pianos and orchestra. It seems not generally to be liked, though it has been admired even by those who find offence in its bold sarcasms, its juxtaposition of the limp and the lively, the funeral itself, and the excited discussion afterwards of the funeral bake-meats. The *String Quartet* (1941) has astonishing writing, the usual hardy facility and pertinent comment. It runs the four strings, as is the modern habit, very hard. There is little enough of the intimacy for which the four instruments used to be considered the prime medium. Judged as construction, as drama more than lyricism, as prose more than poetry, the work has its own strength and achieves its own success. It is many years since an intimate string quartet, greatly conceived, has been written; possibly the times had nothing to offer that would move a contemporary-minded musician to such depths.

Such are the works connected with Britten's visit to America. When he came back to England the first of his latest music the public heard was the charming, evocative *Ceremony of Carols* for boys' voices and harp (1942), and in the next year another choral work, as original, daring, and as successfully reaching its aim, the festival cantata commissioned by St Matthew's Church, Northampton (thus making history in church music), called *Rejoice in the Lamb*. The *Ceremony* seems at first a period piece; it ends by impressing the hearer with a sense of the composer's certainty of movement, his unusual ability to combine the cultures of an old and a new art. *Rejoice in the Lamb* has about it a freshness unlike anything in our music, new in Britten's. The delicate steel-like tension of Christopher Smart's lines is echoed in music that has a similar quality of ageless youth and instinctive unquestioning wisdom. The effect, once it has registered upon the listener, is of music reaching the understanding with a vague, hesitant, yet quite vital touch as from some unexplored region of the mind.

In this year (1943) the *Serenade* for tenor voice, horn, and string orchestra was first heard. Those who held, in the face of a good deal of subjective criticism, that Britten would one day take in the wide visionary scope of the true poetic creative artist were justified in this work. There is still a curious insensitiveness to the inherent rhythm of a verbal phrase which in an artist now so assured can only be deliberate. But that is forgotten (except perhaps by the singer, if he be sensitive) in the larger aspect of the music's supporting, caressing, urging onward the poetic idea of each song. Enshrined within an expanse of solo horn music, by turns lyrical and dramatic, the songs, flooded with the warm tones of that most romantic of all brass instruments, have an extraordinary quality of texture and sentience. The words from various sources (which one imagines as having been chosen by a peculiarly alert connoisseur of poetry) begin with Cotton's *The days grow old* ... and end with Keats's *O soft embalmer of the still midnight* ... for which Britten, by now a singularly aware manipulator of a peroration, writes some of his finest visionary music. There are other things, notably the dirge *This ae nighte*. Indeed, the whole cycle has individuality and is a most original conception.

Britten's first opera, *Peter Grimes*, has a libretto by Montague Slater based on the tale in Crabbe's Letter XXII in *The Borough*. To the bare facts of that tragic situation of the lone fisherman and the apprentices dying on his hands certain material has been added for the heightening of the drama and a general increase of emotional tension. Britten's music is in a rapid conversational give-and-take with some remarkable extended choral passages and impassioned solo writing. The pace is hard throughout. It gives the impression of being immensely effective theatre. *Peter Grimes* was ready for the reopening of Sadler's Wells Theatre on June 7th, 1945. There had been much publicity over this production, and it may be granted that no English opera has ever had such a press. When heard, it was found to be finer as a work of art, less tendentious as a vehicle for ideas, less portentous as a manifesto than friends or enemies had implied. And when the *Four Interludes* from the opera were played at the Cheltenham Festival a few months later, there was no questioning the quality of vision Britten had experienced nor his remarkable success in expressing that vision in music of great emotional power, penetrating beauty, and a completely individual manner of writing.

The foregoing notes are, perhaps, all that it would be allowable to expect in the circumstances, complicated by the fact that this particular composer is remarkably prolific, still young and therefore but at the beginning of a long and rich artistic development. And thus nothing yet is certain. The understanding of new music is a long and hardy study. Of Britten's latest works the *Serenade* may well move some sympathetic listener immediately; but it will take, and should be given, more time than its own present age to penetrate the understanding of even an alert mind. And only when that has happened can an opinion be offered as to its quality or its power to persist. Whoever tries to discover the intrinsic quality of the music of Britten and his generation must take courage from what they possess in only a small degree, sufficient knowledge to form a judgment.

[See notes at end of chapter on Rubbra and elsewhere. Ed.]

CHAPTER XVIII

'What Now?'

ROBIN HULL

*

Howard Ferguson – B. 1908	*Alan Rawsthorne* – B. 1905
Gerald Finzi – B. 1901	*Elizabeth Maconchy* – B. 1907
Gordon Jacob – B. 1895	*Alan Bush* – B. 1900
Lennox Berkeley – B. 1903	*Michael Tippett* – B. 1905

*

IT has been made clear that the music of Benjamin Britten points boldly to the future. The composers now to be discussed are also 'forward-looking' – some, of course, more strongly than others – although each is firmly distinctive in style. Their presence in the onward movement of our national music is due partly to the fact that the revolt against late romanticism has entered upon a second, consolidating phase. The first phase, so memorable for the pioneer work of Arnold Schönberg (now past his seventieth year), was over and done with before Berkeley, Rawsthorne, and others here had touched even the fringe of artistic maturity. Schönberg's personal creed embraced strictly equal treatment of the twelve notes in the chromatic scale, a rejection of the major-minor key-system, and an insistence that music should be exempt from 'romantic' interpretation of its meaning.

Today the results of his work are felt at so distant a remove, owing to the remarkable speed at which the revolution has developed, that it would be wildly misleading to write of any composer in this chapter as being under Schönberg's direct influence. The situation is, rather, that Schönberg enriched the musical language with far-reaching resources which have become part of the expressive means available to later composers. Some of those within our group seem to have found that these resources are much to their purpose; others have evolved or turned to different means for their special needs; but every thoughtful composer of recent times has been compelled to decide his attitude towards this inheritance. A good deal of 'forward-looking' music tends rather to strike a middle course between radical adherence to the major-minor key-system, and unqualified loyalty to strictly equal treatment of the twelve notes in the chromatic scale. The effect is largely to reap the advantages of free tonality while permitting, so far as may be desirable, the near or remote implication of a key-centre. This process, far from being reactionary, has proved a valuable step towards fuller yet disciplined liberty. The distaste for any literary interpretation of their music is every whit as pronounced among 'forward-looking' composers today as it was during the initial stage of revolt against late romanticism. Their standpoint upon this matter has been considerably justified by redirecting attention to music *per se*, and by a welcome asceticism in thought and self-expression.

*

There was every reason to suppose, after so drastic a revolution, that many years must pass before romance could re-emerge in any shape or form. A point of great interest about the work of HOWARD FERGUSON (b. 1908) is his success in proving that there is still ample scope for romanticism which follows a new direction. Writing in a style wholly his own and aloof from passing cults, the roots of his art strike healthily to the depths of Brahms's final works. Some affinity with that composer's Clarinet Quintet may be found, indeed, in the darker hues of Ferguson's rich and mellow Octet for clarinet, bassoon, horn, string quartet, and double bass. This captivating music offers a natural starting-point for anyone not hitherto acquainted with Ferguson's characteristics. The Octet is available upon gramophone records, and also exists in a version for string orchestra under the title *Serenade*. Unless the listener meets with unexpected difficulties even after a careful hearing – and this is unlikely to happen – it is vastly more desirable for him to approach the Octet in its entirety than to pick out single movements. No doubt the slow movement offers a particularly swift approach, but it is the least typical of Ferguson. The construction of the work as a whole is remarkably clear, with beautifully woven texture, and the instrumental colouring reveals an acute judgment of contrast.

Finely wrought though the Octet undoubtedly is, Ferguson does fuller justice to his individuality in the F minor Sonata for Piano, cast in three movements and dedicated to the memory of Harold Samuel. This Sonata, which is intentionally elegiac, strikes one as more concise and in many respects more subtle than the Octet: the subject-matter is tautly delivered and in general the concept is cogently unified. As might be expected from so accomplished a pianist, the keyboard writing shows a close and assured understanding of the instrument. Possibly it could be claimed that Ferguson might well have allowed himself sharper contrasts of mood and figuration; the uniformity of feeling throughout the three movements can become a little oppressive; but that is a relatively modest criticism to set against his powerfully sombre pages. The excellent gramophone recording is invaluable, almost indispensable, for a thorough grasp of the Sonata. Detailed acquaintance with his work will be useful to a more immediate appreciation of Ferguson's *Five Bagatelles* for piano than their highly compact thought might otherwise allow. The *Bagatelles*, expertly written though difficult to play, share with the *Partita* for orchestra the handicap of not yet being recorded for gramophone. The latter work, with its eloquent and strikingly original pages, makes clear that Ferguson is thoroughly at home in handling larger resources, and every opportunity to hear a performance should prove of great assistance in furthering an introduction to his music. The completion of a String Quartet is now awaited (1945).

*

Although it is in his vocal and choral settings that GERALD FINZI (b. 1901) has so far shown himself to be especially remarkable, a beginning may wisely be made with some instrumental works possibly more accessible for listening and performance. The (revised) *Introit* for small orchestra and solo violin gives an excellent idea of the fastidious, yet rarely over-refined, style that Finzi commands so exquisitely in idyllic mood. A somewhat broader impression of his art can be gathered from the *Interlude* for oboe and string quartet. This work ranges from quietude to vigorous, even impassioned, writing and thus has the advantage of revealing the composer outside a strictly reflective vein. The Prelude and Fugue for string trio, a model of skill and economy, provides additional evidence that he can call upon more energetic qualities than might be realised by those chiefly acquainted with his contemplative writings. The foregoing works, though finely varied, all bear testimony to Finzi's very personal and sensitive thought, disciplined utterance and exalted standard of craftsmanship.

Let Us Garlands Bring, a group of five Shakespearean songs for soprano, dedicated to Vaughan Williams on his seventieth birthday, would in itself go far towards placing Finzi among the most significant song-writers of our time. To measure his achievement, it must be stressed that he handles such resoundingly well-known poems as *O Mistress Mine* with a freshness wellnigh inconceivable in the wake of settings by so many other composers. Finzi writes, indeed, as though he had never heard a single note of Quilter. His whole approach to the mood and verbal problems of the texts is not only entirely independent but more closely attuned to Shakespeare than that of any save one or possibly two predecessors. *Come away, Death* is handled as true elegy; *Who is Silvia* is set with an exact touch far removed from the tradition of saccharine coyness; and *It was a lover* shows a scrupulous regard for meaning and accent such as informs Finzi's treatment of each song. It is this really astonishing capacity for identifying himself with the poet, while giving due regard to musical individuality, that carries him easily over the notorious difficulty of setting Thomas Hardy. *Earth and Air and Rain*, ten songs for baritone, makes imaginative demands of the highest order to which Finzi rises with almost invariable mastery. *The Clock of the Years* may be mentioned, perhaps, as outstanding in a group of which none is less than notable. *When I set out for Lyonesse* reveals a freedom and flexibility likely to banish from the listener's mind every setting by other hands. Indeed, the foregoing groups of songs bring out Finzi's gifts more broadly than his very lovely *Dies Natalis*, a cantata for soprano or tenor solo and string orchestra. To be sure, the music here is impeccably suited to the mystical text of Thomas Traherne; there is abundant skill to shape the imaginative vision; yet the necessity to sustain so fully a mood of rapture and ecstasy keeps the work within boundaries from whose strictness the listener may find himself desiring a more ample respite.

*

GORDON JACOB (b. 1895) is so renowned for his infinite skill in orchestration that there has been some danger of his receiving less than rightful due as a composer. The *Passacaglia on a Well-known Theme* (*Oranges and Lemons*) provides a very helpful introduction to certain points in Jacob's style. Far from being a piece of deft frivolity, the *Passacaglia* is a fine, dignified work whose musical growth proceeds inevitably to a noble close by way of changes rung upon the repeated theme with true imagination. We can see here, too, Jacob's very striking faculty for turning ancient means (such as the ground bass) to thoroughly modern purposes – a feature which can be traced more fully in his Suite No. 1 in F for small orchestra. His style takes liberal but not extravagant account of latter-day harmonic resources: at times, indeed, there is a refreshing flavour of acerbity about his pages, whose strongly individual sentiment indicates an equally strong aversion to sentimentality. He possesses the rare

merit of refusing to add a single note to his scores beyond
the exact limits of what he wishes to express. This quality
makes for a satisfying terseness which the reader will find
admirably exemplified in Jacob's concertos for solo instruments and orchestra. The Oboe Concerto, whose slow movement is beautifully pastoral in feeling, may well be the first
choice, though the Concertos for solo piano and solo viola
respectively should be noted for subsequent exploration.
The Violin Concerto has now been withdrawn.

Some major works by Jacob, including a Symphony for
full orchestra, still await completion or first performance at
the time of writing, but a composition for special notice is
his *Variations on an Original Theme* for orchestra. The theme
is not only striking in itself, but replete with possibilities
for musicianly treatment which the composer develops to
outstanding advantage during the course of nine variations.
Whether one turns to the broad and stately third variation,
the fleet but brilliant sixth, or the magnificent fugue at the
close, it is manifest that Jacob has wrought this work with a
strength and depth of invention which must have a profound effect upon the weight of his contribution to the
music of our time. The Variations need no direct comparison with the *Enigma* to justify their standing as one of the
finest sets written by a British composer since Elgar's day.
It must suffice to add, for those wishing to explore Jacob's
most excellent chamber works, that it is a good plan to
begin with his Oboe Quartet, then to take account of the
String Quartet in C, and progress towards the Clarinet
Quintet which won golden opinions at its first performance.

*

LENNOX BERKELEY (b. 1903) 'did not study in France
to procure a Gallic style, but instinctively sought in that
country the kind of musical training most appropriate for
the development of abilities which he already possessed'.
This quotation, besides supplying a reminder for which the
necessity has not yet ceased to exist, may give a serviceable

clue to some of the qualities inherent in this very gifted
composer. His truly representative works are distinguished
by keen perception, flawless logic and an irreproachable
technique. The clearness of his mental outlook, and the
genuine originality informing that mind in its expression,
are among the further characteristics which help to mark
out Berkeley's musical personality as something conspi-
cuous in British composition. A great part of his strength
lies in a flow of inventive thought worth arguing, and an
exceptional skill in maintaining continuity until the final
note of his argument has been stated.

Berkeley's method of self-expression, though flexible in
tonality, is so purposeful as to spare the listener any serious
difficulty in following the necessary implications of key.
The problem of where to begin acquaintance with his
music is made a little complex by purely temporary circumstance. If the String Trio is to be recorded, that work
would be an obvious choice because, up till now, only one
other composition by Berkeley *has* been recorded. On the
other hand, many listeners may already claim familiarity
with his incidental music to the film, *Hotel Reserve*, from
which it is possible that an orchestral suite will be made.
Certainly the film music reveals a warmth in which Berkeley
had hitherto appeared reluctant to indulge, but which he
can safely admit without hurt to the quality of his sentiment.
The String Trio, however, gives a much more abiding view
of Berkeley's style, and also of his success in writing for a
medium notoriously merciless to anything below the level
of uncommon musicianship. Otherwise the wisest choice
for the listener may be to start with the Serenade for Strings,
or the Sonatina for Violin and Piano, the latter being one of
the most uniformly fine works that Berkeley has written up
to the present (1945).

His engaging *Divertimento* for small orchestra suggests a
natural approach (on the score of accessible performances)
to the much larger matter of the Symphony. The latter is a
composition outstanding for elegance, purity of style and

inventive resource. Its four movements, though amply contrasted, are expressed with a restraint deriving from habi-
tual self-discipline. Like everything written at the mature
stage of Berkeley's career, the Symphony reflects a sustained
vigilance for neatness and precision while avoiding exiguity
of material or manner. The second String Quartet is best
deferred until a fairly late stage of the listener's progress
with Berkeley's music. Though ranking among his best
works, such concentrated thought as the composer gives us
there demands a tolerable knowledge of his style and adequate opportunities for repeated hearing. The piano music
most typical of Berkeley is definitely outside the range of
any except an unusually gifted executant, but the earliest
chance to hear his Four Concert Studies is one to be swiftly
taken.

*

We come now to a sequence of composers whose respective music, though sharply dissimilar in style, undoubtedly
makes more rigorous demands upon the newcomer than
some already discussed. Thoughtful readers will welcome,
and are entitled to demand, this plain warning that an especial diligence is required. It is not that these composers
are in the smallest degree wilfully or negligently obscure.
Their methods of self-expression admit a rough analogy
with written language, which has been much enriched by
new words, and in which the traditional method of sentence
construction has become drastically abbreviated. The difficulty for the listener is twofold. He has to familiarise himself with a more extensive musical vocabulary. And he meets
with the further necessity of finding out what 'short cuts'
the composer is taking for granted. It is encouragingly obvious, on the other hand, that these difficulties will recede in
direct ratio to applied efforts in listening, especially if the
listener can fortify his efforts by studying one of the admirable and clearly written books dealing with the main
principles of modern harmony. This is not to overlook the

requisite of performances in sufficient number to give listeners a fair chance. And it must be confessed that, up to the moment of writing, the gramophone catalogues offer much less assistance than is most urgently required. Readers will naturally keep a sharp look-out for any further recordings which may have appeared by the time that these words are in print.

*

The foregoing remark applies, first and foremost, to the Piano Concerto of ALAN RAWSTHORNE (b. 1905), which many people are likely to find the most quickly approachable of his works. In the meantime, a record of the *Four Bagatelles* for piano (supplemented, if possible, by a copy of the piano score) makes a valuable introduction to Rawsthorne's style and method. These *Bagatelles*, except the fourth, move at a considerable pace, and this point has to be allowed for in becoming acquainted with their flow. An important stage of familiarity will be reached as soon as it is found that Rawsthorne is working quite explicitly from a tonal-centre, but that he does not require continually to emphasise this fact. It emerges, in short, that there is a very definite method behind a tonal freedom which at first may strike the ear with surprising harshness. The final *Bagatelle* gives an admirable illustration of the process in 'slow motion', as it were, and possibly some listeners will find it helpful to concentrate particularly upon this piece.

The other recorded work by Rawsthorne is the Theme and Variations for Two Violins. Although the musical subject-matter offers decidedly stern going, the extraordinary skill and musicianship of these pages can go far to grip attention from the outset. This composition is, indeed, a marvellous feat in technique, but the vital point for observation consists in the reality of the invention which grows from the theme. Rawsthorne carries forward his purpose with a range of mood no less resourceful than the mastery of its exposition. The whole work is crystal-clear in the writing and can become equally so to the listener who perseveres with records and music to aid him. Taken in conjunction with the *Four Bagatelles*, the Variations give at least an idea of Rawsthorne's very impressive qualities.

The Piano Concerto brings out more completely the justice of suggesting that this composer, though less spectacularly gifted than Britten, may yet stand in evident range of equality with him. It is important to note that the Concerto, if provoking a hasty demur in those unprepared to take the slightest trouble over their listening, has also met with a good deal of admiration outside as well as within the ranks of musical specialists. Granted a more open choice than obtains up to the present, the listener would be well advised to give this work high priority in his explorations of Rawsthorne's music. The *Symphonic Studies* for orchestra, though undeniably among the finest achievements from this composer's pen, afford a degree of difficulty which enforces the wisdom of postponing their acquaintance until the listener finds himself on good terms with the works already mentioned.

*

Although the music of ELIZABETH MACONCHY (b. 1907) suggests that her main occupation is with forceful, logical arguments rather than emotion, the arguments she states usually command attention as much for their substance as for their expert delivery. Few British composers of her generation are more soundly equipped in every technical regard, and the significance of Miss Maconchy's work has become recognised far afield. Her most engaging composition, a set of six pieces entitled *Puck Fair*, is remarkably well suited to the orchestra, but it does not represent her so strongly as the most characteristic pages among her important output of chamber music. From the listener's point of view, especially if he happens to be a capable pianist, the Impromptu for piano (a Fantasia on One Note) gives a satisfactory impression of Miss Maconchy's style and the notable authority with which she handles her ideas. It is then a natural step to the nine short piano pieces grouped under the heading *A Country Town*. These pieces serve admirably to reveal in miniature, just as the string quartets do on a larger scale, the special flair of Miss Maconchy for genuinely developing a thesis of great originality and conciseness from an inaugural premise. Her gift for intelligent, if sometimes too remorseless, wit must be accounted among the features giving true personality to her art. Of the four String Quartets which Elizabeth Maconchy has written so far, No. 3 (in one movement) is at present the most accessible, and by an excellent stroke of fortune the Third Quarter happens also to serve the listener as a fine introduction to her activities in this sphere. The third String Quartet is not only expertly written, with unexceptionable judgment of effect, but illustrates very markedly that the composer possesses sustained ability to make her points tersely and yet sufficiently. The force of her logic is much advanced by a lucidity of texture, which in general stands high among Miss Maconchy's characteristics as an artist. Again, it would be hard to find any mature work from her pen which fails to carry aesthetic as well as intellectual conviction.

A composition by which listeners may find it useful to test this claim is the Theme and Variations for string orchestra. Certainly first-rate powers of argument are to the fore in those pages, as in everything showing Miss Maconchy's invention at her best, but the variations themselves admit of mood-contrasts which keep the music free from any danger of dry impersonality. This is not to weaken an ability for dispassionate argument, but rather to elucidate the angle from which argument is expressed. For this reason, and others already touched upon, it is apparent that the further recognition of Elizabeth Maconchy's firmly individual output is almost solely dependent upon commensurate opportunities for listeners to appreciate her worth. The works mentioned above offer a fairly substantial beginning, but those who wish to explore further would be well advised to continue their search with the well-wrought Viola Sonata, written in 1937, and remarkably appropriate to its medium.

*

The music of ALAN BUSH (b. 1900) plainly requires, for successful approach, those careful and repeated hearings made possible by gramophone records, or, at the least, by public performances of tolerable frequency. It must be owned that, up to the present, Bush has been very insufficiently served in both these regards. Of course this circumstance may be remedied at any moment, as it ought to be, but meanwhile the problem of access remains needlessly severe. Yet perceptive music-lovers enabled to hear even one performance of a work so boldly individual as Bush's *Dialectic* for string quartet can scarcely fail to be struck by the outstanding force of its intellectual power. The music is conceived with a virility of purpose fully realised in the address. The very urgency of the argument requires tension in its delivery, but this tension is always under drastic control, and never slips in the direction of emotional oratory. An interesting point for the listener is that this refusal to misuse emotion does not involve the smallest loss of variety in Bush's pages. The effect is rather as if different sections or stages of the argument demand a corresponding change of voice, yet such changes are invariably consistent with the whole. So far as the reader finds himself afforded any option in the matter, the *Dialectic* is certainly a first choice in trying to measure Bush's style at its true strength. The main problem in listening is likely to devolve much less upon the nature of the musical language, which is not only extremely direct but very clearly employed, than upon a swift assimilation of such potent subject-matter. It is more than possible, indeed, that a first or second hearing may not reward the listener as quickly as he desires, but there are good grounds for suggesting that any such experience will arise almost entirely from conciseness of Bush's material.

The Symphony in C demonstrates vividly, as those who have had a chance to judge may endorse, that this composer's powers are equal to sustaining invention upon a very big scale. He is one of the relatively few who have mastered the secret of 'going on' when dealing with a large structure; that is to say, he is nowhere thrown back upon the device of skilful joinery to conceal an untoward transition. The day has long been overdue for a revival of this Symphony, and also for a hearing of the Piano Concerto (with baritone solo and male-voice chorus in the last movement), which, through no fault of their own, remain a closed book even to those who would rightly value performances.

*

The unique art of MICHAEL TIPPETT (b. 1905) springs from phenomenal gifts which in their highest application are expressive of sheer genius. His music owes much of its integral character to the fact that the composer has realised, with supreme insight, how exactly his purpose can be fulfilled by the personal development of a technique virtually dormant since the English madrigal reached its apotheosis in John Wilbye. The crux of the matter lies not so much in Tippett's elaborate polyphony, though that is exceedingly important, but in his intricate recourse to polyrhythmic usage. There is nothing even remotely archaic about this process. On the contrary, the musical effect is something which could be achieved only by a composer belonging heart and soul to our own day. The exigencies of concert performance necessitate, indeed, the optical guidance to be derived from the bar-line, and Tippett, as the result of infinite care, has met this difficulty with great skill. The extraordinarily supple quality of his pages arises largely from the circumstances that his music achieves all the freedom to be obtained by a flow *across* the bar-line. Thus the singing, soaring ecstasy so characteristic of Tippett's invention is preserved without the slightest weakening of its inner vitality.

The Oratorio, *A Child of Our Time*,[1] is of such outstanding importance, and has proved so swiftly accessible to listeners even at a first hearing, that this work has an overriding claim for present consideration. In default of opportunities to take the Oratorio as a starting-point, there is much to be said for making a beginning with the Concerto for double string orchestra. The final movement, though not actually the strongest, might be selected for study by those who find that their progress is becoming unduly slow. Of the two String Quartets, No. 2 in F sharp is especially valuable in hastening acquaintance with the essentials of the composer's style. For one thing, the opening movement 'is partly derived from Madrigal technique where each part may have its own rhythm and the music is propelled by the differing accents, which tend to thrust each other forward'. This Quartet also illustrates in a consummate degree Tippett's mastery of musical line carried forward so as to create a large but perfectly controlled span. String Quartet No. 1 in A, which has been much strengthened and compressed by revision, stands very close to its successor as regards purely musical interest and yields little to Quartet No. 2 in F sharp in lucid, admirably balanced writing. *Boyhood's End*, a Cantata for tenor voice and piano, is an exquisitely conceived work than which few more striking examples are to be found, in shorter form, of Tippett's enthralling lyricism.

A Child of Our Time is set for soli, chorus and orchestra with a text by Tippett himself. The actual event inspiring this text was the shooting of a German diplomat by a young Jewish refugee. This act was followed by 'the most severe and terrible of official pogroms in Germany'. Tippett emphasises that the text is concerned with the general significance of these events because they repeat one of the fundamental patterns of human experience. His general plan is

---

[1] A more detailed account of this oratorio, from which some of the following observations are taken, was contributed by the present writer to *Musical Opinion*, March, 1944.

intended to recall the sequence of prophecy, narrative, and commentary in *The Messiah*. Part I deals with the present-day (but also eternal) problem of individuals and minorities unaccepted within the ruling conventions. Part II reveals 'A Child of Our Time' 'enmeshed in the drama of his personal fate and the elemental social forces of our day'. Part III is a meditation upon the significance of this drama and its potential solution. The mood of each Part is established by the opening chorus. Tippett expresses what he wishes to convey by means of narrative recitative, contemplative arias, dramatic choruses and the use of Negro spirituals as an equivalent of the chorale. These spirituals, five in number, are not grafted upon the main body of the work, but arise spontaneously during the course of the invention and establish their integral place in the Oratorio.

The contemplative arias are informed by a great range of expression, not only as between one mood and another but also between the finer shades of closely similar moods. To take examples which are actually conjunct in the score, the very beautiful tenor solo *I have no money for my love*, which makes an unforgettably moving effect while guiltless of exploiting a poignant situation, stands in exceedingly well-defined contrast to the succeeding soprano solo, *How can I cherish my man in such days?* It is this ability to sustain contrast while preserving organic unity which becomes more and more evident as acquaintance with the Oratorio increases. Furthermore, these arias provide irrefutable evidence that Tippett excels in sensitive, lyrical expression whose intensely personal nature makes profitless a comparison with music other than his own.

A remarkable breadth of range, again, is one of the features most prominent in the dramatic choruses. Indeed, the very word 'dramatic' must be considered in a much wider sense than is applicable to the vivid, furious counterpoint of *The Terror* chorus, *Burn down their houses!*. Some of the most impressive drama in the whole Oratorio comes at moments of restraint such as those that give profound dignity to the opening bars of the work. The composer's insight is shown most eloquently by his carrying into music the realisation that those overwhelmed by persecution are prevented, through the very nature of their circumstances, from finding a neatly polished solution to their problems. Thus, towards the close, the words 'It is Spring' call for and receive much more reserved treatment than conventional exultation. The settings of the five spirituals, divorced from all sentimentality, make a much deeper effect than any that may be suggested by the mere fact of their presence. The culmination of the oratorio in *Deep River* is a stroke of imaginative genius. Such universality of address as Tippett achieves in *A Child of Our Time* exalts the work into a realm infinitely removed from controversy about the text. He has written, indeed, what may prove to be the most important oratorio by a British composer since Elgar's *Dream of Gerontius*.

Index of Composers

AND

List of Gramophone Records

*

This index to composers' names includes a list of recordings of all works believed to be available in Great Britain at the time of going to press. It covers those composers whose names are given in the headings of Chapters II to XVIII inclusive. The following abbreviations are used in describing the records mentioned :

Acc.	Accompanist	Cond.	Conductor	Sop.	Soprano
Arr.	Arranged	D.	Decca	Ten.	Tenor
Bar.	Baritone	H.	H.M.V.	Trad.	Traditional
C.	Columbia	Orch.	Orchestra	Unacc.	Unaccompanied
Con.	Contralto	P.	Parlophone	Vln.	Violin
NGS	National Gramophone Society				

Figures in **bold** type indicate the principal reference to the composer in question.

BACH, J. S., 16, 21, 47, 143
BALFOUR GARDINER, H., **185–6**
BANTOCK, Sir Granville, 45, 65, 180, **184–5**, 187
   Adoration
      Orchestra
         The London Promenade Orch.
         1 side Paxton PR419
   Captain Harry Morgan
      Song
         Oscar Natzka (bass), piano acc. Hubert Greenslade
         1 side Col. DB2420
   Circus Life
      Orchestra
         The London Promenade Orch.
         1 side Paxton PR410
   Cobweb Castle
      Orchestra
         The London Promenade Orch.
         ½ side Paxton PR434

BANTOCK, Sir Granville—*continued*

King Lear (dramatic tone poem)
    Orchestra
        The London Promenade Orch., cond. Collins
        1 side Paxton PR500

Love's Awakening
    Orchestra
        The London Promenade Orch.
        1 side Paxton PR420

Lure of the Isles
    Choir and orchestra
        The London Promenade Orch.
        1 side Paxton PR462

O Can Ye Sew Cushions? (Lullaby, arr. Granville Bantock)
    Choir
        Glasgow Orpheus Choir, cond. Roberton
        1 side HMV B9464

Oriental Dance
    Orchestra
        The London Promenade Orch.
        1 side Paxton PR461

Oriental Serenade (Parts 1 and 2)
    Orchestra
        The London Promenade Orch.
        1 side Paxton PR 419

Persian Dance
    Orchestra
        The London Promenade Orch.
        1 side Paxton PR460

Processional, 'King Solomon'
    Orchestra
        The London Promenade Orch.
        1 side Paxton GTR104

Romantic Episode
    Orchestra
        The London Promenade Orch., cond. Collins
        1 side Paxton PR491

Sea Longing
    Choir and orchestra
        The London Promenade Orch.
        1 side Paxton PR460

Sea Sorrow (An Bron Mara) (from *Songs of the Hebrides* by Marjory Kennedy-Fraser, arr. Granville Bantock)
    Choir
        Glasgow Orpheus Choir, cond. Roberton
        1 side HMV C3639

Bax, Sir Arnold—*continued*

Mediterranean (1920)

  Piano, arr. orchestra

      New Symphony Orch., cond. Goossens

      1 side H.C1620

Nonett

  String quartet, double bass, flute, clarinet, oboe, and harp

      Griller String Quartet, Victor Watson, Joseph Slater, Frederick Thurston, Leon Goossens and Maria Korchinska

      4 sides English Music Society, Vol. II

Oliver Twist (incidental music to film)

  Piano and Orchestra

  (*a*) *The Oliver Theme*

      Harriet Cohen with Philharmonic Orch., cond. Mathieson

      2 sides C.DX1516

  Orchestra

  (*b*) *Pickpocketing*

  (*c*) *The Chase*

  (*d*) *Fagin's Romp – Finale*

      Philharmonia Orch., cond. Mathieson

      2 sides C.DX1517

Pæan (*Passacaglia*) (1928)

  Piano

      Harriet Cohen

      1 side C.DB1786

Quartet No. 1 in G (1918)

  String quartet

      Griller String Quartet

      8 sides D.K1009–12

Quintet

  Oboe and strings

      Leon Goossens (oboe) and the International String Quartet – André Mangeot, Boris Pecker, Frank Howard and Herbert Withers

      4 sides NGS76–7

Sonata

  Two pianos

      Ethel Bartlett and Rae Robertson

      5 sides NGS156–8

Sonata (1921)

  Viola and piano

      William Primrose and Harriet Cohen

      7 sides English Music Society, Vol. II

Sonata (*The Phantasy Sonata*, 1928)

  Viola and harp

      Watson Forbes and Maria Korchinska

      6 sides D.K941–3

BLISS, Sir Arthur—*continued*

March 'The Phœnix' (in honour of France)
>Orchestra
>>Philharmonia Orch., cond. Lambert
>>2 sides H.C3518

Polonaise
>Piano
>>Cyril Smith
>>1 side D.K780

Quartet in B flat
>String quartet
>>Griller Quartet
>>8 sides D.K1091–4

Quintet (1932)
>Clarinet and strings
>>F. Thurston and Griller Quartet
>>7 sides D.K780–3

Sonata (1933)
>Viola and piano
>>Watson Forbes and Myers Foggin
>>6 sides D.X233–5

Things to Come (Suite from music to H. G. Wells's film) (1935)
>Orchestra
>>London Symphony Orch., cond. Bliss
>>6 sides D.K810–11 and D.K817 (cond. Mathieson

BOUGHTON, Rutland, **189**

Faery Song (from *The Immortal Hour*)
>Choir
>>(1) Glasgow Orpheus Choir, unacc., cond. Roberton
>>1 side H.B9608
>Song
>>(2) Richard Lewis (ten.), piano acc. Norman Franklyn
>>1 side D.M634
>Song
>>Webster Booth (ten.), harp acc. J. T. Cockerill
>>1 side H.B8947

BRAHMS, 21, 65, 76, 89, 97, 99, 101, 152, 213

BRIDGE, Frank, **74** ff., 103, 132, 205, 206

Come to me in my dreams
>Song
>>Richard Tauber (ten.), piano acc. Percy Kahn
>>1 side P.RO20554

(The) Graceful Swaying Wattle Choir (2-part song)
>Choir
>>County Grammar School in South Wales
>>½ side H.C3527

BRITTEN, Benjamin—*continued*

Peter Grimes, Op. 33*a*

Four Sea Interludes and Passacaglia:

   Orchestra

       (1) Concertgebouw Orch. of Amsterdam, cond. van Beinum
       6 sides D.K1702–4

(a) Dawn. (b) Sunday Morning
       D.K1702

(c) Moonlight. (d) Storm
       D.K1703

(e) Passacaglia (Pts. 1–2)
       D.K1704

       (2) London Symphony Orch., cond. Sargent
       4 sides C.DX1441–2

Quartet in C major, Op. 26, No. 2

   String quartet

      Zorian String Quartet
      7 sides H.C3536–9

Rape of Lucretia, Op. 39

   Opera (abridged recording)

      Peter Pears, Nancy Evans, Joan Cross, Floria Nielsen,
        Norman Lumsden, Dennis Dowling, Frederick Sharp,
        Chamber Orch., cond. Goodall
      16 sides H.C3699–3706

Seven Sonnets of Michelangelo, Op. 22

   Voice and piano

      Peter Pears and Benjamin Britten
      4 sides H.B9302 and H.C3312

Simple Symphony (1923–5), Op. 4

   String orchestra

      Boyd Neel String Orch., cond. Neel
      5 sides D.K245–7

*Variations and Fugue on a Theme of Purcell (Young Persons Guide to the
   Orchestra)*, Op. 34

   Orchestra

      Liverpool Philharmonic Orch., cond. Sargent
      5 sides C.DX1307–8 and DXS1309

Village Harvest, see *Irish Reel*

(The) Sally Gardens ⎫
Little Sir William ⎬ Folk-song arrangements
Oliver Cromwell ⎭

   Voice and piano

      Peter Pears (ten.), piano acc. Benjamin Britten
      2 sides D.M555

DELIUS, Frederick—*continued*

   Appalachia (1902) (*Variations on an old Slave Song for full orch. with final chorus*)

      Choir and orchestra

          London Philharmonic Orch., cond. Beecham, with B.B.C. Chorus

          10 sides Delius Society, Vol. III

   Brigg Fair (1907), *An English Rhapsody*

      Orchestra

          Royal Philharmonic Orch., cond. Beecham

          4 sides H.DB6452–3

   (La) *Calinda* (arr. Fenby)

      Orchestra

          (1) London Philharmonic Orch., cond. Beecham

          1 side Delius Society, Vol. III

          (2) Hallé Orch., cond. Lambert

          1 side H.C3273

   Concerto

      Piano and orchestra

          (1) Betty Humby Beecham and Royal Philharmonic Orch., cond. Beecham

          5 sides H.DB6428–30

          (2) Benno Moiseiwitsch and Philharmonia Orch., cond. Lambert

          5 sides H.C3533–4 and C.S3535

   Concerto (1916)

      Violin and orchestra

          Jean Pougnet and Royal Philharmonic Orch., cond. Beecham

          5 sides H.DB6369–71

   Deux Aquarelles (arr. Fenby)

      String orchestra

          Boyd Neel String Orch.

          1 side D.X147

   Deux Aquarelles (arr. Fenby)

      String orchestra

          Hallé Orch., cond. Barbirolli

          1 side H.C3864

   Eventyr (Once Upon A Time) (1917) *Ballade for Orch., after Asbjörnsen's 'Fairy Tales'*

      Orchestra

          London Philharmonic Orch., cond. Beecham

          4 sides Delius Society, Vol. I

   Fennimore and Gerda (1908–10) – *Intermezzo*

      Orchestra

          London Philharmonic Orch., cond. Beecham

          1 side Delius Society, Vol. II

DELIUS, Frederick—*continued*

Five Songs (No. 1, *Irmelin*)
   Song
      Nancy Evans (con.), piano acc.
      1 side D.F5707

Hassan (1920) (incidental music to James Elroy Flecker's drama)
   Orchestra
   (a) Act 1 : Scenes 1 and 2 ; Serenade
      London Philharmonic Orch., cond. Beecham
      2 sides Delius Society, Vol. I
   (b) Closing Scene
      London Philharmonic Orch., cond. Beecham
      2 sides Delius Society, Vol. I
   (c) Intermezzo and Serenade (arr. Beecham)
      (1) Liverpool Philharmonic Orch., cond. Rignold, solo
         violin Henry Datyner
      1 side C.DX1621
      (2) Halle Orch., cond. Lambert
      1 side H.C3273

In a Summer Garden – A Fantasy
   Orchestra
      London Philharmonic Orch., cond. Beecham
      3 sides Delius Society, Vol. II

Indian Love Song (1891) (from 'Three English Songs' by Shelley)
   Song
      Nancy Evans (con.), piano acc.
      1 side D.F5707

Irmelin, see Five Songs

Irmelin (1890–2)
   Opera
   Prelude
      (1) Royal Philharmonic Orch., cond. Beecham
      1 side H.DB6371
      (2) National Symphony Orch., cond. Beer
      1 side D.K1836
   Intermezzo (Prelude used as an Interlude in Koanga)
      London Philharmonic Orch., cond. Beecham
      1 side Delius Society, Vol. III

Koanga (1895–7): Closing Scene
   Opera
      London Philharmonic Orch. and London Select Choir,
         cond. Beecham
      2 sides Delius Society, Vol. I

Love's Philosophy (from 'Three English Songs' by Shelley)
   Song
      Heddle Nash (ten.) and Gerald Moore (piano)
      1 side Delius Society, Vol. I

DELIUS, Frederick—*continued*

Marche Caprice
  Orchestra
        Royal Philharmonic Orch., cond. Beecham
        1 side H.DB6430

On Hearing the First Cuckoo in Spring (1912)
  Small orchestra
        (1) Royal Philharmonic Orch., cond. Beecham
        2 sides C.L2096
        (2) Royal Philharmonic Orch., cond, Beecham
        (Recorded under the auspices of the Delius Trust)
        2 sides H.DB6923

Over the Hills and Far Away (1895)
  Orchestra
        London Philharmonic Orch., cond. Beecham
        3 sides Delius Society, Vol. II

Paris : the Song of a Great City – A Nocturne (1899)
  Orchestra
        London Philharmonic Orch., cond. Beecham
        6 sides Delius Society Vol. I

Sea Drift (Walt Whitman) (1903)
  Baritone, choir and orchestra
        John Brownlee, London Select Choir, and London Phil-
            harmonic Orch., cond. Beecham
        7 sides Delius Society, Vol. II

Sonata, No. 3
  Violin and piano
        Albert Sammons and Kathleen Long
        5 sides D.M557–9

Summer Night on the River (1911)
  Orchestra
        London Philharmonic Orch., cond. Beecham
        2 sides C.LB44

To the Queen of My Heart (from 'Three English Songs' by Shelley
    (1891)
  Song
        Heddle Nash (ten.) and Gerald Moore (piano)
        1 side Delius Society, Vol. I

Two Aquarelles (arr. Fenby)
  String orchestra
        Boyd Neel String Orch.
        1 side D.X147

(*A*) *Village Romeo and Juliet* (1900–1) The Opera, in 3 acts, with a
    Prologue, recorded complete, twelve 12-inch records divided
    into two sets :

HOLBROOKE, Joseph—*continued*

Children of Don (1911)

  Overture

  Orchestra

      Symphony Orch., cond. Hammond

      2 sides D.X196

  Noden's Song

  Voice and orchestra

      Norman Walker (bass) and orch.

      1 side D.X176

Concerto (No. 1), *Op. 52* – 'The Song of Gwyn Ap Nudd'

  Piano and orchestra

      London Promenade Orch. and Grace Lyndon, cond.
      Hammond

      7 sides Paxton CPR107–10

Dylan (1914)

  Opera

  (*a*) *Prelude*

  Orchestra

      Symphony Orch., cond. Raybould

      3 sides D.X194–5

  (*b*) *Sea King's Song*

  Voice and orchestra

      Norman Walker (ten.) and orch.

      1 side D.X176

Symphony, No. 3, Finale – 'Ships'

  Orchestra

      Symphony Orch., cond. Raybould

      1 side D.X195

HOLST, Gustav, **44** ff., 87, 89, 92, 188

Diverus and Lazarus

  Carol

      Decca Choir

      D.F1566

Hymn of Jesus, Op. 37

  Choir and orchestra

      Huddersfield Choral Society and Liverpool Philharmonic
      Orch., cond. Sargent

      5 sides G.C3399–400 and CS3401

I Vow to Thee, My Country

  Vocal octet and strings

      The Templars Octet with string acc., cond. Dixon

      ½ side H.C3781

HOLST, Gustav—*continued*

Lullay my Liking
    Vocal quartet
        The Celebrity Quartette (Isobel Baillie, Gladys Ripley,
           John McHugh and Harold Williams)
        1 side C.DB2464

(The) Perfect Fool – Ballet Music
    Orchestra
        London Philharmonic Orch., cond. Sargent
        3 sides D.K1561–2

Rig Veda – Hymn to the Waters, Op. 26, No. 2
    Choir
        Nottingham Oriana Choir
        1 side D.M.560

St Paul's Suite, Op. 29, No. 2
    String orchestra
        Jacques String Orch.
        4 sides C.DB1793–4

Suite in E flat
    Military band
        Band of the Royal Artillery, cond. Geary
        3 sides Boosey & Hawkes M2033–4

Suite in F (No. 2)
    Military band
        Band of the Irish Guards, cond. Willcocks
        2 sides Boosey & Hawkes MT2010

This I have done
    Unaccompanied choir
        (1) B.B.C. Chorus
        1 side D.K841
        (2) Fleet Street Choir
        1 side D.K1089

Wassail Song (Folk-song)
    Choir
        B.B.C. Chorus
        1 side D.K841

HOWELLS, Herbert, **188,** 189

Elegy
    Viola solo, string quartet and string orch.
        Boyd Neel Orch. and Max Gilbert, cond. Neel
        3 sides D.M484–5

IRELAND, John, 74, **97** ff., 132, 172, 175, 203
    Comedy Overture
        Brass band
            Black Dyke Mills Band, cond. Mortimer
            3 sides Jamco BD 1206–7

IRELAND, John—*continued*

Concertino Pastorale
   String orchestra
         Boyd Neel String Orch., cond. Neel
         5 sides D.X253–5

Concerto in E flat major
   Piano and orchestra
         Eileen Joyce and Hallé Orch., cond. Heward
         6 sides C.DX1072–4

Downland Suite (*Minuet* only)
   String orchestra
         Boyd Neel String Orch., cond. Neel
         1 side D.X255

(*The*) *Forgotten Rite*
   Orchestra
         Hallé Orch., cond. Barbirolli
         2 sides H.C3894

Holy Boy (from *Four Piano Preludes, Op.* 17)
   Piano, arr. 'cello and piano
         Florence Hooton and Ross Pratt
         1 side D.K900

London Overture
   Orchestra
         Liverpool Philharmonic Orch., cond. Sargent
         3 sides C.DX1155–6

(*The*) *Overlanders* (incidental music to the film)
   Orchestra, arr. Irving
         London Symphony Orch., cond. Mathieson
         2 sides D.K1602

Phantasie Trio in A minor (1908)
   Violin, viola and piano
         Grinke Trio
         3 sides D.K899–900

Piano Trio in E major, No. 3 (1938)
   Violin, 'cello and piano
         Grinke Trio
         6 sides D.X242–4

Sea Fever (1913)
   Song
         Roy Henderson (bar.), piano acc. Ivor Newton
         1 side D.M526

(*The*) *Soldier*
   Song
         Roy Henderson (bar.), piano acc. Ivor Newton
         1 side D.M526

VAUGHAN WILLIAMS, Ralph—*continued*
  Fantasia on a Theme of Tallis (1910)
    String orchestra
        (1) Boyd Neel String Orch., cond. Neel
        4 sides D.K815-6
        (2) B.B.C. Orch., cond. Boult
        4 sides H.DB3958-9
        (3) Hallé Orch., cond. Barbirolli
        4 sides H.C.3507-8
  Fantasia on the Theme of 'Greensleeves'
    String orchestra
        (1) Queen's Hall Orch., cond. Wood
        1 side D.K822
        (2) (arr. R. Greaves) Hallé Orch., cond. Barbirolli
        1 side H.C.3819
        (3) Jacques String Orch., cond. Jacques
        1 side C.DX925
        (4) Hallé Orch., cond. Sargent
        1 side C.DX1087
  Flos Campi – Suite
    Viola, chorus and orchestra
        William Primrose and B.B.C. Chorus, Philharmonia Orch.
            cond. Boult
        6 sides H.DB6353-5
  For all the Saints
    Vocal octet and organ
        Templars Octet, cond. Dixon, with Herbert Dawson
        1 side H.C3784
  How can the Tree but Wither
    Song
        Nancy Evans (con.)
        1 side D.K862
  Hymn Tune Prelude on Song 13 (Orlando Gibbons, arr. Vaughan
    Williams)
    Piano
        Harriet Cohen
        1 side C.DX1552
  I will give my love an apple
    Choir
        Secondary Modern School in N. Midlands
        ½ side H.C3679
  Job (a Masque for dancing)
    Orchestra
        BBC Symphony Orch., cond. Boult
        10 sides H.DB6289-93

VAUGHAN WILLIAMS, Ralph—*continued*

Lark Ascending

Violin and orchestra

(1) Frederick Grinke and Boyd Neel Orch., cond. Neel

3 sides D.K259–60

(2) David Wise and Liverpool Philharmonic Orch., cond. Sargent

4 sides C.DX1386–7

Linden Lea (Barnes)

Song

(1) John McCormack (ten.)

1 side H.DA1791

(2) Astra Desmond (sop.)

1 side D.M522

(3) Heddle Nash, piano acc. Gerald Moore

1 side H.B9719

(*The*) *Loves of Joanna Godden* (incidental music to film)

Orchestra

Philharmonia Orch., cond. Irving

2 sides C.DX1377

On Wenlock Edge (from 'A Shropshire Lad')

Song cycle

Peter Pears, Zorian String Quartet and Benjamin Britten

6 sides D.M585–7

Orpheus with his Lute

(1) Choir

School Choir

½ side H.C3526

(2) Song

Roy Henderson (bar.) with piano acc.

1 side D.M583

'*Scott of the Antarctic*' (from the incidental music to the film)

(*a*) *Prologue*

(*b*) *Pony March*

(*c*) *Penguins*

(*d*) *Climbing*

(*e*) *The Return*

(*f*) *Blizzard*

(*g*) *Final Music*

Orchestra

Philharmonia Orch., cond. Irving

2 sides H.C3834

Serenade to Music

Voices and orchestra

B.B.C. Orch. and soloists, cond. Wood

4 sides C.LX757–8

WALFORD DAVIES, Sir Henry, 24, 28–9
God be in My Head
  Choir
    Tommy Handley Memorial Choir, cond. Woodgate
    ½ side H.C3844
(The) Holly and the Ivy
  Choir
    Large Grammar School in North : 1 side H.C3680
Solemn Melody
  Organ
    (1) Harry Goss Custard : 1 side C.DX1477
    (2) Charles Smart : ½ side H.C3844
WALTON, William, **134** ff.
Belshazzar's Feast (1931) *Choral*
  Choir, brass bands, baritone and orchestra
    Huddersfield Choral Society, Liverpool Philharmonic Orch.,
    Brass bands, and Denis Noble, cond. Walton
    10 sides H.C3330–4
Concerto
  Viola and orchestra
    Frederick Riddle and London Symphony Orch., cond.
    Walton : 6 sides D.X199–201
Concerto (1939)
  Violin and orchestra
    Heifetz and Cincinnati Symphony Orch., cond. Goossens
    6 sides H.DB5953–5
Crown Imperial (1937) *(Coronation March)*
  Orchestra and organ
    B.B.C. Symphony Orch. and Berkeley Mason, cond. Boult
    2 sides H.DB3164
Daphne
  Song
    Dora Stevens (sop.) and Hubert Foss (piano)
    1 side D.M490
Façade Suite No. 1 (1922)
  (1) Recitation with music
    Edith Sitwell and Constant Lambert : 4 sides D.K991–2
  (2) Arranged for ballet
    London Philharmonic Orch., cond. Walton
    4 sides H.C2836–7
Façade Suite No. 2
  Orchestra
    London Philharmonic Orch., cond. Walton : 1 side H.C3042
Four Dances
  Orchestra
    Orchestre Raymonde, cond. Walter : 2 sides C.DX938

'WARLOCK, Peter'—*continued*

Captain Stratton's Fancy
  Song
      Roy Henderson (bar.) : 1 side D.M563

Chop Cherry (from *The Old Wives' Tale*, George Peele, 1590)
  Voice and string quartet
      John Armstrong (bar.) with International String Quartet
      ½ side NGS165

Cornish Christmas Carol
  Choir
      B.B.C. Choir : 1 side D.K827

Corpus Christi
  Choir
      B.B.C. Choir : 1 side D.K827

(The) Curlew (W. B. Yeats)
  Baritone, flute, cor anglais and string quartet
      John Armstrong, R. Murchie, T. McDonagh and Inter-
      national String Quartet, cond. Lambert
      5 sides NGS163–5

Fair and True
  Song
      Roy Henderson (bar.) : ½ side D.M519

Milkmaids
  Song
      Roy Henderson (bar.) : 1 side D.M563

My Own Country
  Song
      Roy Henderson (bar.) : 1 side D.M519

Piggesnie
  Song
      Roy Henderson (bar.) : ½ side D.M519

Rest, Sweet Nymphs
  Song
      Nancy Evans (con.) : ½ side D.K866

Saint Anthony of Padua
  Song
      Nancy Evans (con.) : ½ side D.K866

Sleep (from *The Woman Hater*, Beaumont and Fletcher, 1607)
  Voice and string quartet
      John Armstrong (bar.) with International String Quartet
      ½ side NGS165